Causation

Causation

A User's Guide

L. A. Paul and Ned Hall

OXFORD
UNIVERSITY PRESS

OXFORD
UNIVERSITY PRESS

Great Clarendon Street, Oxford, OX2 6DP,
United Kingdom

Oxford University Press is a department of the University of Oxford.
It furthers the University's objective of excellence in research, scholarship,
and education by publishing worldwide. Oxford is a registered trade mark of
Oxford University Press in the UK and in certain other countries

First Edition published in 2013

Impression: 1

British Library Cataloguing in Publication Data

Data available

ISBN 978–0–19–967344–5 (hbk)
978–0–19–967345–2 (pbk)

Printed in Great Britain by
CPI Group (UK) Ltd, Croydon, CR0 4YY

Contents

Preface

This book grew out of a series of conversations that began at Princeton in the 1990s. As graduate students, we studied causation with David Lewis, and when Lewis ran a seminar in 1996 devoted to the problems and puzzles of counterfactual analyses of causation, it began a discussion about the nature of causation that lasted throughout the process of writing dissertations, to tenure, and beyond. The book was truly co-authored, in the sense that each chapter was written and rewritten by each of us, sometimes as we sat in the same room, and sometimes as we worked together online, and many of the sections of the chapters were developed from conversations in which we developed joint views about the right perspective on the metaphysics of causation.

We owe thanks to many interlocutors over the years. We are especially grateful to David Lewis, who was the best of all possible mentors. We also want to give special thanks to Chris Hitchcock, who engaged in many detailed discussions of causal modeling, and to Jonathan Schaffer, who read the entire book at least twice and gave us extensive, excellent—and spirited—comments each time.

We also thank Robert Adams, Sara Bernstein, Michael Bertrand, Thomas Blanchard, Douglas Ehring, Alvin Goldman, Caspar Hare, Kieran Healy, Marc Johansen, Dan Korman, Christian Loew, Dan Marshall, Tim Maudlin, Stephen Morgan, Alyssa Ney, Agustin Rayo, Raul Saucedo, Bradford Skow, Holly Smith, Eric Swanson, Michael Strevens, Judith Jarvis Thomson, Brad Weslake, Stephen Yablo, the members of Bradford Skow's 2009 causation seminar at MIT, members of our causation graduate seminars at Yale, Arizona and Harvard, two anonymous referees for OUP for discussion and comments, and Peter Momtchiloff for his editorial support and endless patience.

The Frank H. Kenan Fellowship, awarded by the National Humanities Center, with additional support provided by the University of North Carolina, provided crucial support for Paul in 2011–12.

Finally, we'd like to thank our spouses. Although neither of us have wives who typed our manuscripts and corrected our typos, we have something infinitely more valuable: incredibly patient, supportive and loving spouses who provided so much of their time, energy and emotional support during the long and involved process of creating this book. Thank you, Kieran and Barbara.

Annotated list of figures

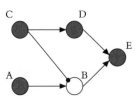

At time 0, **C** and **A** both fire. **C** sends a stimulatory signal to **D**, which fires at time 1. **A** sends a stimulatory signal to **B**, but the inhibitory signal from **C** (symbolized by the line with the blob on the end) blocks it, so **B** does not fire. **D** sends a stimulatory signal to **E**, which fires at time 2.

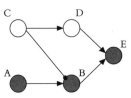

At time 0, only **A** fires. **A** sends a stimulatory signal to **B**, which fires at time 1. **B** sends a stimulatory signal to **E**, which fires at time 2.

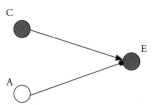

At time 0, only **C** fires. **C** sends a stimulatory signal to **E**, which fires at time 1. If **A** had fired at time 0, **E** would not have fired.

E is a *chancy* neuron: it will not fire unless stimulated by **C**, but even if stimulated, it has only chance 50% of firing. At time 0, **C** fires. **C** sends a stimulatory signal to **E**, which fires at time 1.

See: Chapter 2, §4.3; §4.5; Chapter 3, §4.3.1.

The fat arrow between **C** and **E** indicates that stimulatory signals sent by **C** are probabilistic, having a very small chance of dying out before they reach **E**. **E** has a very low chance of firing without being stimulated, but will (with certainty) fire if stimulated. In the depicted case, **C** fires at time 0, but the signal it sends dies out before reaching **E**; nevertheless, **E** fires at time 1.

See: Chapter 2, §4.3.

A and **C** fire at time 0, sending stimulatory signals to **E**, which fires at time 1. **E** has no chance of firing unless it receives a stimulatory signal from either **A** or **C**. If it receives just one stimulatory signal, then it is certain to fire; but if, as in the events depicted in the figure, it receives two stimulatory signals, then its chance of firing is a mere 0.01. Nevertheless, in this case it does fire.

See: Chapter 2, §4.3; Chapter 3, §5.

C fires at time 0, sending weak stimulatory signals to each of
E1, . . . , **E17100**. Each **E**-neuron has a probability of firing of 0.9, if not stimulated; the signals from **C** raise this probability to 0.901. Exactly 901,000 of the **E**-neurons fire. Given that **C** fired, the probability that at least 901,000 of the **E**-neurons would fire was slightly greater than 0.5. If **C** had not fired, this probability would have been less than 0.0005; the probability would have been greater than 0.99 that not more than 900,700 of the neurons would fire.

See: Chapter 2, §4.3.

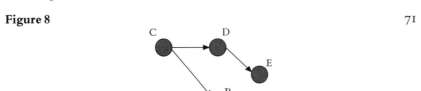

C fires, sending signals to **B** and **D**, both of which fire; **E** fires upon receiving the signal from **D**.

See: Chapter 3, §1.

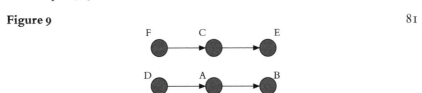

F fires at time 0, sending a stimulatory signal to **C**, which fires at time 1; **C** sends a stimulatory signal to **E**, which fires at time 2. **D** fires at time 0, sending a stimulatory signal to **A**, which fires at time 1; **A** sends a stimulatory signal to **B**, which fires at time 2.

See: Chapter 3, §2.3.1, §2.3.2, §2.3.3.

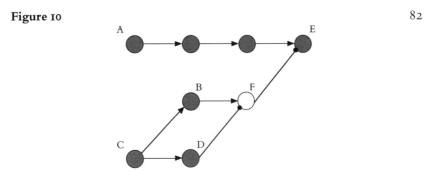

A and **C** fire at time 0. **A** sends a stimulatory signal to **E**, via the unlabeled neurons; **E** fires at time 3. **C** sends stimulatory signals to **D** and **B**, both of which fire at time 1. **D** sends a stimulatory signal to **F**, but **B** sends an inhibitory signal to **F**; accordingly, **F** does not fire at time 2.

See: Chapter 3, §2.3.3; Chapter 4, §3.4.1, §3.4.2; Chapter 5, §1, §1.2; Chapter 6, §1.

Figure 11   87

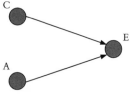

A and **C** fire at time 0, sending stimulatory signals to **E**, which fires at time 1. The firing of **E** is overdetermined, in that either signal from **A** or **C** alone would have sufficed to bring it about. **E** fires in exactly the same way whether it is stimulated by **A** or by **C**.

See: Chapter 3, §5; Chapter 6, §1.

Figure 12   88

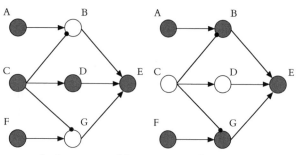

The two diagrams depict two possible sequences of events, within the same network of neurons. On the left, **A**, **C**, and **F** all fire at time 0; the inhibitory signals from **C** prevent **B** and **G** from firing at time 1; the signal from **C** stimulates **D** to fire at time 1. **D** sends a stimulatory signal to **E**, which fires at time 2. On the right, **A** and **F** fire at time 0; the signal from **A** stimulates **B** to fire at time 1; the signal from **F** stimulates **G** to fire at time 1; the stimulatory signals from **B** and **G** overdetermine the firing of **E** at time 2.

See: Chapter 3, §2.3.3.

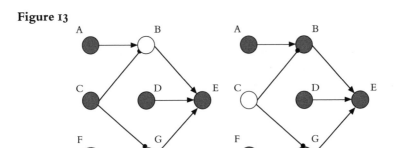

The two diagrams depict two possible sequences of events, within the same network of neurons. On the left, **A**, **C**, and **F** all fire at time 0; the inhibitory signals from **C** prevent **B** and **G** from firing at time 1. **D** fires at time 1 (as the result of causes not depicted). **D** sends a stimulatory signal to **E**, which fires at time 2. On the right, **A** and **F** fire at time 0; the signal from **A** stimulates **B** to fire at time 1; the signal from **F** stimulates **G** to fire at time 1. **D** fires at time 1 (as the result of causes not depicted). The stimulatory signals from **B**, **D**, and **G** overdetermine the firing of **E** at time 2.

See: Chapter 3, §2.3.3, §2.5.

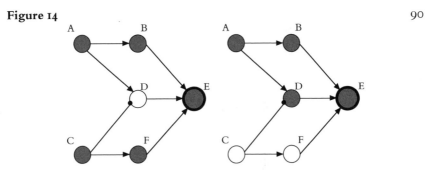

The two diagrams depict two possible sequences of events, within the same network of neurons. **E** is a stubborn neuron, needing two stimulations in order to fire. In the right-hand diagram, it receives both, ultimately, from **A**. In the left-hand diagram, it receives one from **A** and one from **C**; it *would* have received both from **A**, but for the preempting action of **C**.

See: Chapter 3, §2.4, §3.1.

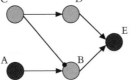

The depicted neurons can fire with different intensities, emitting signals, stimulatory or inhibitory, with corresponding intensities. **E** will fire iff it receives stimulatory signals of combined intensity 10 or greater. **A** fires with intensity 10, and **C** with intensity 5. The inhibitory connection between **C** and **B** does not prevent **B** from firing, but just reduces the intensity of its firing from 10 to 5. Since, as a result of the stimulatory signal from **C**, **D** likewise fires with intensity 5, **E** fires.

See: Chapter 3, §3.1, §3.2, §3.3, §4.3.3.

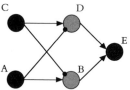

A and **C** send strong stimulatory signals to **B** and **D**, respectively. In addition, **C** sends a weak inhibitory signal to **B** and **A** sends a weak inhibitory signal to **D**. Had **C** not fired, **B** would have fired with intensity 10; likewise, had **A** not fired, **D** would have fired with intensity 10. Instead, each fires with intensity 5. **E** will fire iff it receives stimulatory signals with combined strength of 10 or greater. So **E** fires.

See: Chapter 3, §5; Chapter 4, §2.4.

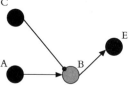

E will fire if it receives a signal of *any* intensity. Had **C** not fired, the signal from **B** would have been of intensity 10. But thanks to *C*, it has intensity 5. **E** fires.

See: Chapter 3, §3.2.

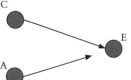

The stimulatory signal from **C** reaches **E** just before the stimulatory signal from **A**; the diagram represents this fact by being a "snapshot" of a time; drawing the arrow from **A** so that it does not quite extend to **E**.

Figure 19   100

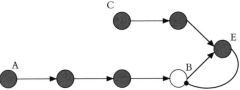

A and **C** fire simultaneously. The inhibitory signal from **E** prevents **B** from firing; if it had not done so, the signal from **A** would have caused **E** to fire. The backup process is *cut short*: neuron **B** is prevented from firing.

Figure 20   109

A duplicate of figure 18, minus **A**.

Figure 21   125

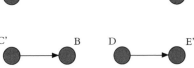

Here *C* causes *E*; the pair (*C*, *E*) perfectly intrinsically duplicates the pair (*C'*, *E'*); yet *C'* does not cause *E'*.

Figure 22   133

The inhibitory signal from **C** prevents **E** from firing, and the inhibitory signal from **C** prevents the stimulatory signal from **D** from causing **E** to fire by somehow interrupting the causal process from *D* to *E*.

See: Chapter 3, §4.3.4; Chapter 4, §1.2, §3.1.

Figure 23   133

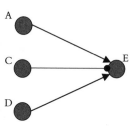

C and *D* interact such that *C* prevents the process from *D* to *E*, thus preventing *D* from bringing about *E*, while *A* independently succeeds in causing *E*.

See: Chapter 3, §4.3.4.

Figure 24   135

See: Chapter 3, §4.3.4.

Figure 25   135

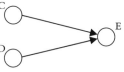

Neuron **C** can fire with various different colors and in various different intensities, as can **D**.

See: Chapter 3, §4.3.4.

Figure 26   136

Virulent late preemption: the *test case*: **D** fires, and **C** fires in triggering grey with intensity I, and **E** fires.

See: Chapter 3, §4.3.4, §6.

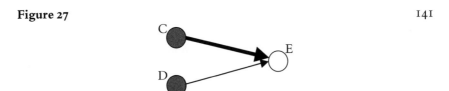

C fires with the inhibiting intensity but not in the triggering shade.

See: Chapter 3, §4.3.4.

See: Chapter 3, §5.

An example of double prevention.

See: Chapter 3, §5; Chapter 4, §1.3, §3.1, §3.3, §3.4.2; Chapter 6, §1.

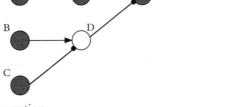

C and D both fire, in the same color—red—but with different intensities; that C fires more intensely is represented by shading its circle more darkly. A short while later, E fires in the color red.

See: Chapter 3, §6.

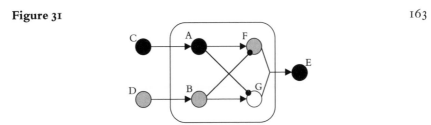

The strong inhibitory signal from **A** cancels out the weak stimulatory signal from **B**, and **G** does not fire; but the weak inhibitory signal from **B** does not cancel the strong stimulatory signal from **A**, so **F** *does* fire (weakly); and so **E** fires.

See: Chapter 3, §6.

Figure 32   164

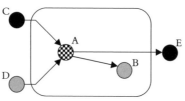

A acts as a kind of "shunt", deflecting the less intense signal into the downward path where neuron **B** absorbs it, and sending the more intense signal along the main path to **E**.

See: Chapter 3, §6.

Figure 33   164

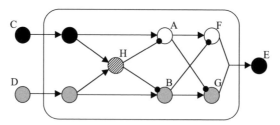

H acts as follows: If there is just one incoming signal (or none), it does nothing. If there are two incoming signals of different colors, it does nothing. If there are two incoming signals of the same color and same intensity, it does nothing. *But*, if there are two incoming signals of the same color and *different* intensities, it emits an inhibitory signal along exactly one of the exit channels, equal in strength to the stronger of the two incoming signals. If the stronger incoming signal came from the "upper" channel, then the inhibitory signal likewise exits from the upper channel; if it came from the lower, then the lower.

See: Chapter 3, §6.

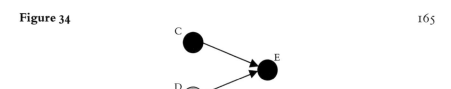

C, D, and *E* exhibit the test pattern as a matter of fundamental
law only.

See: Chapter 3, §6.

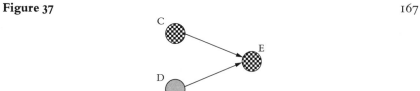

See: Chapter 3, §6.

See: Chapter 3, §6.

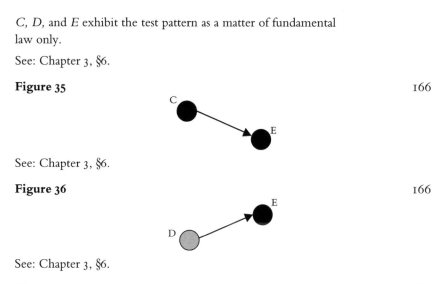

C causes **E** to fire, and that *C* prevents the *D*-process from itself causing
E to fire.

See: Chapter 3, §6.

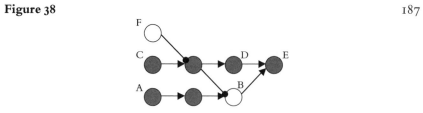

See: Chapter 4, §2.4, §5.

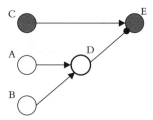

D is stubborn: to fire, it requires both **A** and **B** to fire.

See: Chapter 4, §3.1.

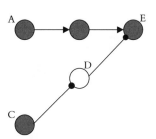

The idle neuron case.

See: Chapter 4, §3.3.

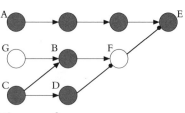

See Chapter 4, §3.4.1, Chapter 5, §1.2.

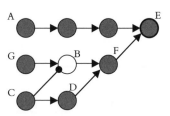

See Chapter 4, §3.4.1.

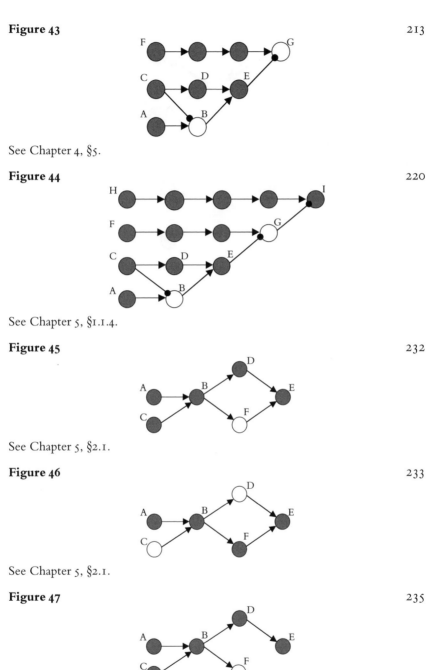

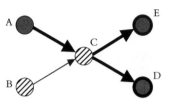

See Chapter 5, §2.2.

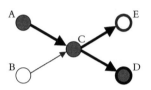

See Chapter 5, §2.2.

1

The scope and aims of this "guide"

1 Introduction

A cause *brings* something *about* or *makes* something *happen*. In this sense, causation is a deeply intuitive and familiar relation, one on which common sense appears to possess a powerful grip. As is typical in philosophy, however, this deep intuitive familiarity has not led to any philosophical account of causation that is at once clean, precise, and widely agreed upon. Not for lack of trying: the last 30 years or so have seen dozens of attempts to provide such an account, and the pace of development is, if anything, accelerating. (See Collins et al. 2004a and Dowe and Noordhof 2004 for some examples.)

It is safe to say that none has yet succeeded. But the effort put into their development has, without question, yielded a wealth of insights. And that is important not merely because of the intrinsic interest of the subject, but because of the myriad ways in which causation works its way into a host of other contemporary philosophical debates: debates concerning (to name a few) mental causation and the nature of mind, epistemology, perception, color, action theory, decision theory, semantics, scientific explanation, the asymmetry of the temporal arrow, and moral and legal responsibility. Philosophically speaking, causation is everywhere. That makes its study—specifically, the study of the prospects for giving a successful philosophical account of the metaphysics of causation—of equally broad interest.

Unfortunately, the literature on the metaphysics of causation conceals its insights within a tangled landscape of conflicting approaches, driven by conflicting motivations and conflicting presuppositions about the very point of providing a philosophical account of causation, and often informed by conflicting intuitions about key cases. Our aim is to sketch a map of this landscape, using a set of examples as landmarks, with special attention given to counterfactual and related analyses of causation. We intend this work to be of use both to the trained specialist and the uninitiated alike.

2 Some remarks on method

A few words about method will help readers to understand the value of working through the many examples to come. (Methodological issues will be discussed in more detail in subsequent chapters.)

The rules seem to have changed in recent years: where once the focus was pretty much only on conceptual analyses of our folk-theoretical notion of "cause," contemporary work cares more about developing and deploying more sophisticated, scientifically informed notions of "cause," sometimes in the service of this or that metaphysical project (e.g., discovering which fundamental ontological facts in the world are involved in causal relations), and sometimes in the service of cleaning up or illuminating some aspect of scientific inquiry (e.g., discerning the proper methods for drawing causal conclusions from statistical data, or articulating what it is to provide a scientific explanation of some phenomenon) or pinpointing some notion of "cause" already in use in scientific inquiry.

These projects differ dramatically. Analyses of our folk notion of "cause" succeed only to the extent that they accurately discern the structure of that notion, and so need to take commonsense intuitions (firm ones, anyway) as a kind of nonnegotiable data; they should likewise pay attention to empirical work on such intuitions conducted by psychologists and experimental philosophers. By contrast, analyses that aim to develop a more theoretically useful notion of "cause" (useful, again, either to metaphysicians or to scientists) should take causal intuitions as defeasible guides to potentially interesting and important features of our causal concept or a causal relation, while being quite prepared to jettison those intuitions in the event that they are discovered to lead nowhere interesting.

We favor the second approach. But we favor it in a way that places a premium on close attention to the full range of our intuitive causal judgments. Yes, it might be the case—in fact, it almost certainly will be the case—that at the end of philosophical inquiry we will see that various of these judgments must be set aside. (We will, in fact, provide specific examples of intuitions that, in our considered view, ought to be ignored.) But that is a verdict to come to after careful deliberation. First, we should use our causal intuitions to tease out interesting wrinkles in the way we think about causation, to identify often-overlooked or newly noticed features of the causal relation, to develop puzzles about cases of causation, and to discover new problems for extant accounts of the causal relation—all as a means of figuring out how to usefully develop and apply a causal concept or concepts, and to construct a theory of the causal relation. One of the aims of this book is to show you how to do this.

One upshot is that the method we favor can superficially appear to be just like the good old proposal-and-counterexample method of conceptual analysis familiar in so many areas of philosophy. But dig deeper, and you'll see that the proposal-and-counterexample method takes a very different attitude toward "ordinary intuitions," one nicely captured in this passage from Lewis (remarking here about a certain class of cases involving "redundant causation," which will be examined in more detail in chapter 3):

If one event is a redundant cause of another, then is it a cause simpliciter? Sometimes yes, it seems; sometimes no; and sometimes it is not clear one way or the other. *When common sense delivers a firm and uncontroversial answer about a not-too-far-fetched case, theory had better agree. If an analysis of causation does not deliver the common-sense answer, that is bad trouble.* But when common sense falls into indecision or controversy, or when it is reasonable to suspect that far-fetched cases are being judged by false analogy to commonplace ones, then theory may safely say what it likes. Such cases can be left as spoils to the victor, in D. M. Armstrong's phrase. We can reasonably accept as true whatever answer comes from the analysis that does best on the clearer cases. (Lewis 1986c, p. 194, italics added)

We disagree, particularly with the italicized sentences. More carefully, given that the aim is to produce one or more precise causal concepts, of use either to science or metaphysics, the appropriate rule is really this one: if an analysis of causation does not deliver the common-sense answer, that is certainly *prima facie* trouble, since it is evidence that something of importance has been overlooked. So it may make sense—but only up to a point!—to proceed as if your analysis has been refuted, when it runs afoul of common sense. But the "as if" here is essential, for running afoul of common sense is not an automatic disqualifier in the new approach. Instead, the theory as a whole needs to be examined before the cost of departing from common sense can be fully weighed.

So many specific maneuvers philosophers make can look just the same, whether they are pursuing Lewis-style conceptual analysis or the more constructive project we prefer. (Many, but not all, as we will see.) But the overarching point of our exercise is profoundly different from the Lewisian analysis. We will return to these topics in chapter 2. (For more discussion, see also Hall 2006, 2007; Paul 2010*a*, 2010*b*, and 2012.)

3 Overview of the project

On to the project. Starting with some groundwork: we seem to be able to recognize certain basic facts about causation. Causation seems, at least in the first instance, to relate *events*: while Suzy might cause a window to break, she does so only in virtue of the way she is involved in an event—her throwing of a rock, say—that causes the breaking. Causation seems to be *transitive*: if C causes D and D causes E, then C thereby causes E. Causation between distinct events seems to be the very paradigm of an *intrinsic relation*: when a causal process connects event C to event E, what makes this process have the causal structure it does depends only on its intrinsic character (and perhaps the "governing" laws of nature), not on any of its surroundings: whether Suzy's rock causes the window to break does not depend on whether, thousands of miles away, the Queen of England is enjoying a cup of tea. *Counterfactual dependence* seems sufficient for causation: if it's true that had C not happened, E would not have happened, then it seems that C must for that reason be among the causes of E. Assuming determinism, causes seem also to guarantee the occurrence of their effects, in some sense. Causation can also, apparently, involve absences, also known as *omissions*: the absence of rain in spring can cause the crops to die in summer. (If you smell trouble here—because, as just noted, another basic fact is that causation relates events, and it is far from obvious that an absence is an event—then your nose is in good working order. We will take a closer look at this in chapter 4.) And causation is *law-governed*: minimally, what causes what is fixed not merely by what happens, but also by what the fundamental laws of nature are, which govern what happens. These theses (and perhaps others that we have not mentioned) have served, in various combinations, as prominent landmarks guiding extant philosophical analyses of causation, and some of the most important questions we will confront include whether we can develop an analysis of the causal relation that respects all of these seemingly uncontroversial theses about it, and indeed, whether all of these theses need to be respected.

The prospects for a comprehensive analysis are unclear, precisely because of the wealth of examples to which any good account must attend. The causation literature is inhabited by a thick undergrowth of such examples, combinations of which can be used to spell trouble for any of the theses mentioned in the previous paragraph. What to do? We won't aim for a firm verdict, but rather will try to aid you, dear reader, in coming up with your own verdicts by providing an opinionated "user's guide" proceeding largely by using a technique we describe as the "method by counterexample." Our method employs a detailed exploration of the main versions of analyses of causation by focusing on the wide range of examples and counterexamples that have been used both to motivate and to undermine them. Some of the examples create problems for particular types of analyses. Some illustrate much more general problems that almost any account of causation must face. Some bring out subtle distinctions and perhaps even contradictions within our "ordinary" conception of causation. Frequently, the examples preserve one causal desideratum at the expense of another—and different examples favor different such desiderata. Some examples, finally, appear on inspection to be far more equivocal than their prominence in the literature would suggest.

We divide the examples into three broad (and partially overlapping) classes. Chapter 3 focuses on those that involve some sort of *redundant causation*; including cases of early and late preemption, and overdetermination. Chapter 4 focuses on those that feature *omissions* in some sort of causal role, including cases where omissions are causes and where omissions are effects, and cases of double prevention. And chapter 5 focuses on those that pose various sorts of threats to the *transitivity* of causation, some of which seem essentially to rely on causation involving omissions, some on alternative potential causal pathways, and some on certain key assumptions about the nature of the causal relata. The number and variety of these examples can seem bewildering and frustrating to all but the most hardened metaphysicians of causation; read through too many, and your intuitions may begin to go numb, leaving you tempted to dismiss the literature that has grown up around them as some sort of pointless philosophical game. While we recognize this temptation, we also intend this guide as a caution against it: the probative value of the examples should not be underestimated, even if navigating the terrain is difficult and complex.

Our guide aims to make this job easier for the reader, by presenting as systematically as possible those examples that we think have the most to teach us about causation, by discussing and developing many of the intuitive responses we have to these examples, and by drawing out as carefully as we can the lessons to be learned. The concluding lesson will take the form of a tentative and somewhat bleak view about which approaches to providing a successful philosophical account of causation remain, at this stage, at all promising. But it is our hope that even those who would abandon the search for such an account will still, by undertaking with us a close study of this philosophically fertile terrain, come away with a deeper and broader understanding of causation and its attendant concepts.

2

Framework and preliminaries

We indicated in chapter 1 that our map of the terrain would be partial, because we will be making some choices up front, lest our guide need its own guide. This chapter outlines those choices, takes care of a few other preliminaries, and considers in more detail the methodological issues broached in chapter 1.

1 Framework

1.1 Some metaphysical assumptions

We will assume, unless otherwise indicated, that the causal relata are events.[1] These events are particulars, located in spacetime. We will not treat causation as a relation between types of events, although we grant that general causal claims can be made that apparently concern event types, viz. "overexposure to the sun causes sunburn." We distinguish such general causal claims from the singular causal claims that are our focus, such as "Suzy's overexposure to the sun caused her sunburn."[2]

We will also assume a broadly *reductionist* outlook, according to which facts[3] about which events cause which other events are fixed, somehow, by (i) the facts about what happens, together with (ii) the facts about the fundamental laws that govern what happens. Minimally, that's a

---

[1] In fact we are both skeptical about this assumption. We assume it merely for simplicity and uniformity, as the vast majority of analyses treat causation as a relation between events. We will flag specific reasons for skepticism as we go along, but see especially chapters 4 and 5.

[2] You should bear in mind that it is a wide-open question whether general causal claims express some genuinely type-level causal relation, or whether we should understand them more prosaically, as expressing some kind of generalization about token-level causal relations among events. For what it's worth, we prefer the latter view, although this guide won't argue for it.

[3] We use the term "facts" to denote things in the world, such as property instances or states of affairs.

supervenience thesis: no two possible worlds differ with respect to what causes what without differing with respect to what happens or with respect to what the fundamental laws are that govern what happens. But, as will become apparent, the most important philosophical approaches to causation aim for something arguably stronger, namely, an account of causation that lays bare the causal ontology in terms of how causal facts are *grounded in*, *reduce to* or *depend upon* these more basic facts. We will come back to this point as we proceed.

As to (i), we take this to include all facts about what particulars exist at what times, and what categorical properties and relations these particulars instantiate. (Perhaps we can be bolder still, and take (i) to be exhausted by the facts about the total history of complete physical states that the world occupies; we won't need to take a stand on this.) As to (ii), the laws we have in mind are the fundamental dynamical laws of the sort that, we can hope, current physics is in the process of revealing to us. (These are to be distinguished from the so-called "laws" of the special sciences.) Taking such physics as our model, we think of these laws as something like rules that determine how complete physical states of the world generate successive physical states (see Maudlin 2007a). We will assume that a successful philosophical analysis of the causal relation ought to show exactly how facts about what happens, together with the laws, fix the facts about event causation (though see §4.5 for a brief defense of this assumption). We will introduce some of the most influential candidates for such an analysis in §2.

We will not investigate the metaphysical nature of these laws, although we will assume, purely for the sake of simplicity, that they are deterministic, and that they permit neither backwards causation nor causation across a temporal gap (see §§4.3–4).[4] Perhaps they somehow consist in mere regularities; perhaps they rest on firmer metaphysical foundations—e.g., necessary connections between universals (Armstrong 1983); perhaps they are

---

[4] Despite appearances, these constraints on the laws do not require causal notions for their articulation. Determinism is just the thesis that two nomologically possible worlds that agree on their histories up to time t agree simpliciter. The prohibition on backwards causation can be understood as the requirement that spacetime contain no closed time-like curves. And the prohibition on causation at a temporal distance can be implemented by requiring that, for any two nomologically possible worlds w_1 and w_2, if the complete physical state of w_1 at t_1 is the same as a complete physical state of w_2 at t_2, then the t_1-probability distribution over possible futures at w_1 is identical to the t_2-probability distribution over possible futures at w_2. (In other words, the present state of the world renders facts about the past irrelevant to what happens in the future.)

metaphysically primitive (Maudlin 2007a). Any philosophically respectable account of laws that does not build on an antecedent notion of cause can serve as background for the sorts of issues confronting reductive analyses that we will be considering. (For the record, we are skeptical of the claim that laws are mere regularities. See Hall forthcoming.)

1.2 Neuron diagrams

In laying out the examples, we will make extensive use of "neuron diagrams" (popularized by Lewis: see in particular his 1986c). Here is a sample:

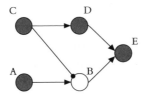

Figure 1

Circles represent neurons; arrows represent token-level stimulatory connections between neurons; lines ending with black dots represent token-level inhibitory connections. Shading a circle indicates that the neuron fires. The temporal order is represented by reading from left to right. We will use these neuron diagrams fairly freely to represent causal connections between events and, throughout, bold capitals will name neurons and italicized capitals name events of their firing. Thus, in figure 1, neurons **A** and **C** fire simultaneously; **C** sends a stimulatory signal to **D**, causing it to fire, while **A** sends a stimulatory signal to **B**. But, since **C** also sends an inhibitory signal to **B**, **B** does not fire. Finally, **D** sends a stimulatory signal to **E**, causing it to fire. Figure 2 shows what would have happened if **C** had not fired:

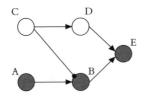

Figure 2

Neuron diagrams earn their keep by representing a complex situation clearly and forcefully, allowing the reader to take in at a glance its central causal characteristics. However, they can also mislead: used carelessly, they can oversimplify an example, draw unwarranted attention to certain features of a case and underemphasize others, and even outright misrepresent the causal structure of the case. In addition, there are interesting problems, some of which we will mention later, that their use may obscure from view. So their prominence in this guide should not suggest to the reader that we think that every interesting and important feature of an example can be boiled down to a neuron diagram, and where necessary we will take pains to highlight those features that cannot. These reservations notwithstanding, the reason for their prominence is also clear: they do a fantastic job of laying out most of the central issues involving redundancy, omissions, and transitivity in a clear and immediately graspable way.

1.3 A subtlety about metaphysics and reduction

We have indicated that we will focus almost exclusively on philosophical treatments of causation that see causal relations among events as somehow metaphysically dependent upon more metaphysically basic facts (concerning what happens, and what the fundamental laws are). That is, we are interested in reductive accounts of causation. That can raise a puzzle, though, concerning what the points of disagreement could be between rival such accounts. Now, this puzzle is in fact quite general, and has nothing per se to do with causation. All the same, it is important to get it out on the table, since attention to the philosophical issues it raises will frequently matter in what follows.

Here it is, in the (very!) abstract. Billy and Suzy, let us suppose, are having a dispute about the nature of some philosophically interesting category X. (X might be free will, or identity through time, or the nature of moral facts, or causation . . .) They have what is, apparently, a factual disagreement about X: Billy says it's one thing, Suzy says it's another. But let us further suppose that they agree completely on what belongs to the fundamental structure of reality: say, they both think that reality consists in a succession of complete physical states in space and time, which succession is governed by certain fundamental laws. And just to be clear, they have no disagreements about what the structure of these states might be, or what space and time are, or what the metaphysical nature of fundamental laws is, etc. (Maybe they both think it's all fundamentally atoms in the void, moving about under the direction of Newtonian laws.) And yet they disagree about the nature of X.

The puzzle, at this point, is that it can seem that there is no longer anything substantive for this agreement to be about. "You both agree on the fundamental facts," one wants to say, "Isn't the rest just talk?" Compare an argument Billy and Suzy might have about whether viruses are alive. Neither is a vitalist: both agree that facts about what is alive and what is not somehow reduce to biochemical facts—about which, in turn, they have no disagreement. Then how is their dispute about viruses genuinely substantive or factual?

Maybe it isn't. That is certainly one intelligible, defensible view. Quite generally, one might adopt the following meta-metaphysical principle:

Any metaphysical dispute over the nature of some feature of reality X must, in order to be genuinely substantive and non-terminological, trace to a dispute over the nature of fundamental reality.

Maybe X itself is recognized to be a feature of fundamental reality, in which case the principle obviously holds. Maybe X is some not-very-philosophically-interesting feature—for example, the dispute might be the (from our perspective!) boring question of whether it is raining outside. Again the principle holds, since we can reconstruct this dispute, in a rather labored fashion, as a dispute about whether the detailed disposition of the fundamental facts is such as to make it the case that it is raining outside. But maybe X is some vastly philosophically significant feature of reality, nevertheless recognized to be non-fundamental; and here, the thought goes, the principle yields something of value, by showing us that if we want our dispute about the nature of X to be genuine, then we had better figure out how it hinges on a disagreement about fundamental reality.

We will not attempt to ascend the meta-metaphysical heights from which one might just be able to discern whether this principle is correct (although Paul, at least, is quite skeptical about it). All we wish to urge here is that however attractive and obvious this principle may seem when one looks at some debates—e.g., Billy and Suzy's debate about whether viruses are truly alive—one should not automatically assume that it holds across the board. There is legitimate room for doubt. Suppose, this time, that Billy and Suzy are arguing over whether the statue is identical to the lump of clay that it is made from.[5] Once again, they agree that all that exists, fundamentally, are atoms in the void, subject to such-and-such fundamental laws. What they may disagree about is how many ways those atoms combine to compose nonfundamental objects. (On this view, the different modes of composition are not fundamental because composition is understood to be a many-one relation between fundamental entities and nonfundamental entities.) In cases such as this, we think it is hasty to hold that their debate cannot possibly be substantive or non-terminological—to treat the foregoing meta-metaphysical principle, that is, as an obvious a priori constraint on how to understand their debate.

The obvious—and perfectly apt!—rejoinder is this: "Fine. Maybe their debate is substantive, after all. But how? Explain, please." Here's why, in our view, the rejoinder is apt: even though (we think!) the meta-metaphysical principle cannot reasonably be assumed a priori, it can be used to locate the burden of proof, in that one who rejects it, in a specific case, owes an account of exactly how a debate about non-fundamental feature X can be substantive, in the face of full agreement about what is fundamental. Is it a dispute about ontology or ontological structure? A dispute about metaphysical emergence? Or is it a dispute about the right ways to describe and categorize the world? Or is it merely a matter of being choosy about what we are paying attention to? One way or another, we need to know.

Example. Return to Billy and Suzy's statue/clay debate. The meta-metaphysical argument that this debate is substantive, even though both parties agree that at the "fundamental level" it is all just law-governed atoms in the void, might proceed as follows: statues, and lumps of clay, are not themselves fundamental entities. Rather, they are *constituted* by such entities. But (and here comes the crucial move) there can be substantive disagreement about what is required for genuine constitution. More specifically, Billy and Suzy might both hold that the statue and lump of clay are constituted by being mereological fusions of particles. (On mereology—the theory of parts and wholes—see Simons 1987, Lewis 1991.) And they might agree that the particles that are ultimate parts of the statue are all and

---

[5] See for example Fine 2003.

only the particles that are ultimate parts of the piece of clay. But they might disagree over a basic question of mereology: namely, whether, entities (the particles, in this case), have a unique mereological fusion. One of them might hold that the statue and lump of clay are each constituted by being mereological fusions of particles, but the mereological fusions of those particles are different. It is because that disagreement is substantive that their disagreement about whether the statue and the piece of clay are one and the same object is substantive too. (See Paul 2006 for related discussion.)

We fully recognize that those attracted to the meta-metaphysical principle will be able to find grounds to grumble. Maybe they will want to say that it's just a confusion to think that the correct principle about the uniqueness of mereological fusions is at all controversial. In any case, we will not advance a step further in this debate. Instead, we wish only to caution you, the reader, that it is philosophically naïve to think, without further argument, that agreement over fundamental reality must render any disagreement over the nature of causation purely terminological.

Finally, suppose some such disagreement is terminological: really, it concerns not the facts about what causation is, but rather which of the many aspects of reality one wants to call "causation." (Compare the debate about viruses.) For all that, it may be a disagreement well worth having— and so not at all "terminological" in the dismissive sense that might apply to saying a debate was "merely verbal," as when we might debate whether whales were fish (see Chalmers 2011). In general, it matters for our intellectual aims—especially our explanatory aims—that we categorize things well. And so it might matter quite a lot what we choose to call "causation." The dismisser says, "You agree on what's fundamental; the rest is just talk." To which the right reply is, "Yes—but it can sometimes matter quite a lot that we construct our talk well."

2 The rival approaches

This section sketches some of the most significant approaches to providing a philosophical account of causation. We start with an examination of regularity theory, an approach that has unjustly fallen into disfavor in some quarters.

2.1 *Regularity accounts*

What have been called "regularity" accounts of causation have traditionally been guided by two quite distinct ideas, a distinction unhappily obscured by use of the single term. The first idea is that causal relations between events should be analyzed as instances of lawful regularities. Davidson (1967) provides perhaps the best known example of such an account: he suggests, roughly, that when *C* causes *E*, there must be some suitable descriptions of these events—as, say, the C-event and the E-event, respectively—such that there is a description of a law connecting C-events with E-events. (Note that Davidson's own candidate for such a law-description includes the word "cause" in its statement, but the paradigm descriptions of fundamental laws provided by physics never do so.)

The second idea is that what is distinctive of the causes of some event is that they lawfully suffice for it, at least in the circumstances (and: given determinism). Probably the best known account along these lines comes from Mackie (1965), although we will present it here in a somewhat different form (borrowed from Lewis 1973*a*): *C* causes *E* iff *C* and *E* both occur, and there is some suitably chosen auxiliary proposition F describing the circumstances of *C*'s occurrence such that (i) in any nomologically possible world in which *C* occurs and F is true, *E* occurs; (ii) in some nomologically possible world in which F is true, and *C* does not occur, *E* does not occur. In short, *C* is an essential part of some set of ontological conditions that are lawfully sufficient for *E*.

The two guiding ideas should have been kept carefully separate. The first has serious problems, which we will return to later (§3.3.1). The second has more merit. But it also needs a more careful expression than that given so far, since the way in which the auxiliary proposition F is to be picked out is too unclear. A better way to proceed is to start with the observation that F must, presumably, include a description of the other causes with which *C* combines to bring about *E*. That leads to the suggestion that what is key is that the set S of causes of an event *E* should *collectively suffice* for that event, but should do so *non-redundantly*: i.e., no proper subset of S should suffice for *E*. Then S had better not include all the causes of *E*, occurring at any time, since later ones will render earlier ones redundant, and vice versa. So let us require merely that the set of causes of *E* that occur at some given time (before *E* occurs) non-redundantly suffice for E.[6] That amendment still clearly does justice to the guiding idea. Then we have the following provisional analysis: C is a cause of E just in case for some time t earlier than E, C belongs to a set of events occurring at t that non-redundantly suffices for E. Note that this sort of sufficiency account may be understood as having a counterfactual element, viz., the nonredundancy constraint.

What remains is to say what "suffice" means. Here is a first pass: a set S of events suffices for (later) event E just in case the occurrence of those events lawfully guarantees that E occurs: in any nomologically possible world in which all the members of S occur, E occurs.[7] Notice that on this reading, our account does not in any interesting sense view causal relations as "instances" of "covering laws," in the way that Davidson's account did; rather, all that is required of the laws is that they draw a distinction between the nomologically possible and impossible by being the laws of the nomologically possible worlds. For that task, the laws of fundamental physics will do just fine.

Still, this account of sufficiency obscures an important issue, since it will in general be possible for the events in S to occur jointly with some other "inhibiting" events that act so as to prevent the occurrence of E. In figure 3, for example, it obviously doesn't follow from the fact that **C** fires, together with the "neuron laws," that **E** will fire (for what if **A** had fired?).[8]

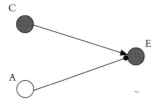

Figure 3

---

[6] Recall that we are assuming causes precede their effects.

[7] We are glossing how event-identity works across possible worlds. If this worries you, replace "in any nomologically possible world in which all the members of S occur, E occurs" with "in any nomologically possible world in which perfect intrinsic qualitative duplicates of all the members of S occur, a perfect intrinsic qualitative duplicate of E occurs." Perform the same maneuver elsewhere when we make assumptions about event identity across possibilia unless you are expressly barred from doing so.

[8] We have often encountered, both in conversation and in print, the view that determinism entails (or even just is) the thesis that the causes of any event guarantee that event's occurrence. Not so: for even under determinism, the causes of some event do not guarantee that nothing occurs that could prevent those causes from bringing about that event.

A better idea is to say that S suffices for *E* just in case, were the events in S to occur without any interference, *E* would occur. If we agree that such interference would require the occurrence of at least one other, contemporaneous event, then we can simplify as well as remove any residual taint of nonreductivity: a set S of events occurring at some time *t* suffices for (later) event *E* iff, were the events in S the only events occurring at *t*, *E* would (still) occur. Calling a set *minimally sufficient* just in case it is sufficient, but no proper subset is, we thus update our regularity account to a *minimal sufficiency account*: *C* is a cause of *E* iff *C* belongs to a set of contemporaneous events that is minimally sufficient for *E*. As we will see in the following chapters, this updated regularity account will need amending if it is to have any hope of success. But in the simple form displayed here, it is an attractive and useful example of the type.

2.2 *Counterfactual accounts*

Counterfactual accounts of causation begin with the idea that, when *E* counterfactually depends on *C* (or for short, just "depends")—when, that is, it is the case that if *C* had not occurred, *E* would not have occurred—then *C* must be a cause of *E*. Promoted to a sufficient and necessary condition, that clearly won't do: it is easy enough to have circumstances in which *C* causes *E*, even though backup processes would have brought about *E* in *C*'s absence (as figure 1 already shows, and as we will see in much more detail in chapter 3). But as a sufficient condition on causation, it has struck many philosophers as exactly right—and therefore as an excellent starting point for a full-blown analysis of causation. Scan the literature on causation, and you will find a profusion of such analyses, departing in myriad different directions from this leading idea. We will by no means try to provide a comprehensive survey, but will sketch here what seem to us to be four especially interesting avenues. (Other counterfactual approaches will be mentioned in the chapters ahead.)

The alert reader may be wondering how an account of counterfactuals can be developed that does not in some way rely on causal notions. This is an excellent question, which (along with related questions) we will defer until §§3.3.2 and 3.3.3 in this chapter.

2.2.1 *Chains of dependence*   Probably the simplest and most elegant approach comes from Lewis (1973*a*), who analyzes causation as the ancestral of counterfactual dependence: *C* causes *E* just in case there is a (possibly

empty) set of events $\{D_1, D_2, \ldots, D_n\}$ such that D_1 depends on C, D_2 depends on $D_1, \ldots$, and E depends on D_n.

Figures 1 and 2 display a natural motivation for this approach. For it is clearly the case that C causes E; yet E does not depend on C. So it won't do simply to identify causation with counterfactual dependence. On the other hand, D clearly depends on C, and—provided we understand the counter-factual in a certain, specific way—E likewise depends on D. What way is that? As non-backtracking. We will look in more detail at what this amounts to in §3.3.2 of this chapter, but for now we will make do with the following idea: we are not to reason that if D had not occurred, that would have to have been because C did not occur, whence E would still have occurred (thanks to the uninhibited process begun by A). That is the kind of "backtracking" reasoning that our intended understanding of the counterfactual rules out.

Notice that by taking the ancestral, the chains of dependence approach analytically guarantees that causation is transitive.

2.2.2 Influence   The second account comes from Lewis's later work (2000, 2004a). The key idea is to replace the simple relation of dependence with a more complicated relation of what we will call counterfactual covariation. Very roughly, E counterfactually covaries with C just in case (and to the extent that) variation in the manner of C's occurrence would be followed by corresponding variation in the manner of E's occurrence. The situation in which C's absence would be followed by E's absence can be seen as a kind of limiting case. Following Lewis, say that C influences E just in case E counterfactually covaries with C to a sufficient extent. (Also following Lewis, we will leave vague what counts as "to a sufficient extent.") Then Lewis's proposal is that causation is the ancestral of influence.

2.2.3 De facto dependence and causal modeling   The third approach has been championed by Yablo (2004), and by advocates of the causal modeling approach (of which more in a moment). The key idea is to identify causation with what Yablo has called "de facto dependence": E de facto depends on C just in case had C not occurred, and had other suitably chosen factors been held fixed, then E would not have occurred. The trick is to say what "suitably chosen" means, and to give clear and systematic truth conditions for this more complex kind of counterfactual. We will return to the second of these issues in chapter 3; here, we will elaborate briefly on the first, by considering one clear example of a de facto dependence account.

We will draw our example from causal modeling (or "structural equations") literature, partly because causal modeling approaches to causation enjoy enormous popularity (see for example Woodward 2005 and Pearl 2000). Accordingly, laying out the example requires a digression in order to explain what is distinctive about the causal modeling approach. According to advocates of this approach, in order to analyze the causal structure of any situation, we must first provide a "causal model" for it. The causal model, in effect, models patterns of counterfactual dependence. The elements of this model consist of variables, a range of possible values for each of the variables, a specification, for each variable, of which other variables (if any) it immediately functionally depends on, and finally, "structural equations" that describe this dependence. Thus, if the situation we are modeling is one in which Suzy throws a rock at a bottle, breaking it, we might construct a simple causal model by assigning a variable to the bottle whose values represent its different possible states (e.g. broken, fractured, unharmed), and assigning a second variable to Suzy's throw whose values represent the strength of the throw (and whether it happens at all). Our model will represent the first variable as functionally depending on the second, according to an equation that says, in effect, that the bottle will break (the bottle-variable will take the value "broken") iff Suzy throws with a strength above a certain threshold.

Causal modeling approaches do an excellent job of representing causal dependency structures, and for this reason, they are enormously influential. The main virtue of causal modeling is that it gives us a way to use known causal structure to discover or determine further causal structure and to predict the results of certain interventions on a system. This is all predicated, of course, on the accuracy of the original representation by the model of the causal system. Assuming the model is accurate, however, we can use causal modeling to in effect show us how a certain causal structure produces results, given a specified input. Causal modeling has been proven to have enormous value, especially when it is deployed in the social sciences to represent complex causal structures or to develop sophisticated causal explanations. Advocates of this approach have made an invaluable contribution to the overall literature on causation.

That said, the contribution to a reductive metaphysics of causation is less clear. It is an excellent question, inadequately addressed in the literature, precisely what principles should guide the construction of a causal model. One could be forgiven for suspecting that these principles really require one to figure out what causes what, in the situation to be modeled, and then to select variables and functional relationships among them to fit. (See Hall 2007 for further discussion.) Let us hasten to add that in some cases the contribution is clear and obviously important; especially in cases where a nonreductive metaphysics of causation nevertheless advances our understanding of the causal relation. We find the work of authors like Hitchcock and Woodward especially valuable in this regard.

Given that we are going to be confining ourselves mostly to examples represented by neuron diagrams, it will in general be obvious how to construct an appropriate causal model: first, assign a variable to each neuron, which can take on a range of values corresponding to each different way that that neuron can fire, reserving one more value for the situation in which it does not fire at all. Next, stipulate that each such variable immediately functionally depends on the variables for those neurons that have a direct "incoming" connection to it, either stimulatory or inhibitory. And finally, write the functional equations down so as to capture exactly how the various possible firing patterns for the input neurons to a given neuron will determine whether and how it fires. (In chapter 3, we will dwell on some important examples that have no handy neuron-diagram representation; it will come as no surprise that they spell trouble for causal modeling approaches.)

Here is the crucial innovation: with causal model in hand, you are in a position to give systematic truth-conditions for a novel sort of counterfactual: namely, one whose antecedent specifies values for arbitrarily many variables. And this expanded set of counterfactuals provides the tools for correspondingly novel treatments of causation.

Suppose for example that we have a causal model for the events depicted in figure 1.

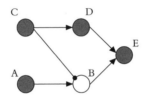

Figure 1

Starting simply, consider how we could use the model to construct a counterfactual situation in which **C** does not fire. We take the actual value of the C-variable (1, for firing) and change it to 0 (non-firing). We make appropriate adjustments downstream, recalculating the values for every variable that depends, either immediately or remotely, on this variable. In doing so, we do not change the actual value of the A-variable. We thus get a situation in which the counterfactual value of the D-variable is 0, the value of the B-variable is 1, and the value of the E-variable is 1. In words: if **C** had not fired, then **D** would not have fired, but **B** would have fired, and therefore so would **E**. So far, so good. (And so far, nothing new—you would be forgiven if, at this point, you were wondering what all the fuss is about.)

Now suppose we want to consider a situation in which **C** does not fire, but **B** also fails to fire (never mind why). When, as here, the antecedent stipulates the value for some "endogenous" variable (i.e., a variable whose value functionally depends on other variables explicitly represented in the model), then in constructing the counterfactual situation we simply ignore those functional equations that would otherwise have fixed the value of this variable. (It helps to imagine that the endogenous variable gets tweaked by an outside intervention that breaks that variable's connection to its input variables—hence the common label "interventionist" for accounts of causation like the one we are considering.) Thus, we set the value of the C-variable to 0, of the A-variable to 1 (its actual value), and the B-variable to 0. We then calculate the values for the D- and E-variables according to the appropriate functional equations, with the result that the D-variable has the value 0 and the E-variable also has the value 0. In words: if **C** had not fired, and **B** had (still) not fired, then **E** would not have fired.

Observe that this counterfactual allows us to say that in a sense, E in figure 1 does depend on C; for in fact **B** does not fire (the B-variable has the value 0), and if we hold this fact fixed, then E depends on C. More generally, it is by means of such counterfactuals that those who pursue a causal modeling version of a *de facto* dependence account of causation aim to analyze that relation.

Here, finally, is one specific proposal, drawn from Hitchcock (2001): Suppose that we have two events, C and E, and associated variables C and E. And suppose that we have some appropriate causal model of the situation in which C and E occur. Say that there is a "path" from C to E just in case there is a possibly empty set of variables $\{D_1, D_2, \ldots, D_n\}$ such that D_1 immediately functionally depends on C (and possibly other variables; we omit this qualification henceforth), D_2 immediately functionally depends on $D_1, \ldots$ and E immediately functionally depends on D_n. Now (departing slightly from Hitchcock for ease of exposition) suppose that there are one or more variables that are not on this path, such that if we hold them fixed at their actual values, then E depends on C. More exactly, the counterfactual circumstance we represent by setting the C-variable to 0, and holding those other off-path variables fixed at their actual values, is one in which the E-variable also gets set to 0. Then, adopting Hitchcock's terminology, we can say that the given path from C to E is an "active route." A simple proposal results: C is a cause of E iff there is an active route from C to E. For example, in figure 1 the C–D–E route is active, as witness the fact that if **C** had not fired and **B** had also not fired, then **E** would not have fired. By contrast, there appears to be no active route from A to E: for the only candidate is the A–B–E route, and holding fixed any combination of the actual values of the C- and D-variables fails to make it the case that E depends on A.

This is not the only way to construct a de facto dependence approach, or even a structural equations variant thereof. But it will provide an attractively simple illustration of the approach in the pages ahead; observe in this regard that it is crystal clear what constrains the choice of factors to be "held fixed" (at least, *modulo* the provision of an appropriate causal model). An interesting alternative approach comes from Yablo (2004), which we will discuss in detail in chapter 3.

2.2.4 Contrastivism   Our fourth approach builds contrast into the causal relation itself. *Contrastive* theories of the causal relation deny that that the causal relation is a two-place relation between event C and event E. Instead, the causal relation has additional relata: for example, in Jonathan Schaffer's version, C rather than C^* causes E rather than E^*, where C^* and E^* are sets of non-compossible events (Schaffer 2005). The idea, at bottom, is that causation is a complex relation involving far more events than just the original C and E. Causation is metaphysically embedded in a causal context or frame, or (speaking roughly) is like velocity in that it is an objective relation that is relative to, or in some sense indexed to, a causal context that specifies which events count as the contrast events. One popular move is to embed a contrastive account into a causal modeling account with values of variables corresponding to a range of contrast events; but a wide range of causal theories can be modified with a contrastive causal relation.

Some proponents of contrastive accounts, most notably Schaffer (2005), do not defend C rather than C^* causes E rather than E^* as a reductive analysis of causation, and do not take it to provide a solution to what are arguably the most central problems with causation, problems with preemption (see chapter 3 for a detailed discussion of preemption).

But even if one does not put forward a contrastive account as a reductive analysis, one might wish to add contrasts to a reductive account, and so need to give an account of how the set of contrast events is determined. If token causal relations, on the contrastive account, are enormously complex, have infinitely many relata, or are turned into human-dependent relations (if the specification of the set of contrast events is determined by human interests, the causal relata and hence the metaphysical character of the causal relation is thus determined by human interests), then we need an account of why contrasts should be built into the causal relation itself, instead of being relegated to merely explanatory or pragmatic domains. Fans of contrastive causation also need to explain why we should reject the intuition that causation is intrinsic to pairs of events at worlds, and versions that take the causal relata to include sets of contrast events need to make palatable the view that causation is a relation that, at least in part, can obtain either between abstracta like sets, or between an enormous number of concrete contrast events. That said, if contrastivism adds enough explanatory elegance and results in more overall success when added to reductive accounts of causation, these concerns, while substantial, could be mitigated.

Most proponents of contrastivism understand it in terms of counterfactual dependence involving contrasts, and argue that contrastive dependence or its ancestral should replace the more usual two-place relation of counterfactual dependence between C and E. (See, for example, Hitchcock 1996, Maslen 2004, Northcott 2008 and Schaffer 2005.) The argument for this move is that contrastive dependence provides much-needed resolutions of problems involving omission-involving causation, event individuation, and—especially—transitivity, since indexing causation to a causal context adds a dimension that explains the root of the concerns these problems raise.

We will touch on how contrastivism handles cases of omissions in §2.1.2, §3.2 and §5 of chapter 4, and will take an especially hard look at the arguments made for contrastive accounts in chapter 5, §1.2, when we discuss transitivity. Our focus will be on evaluating the contributions made by making the causal relation contrastive as part of a reductive account of causation. The contrastive approach provides rich, satisfying explanations for many of the sorts of causal claims we want to make, and surely gets something right about the basis for our causal judgments in many contexts. But as we will see, while making the causal relation contrastive can do this sort of work, it isn't clear it can do all of the heavy lifting that its proponents hope for.

2.3 Probabilistic accounts

Probabilistic accounts of causation are closely related to counterfactual accounts, although they are more naturally suited to treating causation in the indeterministic domain. Consider what each account takes as the central feature of the causal relation: for counterfactual accounts, it is that the effect counterfactually depends on the cause; for probabilistic accounts, it is that the effect probabilistically depends on the cause—that is, the probability that the effect occurs, given that the cause occurs, is higher than the probability that the effect occurs, given that the cause does not occur. (For sophisticated examples of probabilistic accounts, see Eells 1991, Kvart 2004, and Ramachandran 2004.)

We will have only a little more to say about probabilistic accounts in this guide. Not because we consider them unimportant. Rather, we overlook them in part because our focus is on causation in the deterministic domain—making probabilistic relations too crude an instrument for understanding causation[9]—and in part because the relations between probabilistic and counterfactual accounts are so close that problems for one often carry over to the other. We will give just one illustrative example. In figure 1, it is obvious that E does not depend counterfactually on C, since if C had not occurred, the backup process initiated by A would have brought about E. But for exactly the same reason, E does not depend probabilistically on C: the probability that E occurs is independent of whether C occurs (understanding the example now to involve appropriately "chancy" neurons). So each account will have to adopt some strategy for circumventing this and other kinds of examples. And what one finds when one surveys the problem cases is that the available strategies are remarkably similar.

---

[9] This assumes, as is surely appropriate, that the probabilities are understood as objective chances, and not identified with or constructed out of subjective credence.

One final remark. Our claim about carry-over notwithstanding, causation in the probabilistic domain raises several fascinating puzzles that have no obvious analogues in the deterministic domain. These are not puzzles about probabilistic accounts per se; but they are interesting enough to deserve brief mention, so we will sketch a few of the most important ones later in this chapter (see §4.3).

2.4 Transference accounts

The recent literature has seen some interest in accounts of causation according to which it essentially involves the transfer of some sort of quantity from cause to effect. Typical accounts turn to physics in search of the right quantity. For example, Fair (1979) takes it to be energy, while Dowe (2000) and Salmon (1994) allow it to be any sort of quantity that is, according to the fundamental physical laws, conserved. Other "transference" accounts (as we will call them) are more metaphysical: Ehring (1997), for example, takes causation to consist (at least in part) in the transfer of tropes, i.e. particularized properties.

We very much doubt that pure versions of such accounts—ones that contain no admixture of ideas borrowed from regularity or counterfactual approaches—will work: for reasons that will be reviewed in §3.3.5, it simply won't do to identify causation with the transfer of some special quantity. Still, it is possible that a fully adequate account of causation should incorporate elements of some transference account. For example, perhaps the best way to deal with cases of preemption such as figure 1 (as well as other, thornier cases that we will consider in chapter 3) is first to discern the patterns of transfer of the relevant quantity or quantities, and then to look at more abstract relations of counterfactual dependence or sufficiency, etc., that these transfers exhibit. We will also see that transference accounts prove very useful as a foil for drawing out a variety of issues having to do with causal relations that essentially involve omissions (chapter 4).

3 Methodological redux

In chapter 1 we dipped a toe ever so gently into the deep methodological waters that surround philosophical investigations of causation. With sketches of some of the most important accounts of causation in hand, it's time to jump in full force. Doing so isn't especially fun. As is so often the case, it's hard but it's healthy. If all goes well, we'll emerge with a much cleaner understanding of what an account of causation ought to be aiming to accomplish, and, consequently, a better appreciation of the point of the close, examples-based kind of analysis featured in the next three chapters.

3.1 Varieties of analysis

Let's start slowly.

Suppose a philosopher offers up, as part of some philosophical theory (about causation, or some other topic), some biconditional[10] "A iff B." Of course, in typical cases she will really be presenting a schema. It might have the form "C is a cause of E iff—," or "S knows that P iff—," or "F is an intrinsic property iff—," etc., with the blank filled in in some interesting way; you're no doubt familiar with many, many examples of the type. Now, what exactly do we expect from such a schema? What are the standards of success that our philosopher is trying to meet?

You might say, naïvely, "truth": i.e., every instance of the schema ought to turn out to be true. As an attempt to capture what it is we're after in producing such biconditionals, that's not very helpful, for more or less obvious reasons. The instances of the biconditional might be true but entirely uninformative ("C is a cause of E iff C is a cause of E"), or might merely happen to be true (as opposed to being true a priori, or true with some kind of analytical or metaphysical necessity). But even if we are content to say that we expect instances of the biconditional to be informative (without saying precisely what this means), and that we expect them to hold with some kind of necessity (without saying precisely which kind), we are missing further distinctions—some of which are, for the purposes of this guide, rather important to highlight. Here they are.

3.1.1 Mere necessary connection First, our philosopher might merely be aiming to highlight an interesting (and suitably "necessary") connection between the right and left sides of her biconditional—without claiming, further, that either side can in any sense be "explained away" in terms of the other. Here is an example: many philosophers find it plausible that a

---

[10] Or maybe, less ambitiously, just a conditional, in one direction or the other.

property F is intrinsic just in case, for any two possible objects x and y that are perfect duplicates of each other, either both have F or neither has F. Someone might offer this biconditional up as a moderately informative, useful connection between intrinsicness, duplication, and modality—without any aspiration to turn it into a reductive analysis or definition of "intrinsic property."

One sometimes finds, in the literature, philosophers of causation who are clear that this is precisely what they are up to. For example, James Woodward (2005) offers an account of causation in terms of "interventions," which are themselves explained in explicitly causal terms. Of course the account is nonreductive. But Woodward aims to put on display an interesting and important connection between causation and intervention, and nothing more. (Which is not to say that what he aims to do isn't a lot—it is.) Granted, some circular accounts—"C is a cause of E iff E is an effect of C"—do not succeed in putting any interesting or important connection on display. But Woodward's work is a proof by example that some non-reductive accounts succeed.

Still, if our philosopher is insufficiently clear about what her aims are, there is a real danger here of an unintentional "bait and switch": She presents her account as much more ambitious in one context, but then retreats to a "this is just an interesting connection" portrayal in another context. We'll see examples of this kind of unclarity of purpose in the pages ahead. In addition, while we do not for a moment doubt the value of the kind of exercise Woodward is engaged in, we also think that it provides no substitute for the much deeper understanding of the nature of causation that the more ambitious project of exploring a reductive metaphysics of the causal relation can give us.

3.1.2 *Stipulative definition* A second thing our philosopher might be doing in offering up some biconditional is presenting a stipulative definition. In some contexts, this move is just fine—e.g., when one is introducing explicitly technical vocabulary, and explaining how it is to be understood. But in other contexts it's not so fine, especially if it was designed merely to allow one to avoid seriously grappling with counterexamples. Suppose, for instance, that you have become deeply enamored of a simple counterfactual analysis of causation: C is a cause of E iff C and E both occur, and if C had not occurred, E would not have occurred. You're perfectly aware of cases of preemption that seem to spell doom for this analysis. (Figure 1 will do.) But rather than tinker with your analysis, you decide to offer it up as a stipulative definition of what you shall henceforth mean by "cause." Then granted, no one can complain that preemption presents you with a counter-example.[11] But, quite obviously, all you've done is force the complaint to be registered in a different mode: Now the worry will be that you have drawn a useless distinction (not to mention that you have drawn it using familiar words in wholly misleading ways)—or, at any rate, that you have over-looked a valuable distinction (viz., the distinction we mean to be drawing by our use of the word "cause").

Having said all this, it's worth emphasizing that there can be real value in reframing the challenge that a counterexample poses to an account in this latter way, rather than in the apparently more direct way that treats the counterexample as a straightforward refutation. That is, it can sometimes be a valuable exercise to ask (non-rhetorically!), of an analysis that runs afoul of some example, "What would be wrong with avoiding the counterexample, simply by treating this analysis as a stipulative definition?" We will come back to this point later.

3.1.3 Conceptual analysis   A third thing our philosopher might be doing is offering up a good, old-fashioned conceptual analysis. Now, we doubt that there is any clear, widely agreed upon conception of just what conceptual analysis is, or what its standards of success are. We'll discuss two ways of thinking about conceptual analysis, just to get a grip on the sort of project it might be. You might have a Fregean view of concepts, according to which they are a kind of abstract object the mind grasps in having thoughts. You might, in addition, think that concepts (some of them, anyway) are structured, in ways that involve other concepts as constituents. Against such a background of (pretty substantial!) philosophical commitments, it will be quite natural for you to treat conceptual analysis as aiming to put on display the way in which one concept is constructed out of other, more basic concepts.

Taking this Fregean view, you might see the task of your conceptual analysis as an account of how our ordinary "folk" notion of causation is

---

[11] Compare Goodman's (fictional!) "proof that *P*." "Zabludowski has insinuated that my thesis that *P* is false, on the basis of alleged counterexamples. But these so-called 'counterexamples' depend on construing my thesis that *P* in a way that it was obviously not intended—for I intended my thesis to have no counterexamples. Therefore, *P*."

constructed from more basic concepts. Or, you might see your conceptual analysis as more prescriptive: an attempt to elucidate the concept of causation that we should have, and to give an account of how such a concept would be constructed out of other, more basic concepts.

Another way is to treat the provision of a conceptual analysis as a kind of project in empirical psychology. Start with the view of concepts—strikingly different from the Fregean view we just described—as merely psychological structures realized in the brain that enable specific kinds of psychological activity. (Example: an agent who possesses the concept *cat* is thereby able to have thoughts about cats. To possess the concept *cat* just is to have realized in one's brain a certain kind of structure with certain distinctive functional relationships to the rest of one's psychological economy, and to the outside world.) Then an analysis of a concept can be thought of as a theory of how that concept functions in actual human psychological economies.

If a philosopher presents herself as engaged in "conceptual analysis," it is a very good idea to ask her what sort of conception of conceptual analysis she has in mind. And then ask her if it is a descriptive or a prescriptive analysis. And if she wants to tie her view to empirical psychology (and, in our judgment, there is plenty of worthwhile empirical investigation to be done into how humans actually engage in causal reasoning), ask her what armchair philosophical speculation has to contribute to such an investigation. (For a small sampling of psychological literature on the topic, see Gopnik et al. 2004, Lombrozo 2010, Newman et al. 2008, Saxe et al. 2005, Sloman 2005, Wolff 2007, and for an example of experimental philosophical literature, see Hitchcock and Knobe 2009.)

We think there is a good answer that many psychologists themselves would happily accept: armchair speculation can, done with sufficient care and creativity, generate hypotheses worth testing against empirical psychological data. Can generate, and has generated: for example, the distinction, now common in the causation literature, between causation that proceeds by "double prevention" (*C* prevents something from happening which, had it happened, would have prevented *E*) and causation that is more direct, has already been used by psychologists to generate testable hypotheses concerning the structure of human causal reasoning.[12] Still, it is safe to say that the more success psychology achieves at uncovering the structure of such

---

[12] Lombrozo 2010.

reasoning, the less room there will be for philosophers, *qua* philosophers, to contribute to this particular empirical endeavor.

There is another role for empirical psychology in a very different kind of philosophical project; one involving ontological reduction. We will come back to this after we discuss ontological reduction.

3.1.4 Ontological reduction A fourth kind of analysis our philosopher might be presenting is an *ontological reduction* of causation. That is, she might be intending that one side of her biconditional puts on display how facts about what causes what reduce to ontologically more basic facts. Now, this notion can be tricky. So it will help to have a nice, clear example of an ontological reduction. As follows: forget about causation for the moment, and focus on the direction of time. Suppose we are taking for granted—perhaps even treating as ontologically fundamental—relations of temporal betweenness. That is, we are not looking to analyze "time t_1 is between time t_2 and time t_3." But we are looking to analyze "time t_1 is earlier than time t_2." What's more, we seek analysis-as-ontological reduction, in that we think that what it is for one time to be earlier than another can be explained in more ontologically basic terms. Then here is an ontological reduction that many have found attractive (see for example Albert 2000 and Loewer 2012): first, we hold that our universe has one low-entropy temporal end.[13] Then we hold that, in the temporal direction that proceeds away from this end, global entropy always increases.[14] And now we can say: time t_1 is earlier than time t_2 iff t_2 lies, relative to t_1, in the direction of global entropy increase.

There are a few things to notice about this example.

First, our biconditional, "time t_1 is earlier than time t_2 iff t_2 lies, relative to t_1, in the direction of global entropy increase," doesn't carry reductive intent on its face, even if we add "it is necessary that" to the front of it. Suppose you think that the direction of time is just a primitive metaphysical fact (cf. Maudlin 2007*b*). You might agree to the biconditional all the same—you will just take it to state a substantive fact about entropy (namely, that it globally increases toward the future). You might even think this fact is related to other facts so deep that, while it is strictly speaking nomologically

---

[13] Equipped with a notion of temporal betweenness, we can easily say what it is for one time to be a temporal end: it is not between any other two times.

[14] Or: sometimes increases and never decreases. Or maybe we get fancier still, and allow for very short-lived, occasional decreases, so long as the general trend is that it is increasing.

possible for global entropy to decrease toward the future, this is so object-ively unlikely as to be deemed impossible, for all practical purposes. So if, by contrast, you view the biconditional as laying out how facts about the past/future direction are reducible to other, more basic physical facts, then you should just say so explicitly—and not try to pretend that your intent can be adequately captured by insisting that the biconditional holds with some kind of necessity.[15]

Second, it's actually not so clear what kind of necessity this biconditional holds with (according, that is, to those who take it to display a genuine ontological reduction). You might claim that the fact that one time being earlier than another just is the fact of that time lying in the direction of lower global entropy, that is, you might claim that the necessity holds in virtue of identity. Or, you might just claim that, as a matter of metaphysical necessity, one time is earlier than another iff it lies in the direction of lower global entropy. Alternatively, you might hold that the biconditional holds in all possible worlds with laws of nature that allow for facts about entropy,[16] but not in some especially outré worlds. Or you might be suspicious of such a notion of metaphysical possibility, as distinct from nomological possibility, and be willing only to say that it could have turned out (but didn't) that the past/future asymmetry was not grounded in the direction of global entropy increase.

The issues here—about how exactly to understand metaphysical necessity and its relation to ontological reduction—are subtle, and obviously we don't pretend to have settled them. But we insist that it is not an effective dialectical maneuver against a proposed ontological reduction merely to devise a conceivable scenario that violates it. Imagine the following conversation:

> **SUZY:** I think that the direction of time reduces to the direction of entropy increase; what it is for one time to precede another is for the second time to reside, relative to the first, in the direction of entropy increase.
>
> **BILLY:** But that can't be. For it is surely conceivable that entropy decreases toward the future. And what is conceivable is metaphysically possible. And if

---

[15] Which is not to say that it doesn't. It's just that it seems to us more accurate to say that you take the biconditional to be necessary because you take it to describe a relation of ontological reduction, and not that you take it to describe a relation of ontological reduction because you take it to be necessary.

[16] Note that the notion of entropy is not tied to any particular physics.

you are right that temporal direction is reducible to the direction of entropy increase, then this must be so necessarily—which it is not. So your view stands refuted.

SUZY: No, it doesn't.

(Pause.)

We side with Suzy.[17] We think, in fact, that this is one of those cases where dodging an apparent counterexample by means of stipulative definition can be a very helpful tactic. That is, what Suzy should go on to say is this:

> **SUZY:** I'm not giving an account of what *you* mean by "the direction of time." But I stipulate that this is what *I* shall mean by that expression so that I can go on to develop an account of the metaphysical nature of the direction of time in this world—the world we are in. And I now challenge you to show why, by doing so, I'm making any sort of serious mistake, or missing something of importance.

If, in reply, the only things Billy can point to are off-the-cuff intuitions about outré cases, then Suzy should remain unimpressed.

Third, there is really no hope of viewing this reduction of facts about past and future to facts about entropy as conceptual analysis—at least, not of the second, psychological type, and plausibly not of the first, Fregean type either. It is striking that this fact does not impugn the philosophical interest of the analysis in the slightest.

Fourth, there may still be a role for empirical psychology in this sort of analysis. In particular, to the extent that one relies on experience in one's arguments ("time seems to pass from earlier to later" or some such), one needs to take account of any relevant psychological literature. For example, in our test reduction of temporal direction to the direction of entropy increase, psychological literature that suggests that our experience of temporal direction is illusory in some way or subject to certain sorts of misinterpretation needs to be taken into account before relying on any premises about the nature of our ordinary experience. (See Paul 2010*c* for more discussion of our experience of temporal direction and passage and the metaphysical implications of such experience, and Paul 2010*a* and 2012 for ways to understand the contributions that empirical psychology can make to ontological reductions.)

---

[17] In saying this, we're objecting to the view that a merely conceivable scenario could function as a counterexample to an ontologically reductive theory.

Finally, the clarity and interest of the example ought to help allay fears about the philosophical coherence or legitimacy of talk of "ontological reduction." It's perfectly reasonable to wonder what exactly is going on when a philosopher announces that what it is for such-and-such a fact to obtain is for such-and-such other fact to obtain; or (equivalently, in our view) that this fact holds in virtue of that fact, etc. We'll happily go further: it's perfectly reasonable to be on one's guard against overly sloppy, cavalier, or mystifying appeals to such notions. But caution should not give way to dismissiveness: there seem to us to be no good grounds for wholesale rejection of the kind of metaphysical inquiry that seeks substantive, illuminating answers to questions of the form "What is it for such-and-such fact to obtain?" And it seems to us that we have a good enough collective grip on the distinction between more and less ontologically fundamental facts to be able to evaluate proposed answers to such questions with respect to how substantive and illuminating they are. Part of the reason for highlighting philosophical positions such as the foregoing one about the direction of time is precisely to remind ourselves, by means of a vivid example, that we do indeed understand what is being asked by a question such as "What is it for one time to be earlier than another?" and can indeed recognize a substantive and illuminating answer when we see one. And we can recognize this despite the fact that we may have no explicit theory of the "in virtue of" relation.

Now for the punch line. In the case of causation, what is of primary interest to us is whether a philosophical account of causation, understood as an ontological reduction, can be given, and if so, what are the plausible forms it might take.

Ontological reductions take at least two forms in the literature. The first one, the strong form of reduction, understands reduction in terms of identity. On such an understanding, when one reduces causation, one is making an identification. The causal relation just is a certain sort of counterfactual dependence between events, or just is a minimal sufficiency relation between events, etc. Here, "just is" picks out the identity relation: each causal relation is strictly identical to some thing or things in the reductive base. We might compare this to a strong version of composition as identity, according to which a plurality is strictly identical to its sum, or, perhaps less controversially, we might compare it to a view that reduces a sum to its plurality by holding that every time the term "sum" is used, it simply refers to a plurality of some sort.

A weaker form of reduction may be understood in terms of a biconditional, as we discussed earlier, or perhaps as a kind of ontological dependence. Neither of these weaker forms entail identity. On the ontological dependence understanding of reduction, one argues that causation depends on something, such that a causal relation depends on a certain sort of counterfactual dependence between events, or depends on a minimal sufficiency relation between events, etc. Here, "depends" picks out a relation that is something less than strict identity: a kind of ontological grounding or in virtue of relation between the entities in the ontological base and the causal relation. On such a view, the dependent causal relations are best thought of as derivative entities of some sort that are not identical to the more fundamental relations of counterfactual dependence or minimal sufficiency, or whatever the reduction base includes. We can compare this to a weak version of composition as identity, according to which a plurality is not strictly identical to its sum, although the sum is also not "an addition to being," whatever that means. We will not distinguish between the weaker and the stronger forms of reduction unless it matters for the case at hand, although we admit a preference for investigating the "stronger" form of reduction, other things being equal.

Reductive accounts should also be distinguished from eliminative accounts, according to which there is no causal relation (nothing in the world is the causal relation), and emergent accounts, according to which the causal relation is somehow created *ex nhilo* and is an entirely new, irreducible and numerically and ontologically distinct entity, one that is an "addition to being." Neither of these two sorts of views are our focus here, since one eliminates causation altogether, and the other, if we can even make sense of it, is insufficiently reductive.

With this in mind, we can now point out the importance of guarding against three sorts of philosophical bad habits in the quest to give a suitably reductive account of causation.

The first sort of bad habit is the failure to distinguish the metaphysical thesis that causation is an ontologically primitive relation that does not admit of reduction to anything ontologically more fundamental, from the thesis that, in a particular context, we may make assumptions about the causal structure of the case under consideration. The first thesis is a substantive metaphysical claim, and is compatible with an exploration of various sorts of causal puzzles and an account of how the nature and structure of the causal relation can be developed by this exploration. Schaffer (2005) is a good example of the type. The second thesis comes into play when designing causal models, for such models often make assumptions about causal structure that are then in play when the model delivers a verdict about further causal structure.

The second thesis, when stated explicitly and clearly, can play an important methodological role in a reduction. But problems arise if, instead, one is subject to a second sort of bad habit, a habit of making unstated assumptions about causal structure or event identity conditions that are implicitly grounded in assumptions about the causal structure of the very case at hand. The second habit must be guarded against. The trouble is, as we shall see, that it is not always obvious when such assumptions are being made, for they can simply appear to be innocuous assumptions that subtly guide decisions about which event counts as a counterpart, or which sort of intervention to perform, or which sort of situation is chosen as a case study. Such assumptions need to be ruthlessly hunted down and exposed, for they threaten the viability of any account that claims to give ontologically reductive conditions for causation. Make no mistake: such assumptions are perfectly fine when explaining a causal theory or limning the causal features of an example that illustrates a causal feature. But the assumptions can be objectionable when relied upon as part of a reductive account, for if a theory is to reduce causation to something more fundamental, then we must ensure that causal facts are not part of the reductive ontological base.

Moreover, such assumptions prevent the reductive theory from performing one of its most valuable tasks: forming part of the arsenal that we can use to attack a black-box case in order to determine, given some fundamental ontological structure, what causes what. If we don't know what causes what in a particular case, we need the theory to be able to tell us whether the ontological structure exhibited by that case is causal structure. In chapter 3, we will look at work by Lewis and Yablo that makes just this sort of objectionable causal assumption, with consequent implications for their proposals.

A theory that does not claim to be completely reductive has problems with black-box cases unless it has a fail-safe method for marking off known causal structure from unknown causal structure. For we can be mistaken about the overall causal structure of a case when we only have access to part of the structure of events, since embedding a partial structure of events in a larger structure can dramatically change our judgments about the overall causal pattern. This will be demonstrated in chapters 4 and 5 when we discuss omissions and transitivity. Causal modeling accounts based on structural equations and other dependence-based accounts of causation are particularly vulnerable to this sort of problem.

The third sort of bad philosophical habit is the conflation of different sorts of "pragmatic" moves one can make when constructing a model of causation. One sort of familiar, perfectly justifiable pragmatic move is familiar from Mackie (1965), where we gloss certain events or other features of a case as part of the background context. Take a case where lightning strikes a barn, causing a fire. It seems perfectly right to hold that the lightning was a cause of the fire and that the oxygen in the air was not, for the oxygen was simply part of the background causal conditions needed for the fire to occur. Of course, if we changed the explanatory context, say, to one where a elementary school science teacher is lecturing her students on how combustion occurs, it could be perfectly right to say that the presence of oxygen was a cause of the fire. The change in context moves an event from the background into the foreground, hence changing what counts as an appropriate or correct causal explanation of the case.

The important distinction here is between explanation and ontology. Pragmatics applies to successful communication and thus to explanation, not to ontology. While changing contexts can change what we should use in an explanation, and so changes explanatory salience, it does not change the basic causal facts. In our example of the fire, no matter what the context, the domain of causal facts includes all the causal facts (e.g., the fact that oxygen is among the causes of the fire), whether or not it is always explanatory or contextually appropriate to refer to some of these facts. The pragmatic move effectively restricts the quantifier relative to different contexts. It does not change what exists.

An interestingly different approach, that we think is misleading to label as "pragmatic", takes causation to be relative in the way that velocity is relative: the basic causal facts are understood to involve relations to states of affairs as part of their constitutive structure. This in no way makes what the causal facts are into a merely pragmatic affair. (One could understand some of the contrastive approaches to causation in this light.)

Neither the relatively uncontroversial explanatory pragmatic move, nor the controversial but interesting relativist (not pragmatic in our sense!) approach to causation, should be conflated with a much more controversial sort of pragmatic move which takes pragmatics to apply to ontology, and uses pragmatic contexts to change the causal facts. Such a move would, for example, make it the case that the existence of the fundamental causal facts—as opposed to whether and how we pay attention to them—were somehow indexed to pragmatic contexts. On this sort of pragmatic view, one could take the ontological causal status of the presence of oxygen and any other basic causal facts to ontologically depend in part on the explanatory or theoretical context in question.

While such a view is certainly coherent, it is clearly a mistake to think that causal modeling or other causal theories built on such a premise could have widespread application in the natural or social sciences, or even in legal or historical narratives that take themselves to be making factive causal claims. For what value could such a model have for any approach that laid claim to describing the real causal structure of the world? For example, how could such a model have acceptable policy implications? To look at an example, consider recent sociological research suggesting that female applicants whose personal details suggest they have children are less likely to be offered job interviews, are ranked lower in competence, and are held to a stricter performance standard than male applicants with identical applications (Correll et al. 2007). Different assumptions might create different contexts that allowed for different sorts of "interventions" to be evaluated. But if these interventions gave us counterfactual scenarios that suggested that, say, being female and being involved in a school's PTA was not objectively a dependence-lowering event, then either the model is misrepresenting the facts or the causal fact of such discrimination does not exist in the way we think it must. Being able to make objective claims about the world is essential to the role such models play in science and in ways science is extended, e.g., to develop or encourage governmental and corporate policy.

Perhaps another sort of approach, which should also be distinguished from the pragmatic moves described above, could take structural facts about counterfactuals to be objective facts about dependence relations in the world, but relegate *causal* facts to the realm of the merely pragmatic or human-interest-dependent.[18] Such an approach should be considered as an interesting and rather promising contender, as long as one is clear about how one's pragmatism or relativism does not threaten the sorts of factive claims about objective causal dependence we want to make in the natural and social sciences.

In any case, for reasons like these, when pragmatic moves are made, one must be clear about which sort of pragmatic move one is endorsing, and must also use caution when modifying or constructing a causal model and performing interventions. Unless one is explicitly setting aside the possibility that one's view is making objective claims about the world, and (not or!) one is also explicitly setting aside the possibility of implications for reductive metaphysics, one cannot simply claim, without argument, that some ways of intervening are acceptable while others are not, nor can one simply claim that any old intervention is acceptable as long as it is done relative to some sort of context. Moreover, if we are developing a view that is supposed to show us how to uncover the causal structure of a real-world case where we don't know what causes what, we need rules for intervening, for assigning values to variables and for changing contexts, where such rules do not assume that we have antecedent knowledge of the causal structure in question.

Again, some causal modeling theorists face explicit problems here, since their theories underspecify the rules for determining causal structure, yet they take themselves to be providing a methodological underpinning for understanding and developing certain sorts of "black box" causal claims in the natural and social sciences. Don't get us wrong—causal modeling accounts are of significant value, when used according to instructions, and they can provide important methodological underpinnings. But these accounts do not always give us as much information about the objective causal structure of a case as some seem to think—and when they are employed without appropriate constraints, their warranties are invalid.

One final way in which we might have different fundamental causal claims in different contexts is less destructive. There seem to be certain sorts of cases in which the objective causal structure of the cause seems to change depending on which features of the case we attend to. We have in mind certain sorts of difficult cases involving omissions and transitivity,

---

[18] Thanks to Christopher Hitchcock for discussion of this possibility.

especially cases involving double prevention and seeming transitivity failure discussed in chapter 4. Here, we suggest, the problem is not with pragmatics, but rather involves a conflation of two different sorts of causal structure: causation by dependence and causation by production. It really is the case that relative to certain features of the case, C causes E, but relative to some other features of the case, C does not cause E, but this is because C produces E, even if E does not depend on C (or vice versa). Such cases do not threaten the idea that there is an important distinction to be made between explanation and context-independent causal structure. Rather, they highlight the importance of distinguishing two different kinds of context-independent causal structure.

What we will take up next are the rules that we think should be followed in constructing a suitably reductive and suitably ontological account of causation.

3.2 The Book of Rules

Five of the most important rules will be described here.

3.2.1 Rule one: "Thou shalt not smuggle the causal in with the basic."

A traditional conceptual analysis of causation cannot make use of explicitly causal concepts, such as the concept of "intervention" or "manipulation." In a similar fashion, an ontological reduction cannot successfully reduce causal facts to ontologically more basic facts if those facts include causal facts. This is obvious. It should be equally obvious that one cannot use in one's account notions or facts that are merely implicitly or indirectly causal.

Sometimes transgressions of this rule can be subtle. Suppose you think that causal facts are to be analyzed as instances of "covering" laws. Does your analysis need, in order to be extensionally adequate, a distinction between causal and non-causal laws? If so, it violates rule one. Or suppose that your analysis makes use of counterfactuals—but you turn around and give these (nonreductive) causal truth-conditions. We will periodically have occasion, in what follows, to highlight points at which an account undercuts its reductive aspirations in just this way.

3.2.2 Rule two: "Thou shalt not be metaphysically extravagant."

Even if you avoid circularity, you can still undercut the explanatory value of your account of causation by characterizing the ontologically basic facts that serve as its ingredients in too metaphysically extravagant a fashion. Example: Suppose your account accommodates causation by omission. But it does so in part by positing a special kind of "negative" event in Meinongian style. Thus, when Billy's failure to water Suzy's plants causes their death, that is in virtue of a relation between one such negative event (Billy's failure to water the plants) and another, more prosaic event (the plants' death). Negative events must not, you insist, be identified with ordinary, "positive" events. You proceed to construct a Grand Metaphysical Theory, in order to answer such questions as these: Where do they take place? How long do they last? When are they identical to or distinct from one another? What are their parts?

We think that, quite regardless of how clever you are in constructing your theory, something has gone wrong. You started with something metaphysically prosaic, and ended up trying to illuminate its nature by appeal to something else that is far too metaphysically extravagant. Now, what counts as metaphysical extravagance is to some extent relative to a domain of enquiry and to some extent a matter of taste. Still, we think that in the context of contemporary discussions of causation, the standards are reasonably high. Here is a good rule of thumb: the basic ontology needed for causation should not exceed that needed for supervenience on the fundamental truths of physics. This rule of thumb strikes us as especially appropriate, given that one of the aims of an ontological reduction of causation is to produce something useful to, and illuminating of, scientific practice. (But don't misunderstand us: there might be quite a lot of basic ontology needed for supervenience on the fundamental truths of physics. This is not some sort of strict naturalistic constraint.) As we will see, even with this relatively generous interpretation of the rule, we will come across several examples of accounts that fail to follow this rule as well as we would like.

3.2.3 Rule three: "Thou shalt not rely upon explanatorily idle notions." A notion is idle in our sense if, in order to reduce or to fully explicate it, one would have to appeal to machinery that would already be sufficient to analyze causation—to analyze it just as well or even better—without any detour through the notion in question. Suppose you think that what it is for C to be a cause of E is for there to be some law that "covers" C and E, under suitably chosen descriptions. C is an F-event, E is a G-event, and E is R-related to C; and there is a law that says that every F-event is followed by a G-event R-related to it: *that* is the kind of "coverage" that your account takes to be necessary and sufficient for causation. Fine. But the "law" in question is almost certainly not a law of fundamental physics. (Suzy's throw caused the bottle to break. What was the "covering" law? Presumably, something like this: every throw in such-and-such circumstances is followed by damage with such-and-such features. That's not a law of fundamental physics.) So you will, at the end of the day, need some account of what it is for this kind of "higher-level law" to obtain. Imagine that you provide an account in terms of certain kinds of counterfactuals—and that it is clear on inspection that you could have applied those counterfactuals directly to the analysis of causation. Then you will have broken rule three.

3.2.4 Rule four: "Thou shalt not be an ontological wimp."   One way to avoid breaking any of the foregoing rules is to say very little. If ontological reduction is genuinely one's aim (as opposed, say, to the mere necessary connection discussed in §3.1.1), then all one gains by saying very little are gains of theft over honest toil.

There is a straightforward way not to be an ontological wimp: show, explicitly, how facts about causation are grounded in facts about fundamental physical states, together with facts about the fundamental physical laws governing their evolution. Granted, that's a tall order. But keeping it firmly in mind, if only as an ideal, helps guard against the overly cavalier use of unexplained concepts that will occasionally be witnessed in the accounts we discuss.

There is a second way to be an ontological wimp: appeal, in one's reduction, to facts too specific to one's own world. Now, we need to be a little careful here. It's not that we think an account needs to be in the business of issuing verdicts about any old conceivable situation that some philosopher can cook up. The literature (including some of our own contributions!) occasionally likes to speculate about the causal structure of worlds in which magical spells can act across a temporal gap, or in which there is backwards causation, etc.; part of the lesson of the little case study concerning the direction of time rehearsed in §3.1.4 was to remind us that it is far from obligatory for an ontological reduction to extend its scope so far. So an otherwise high-quality account that cannot, alas, say anything coherent about backwards causation and other esoterica should not, for that reason, lose our respect. Still, causation is a generic enough relation (and our corresponding concept of it is broad enough) that tying a theory of it too closely to facts peculiar to our actual world manifests a failure of nerve. Accounts that do that should lose our respect.

3.2.5 Rule five: "Thou shalt not enshrine intuitions." We think it is important to take intuitions very seriously, and we will do so throughout this book, paying special attention to places where our intuitions are in tension, since we take intuitions to be important guides to what we think we know about ontological structure, and the existence of said tensions indicate the need for further analysis.

But intuitions must be used with care. Part of the issue here concerns our newfound methodological clarity about the project. Given our reductive project, we must be clear about when we are drawing on these intuitions and what sorts of causal information we may and may not rely on when making intuition-based assessments. And given that we are not performing a conceptual analysis of our folk concept of causation, which intuitions we take seriously will depend on the sort of project we are tackling. Especially now that the project is ontological reduction instead of old-style conceptual analysis, it is no longer acceptable to simply claim, as Lewis did, that "If an analysis of causation does not deliver the common-sense answer, that is bad trouble."

But there is another point in play. Suppose you are interested in what grounds the direction of time. Someone comes along, insisting that it cannot be grounded in the direction of global entropy increase, because such a view fails to do justice to her intuitive conviction that time genuinely passes. Or suppose you're curious about what it is for an object to be solid. Someone comes along, insisting that there are in fact no solid objects, since atomic theory shows that most of the things we mistakenly take to be solid are composed largely of empty space—and it is intuitively clear that if an object is solid and occupies a certain region R of space, then for any subregion of R, some part of that object occupies that subregion. What should you think?

In both cases, you should reflect on whether intuition has been set up as an arbiter of questions it may not be competent to judge. Granted, when investigating some aspect of the ontological structure of the world, it is hugely important to pay attention to ordinary intuitions as a valuable source of clues for where to look. But the process of theorizing can also yield ample opportunities for rejecting some of these intuitions as misguided (though it can often help to supplement the theory in question with an explanation for why we were so easily led astray; see Paul 2010*c* for a discussion of the psychology that may underpin experience of temporal passage).

This methodological point is obvious in the case of the direction of time or the nature of solidity. Thankfully, the literature on causation is beginning to incorporate it as well, although we think more attention to the empirical psychology of causal judgments is in order.

So while we should let our intuitions play an important role in the development of an analysis of causation, in the end, they must be taken as defeasible. If your analysis flouts some clear and firmly held (nonreductively respectable) intuition, while you should certainly worry that your analysis has missed something important, you should not immediately assume that your analysis has been refuted—especially if it does a better job of capturing its subject, all things considered, than its competitors.

3.3   The accounts reconsidered

We are now in a good position to reconsider the accounts sketched in §2. We'll highlight just a few of the most important issues.

3.3.1   Regularity accounts and laws of nature   Recall that we distinguished two varieties of regularity account. One takes as its key idea that for C to cause E is for these events to be covered (perhaps under appropriate descriptions) by a suitable law. The other says that C must belong to a set of conditions minimally sufficient for E. The second idea brings laws in only indirectly, to say what "sufficient" means. And, as we saw, the laws brought in could simply be the laws of fundamental physics.

What about the first idea? A dilemma confronts it. Maybe the covering laws are supposed to be fundamental laws. But these laws relate, in the first instance, complete physical states of the world to subsequent complete physical states. We will search in vain among them for laws that will explicitly "cover" any but an exceedingly narrow range of causal phenomena. Suzy throws a rock at a bottle, shattering the bottle; are we to suppose that there is always some way of describing her throw and the shattering such that, relative to these descriptions, the relation between the two events can be seen as an instance of some fundamental law? On the other hand, maybe the laws are the far-from-fundamental laws of the special sciences. But then the account will almost certainly flout one or more of our rules. It might flout rule one by taking the "laws" simply to be certain kinds of causal generalizations. Or rule two, by treating them as *sui generis*, and irreducible to more basic physical laws. (Cartwright 1999 seems to have a view that is something like this.) Or rule three, by analyzing these laws in counterfactual terms themselves adequate to analyze causation. Or rule four, by saying nothing about what these laws come to (Maudlin 2004, though in other respects quite brilliant, is an example).

We think the best way to avoid the dilemma is to abjure the style of regularity account that gives rise to it; that is why we favor, as a more interesting and fruitful approach, the second of the two ideas sketched in §2.1, and we will focus on the minimal sufficiency version of a regularity account in the chapters ahead.

3.3.2 Truth conditions of counterfactuals   A successful account of causation cashed out partly or wholly in terms of counterfactuals needs a successful account of counterfactuals. (Note that this point applies not merely to the accounts sketched in §2.2, but also to the "minimal sufficiency account" sketched in §2.1.) Moreover, such an account must be reductive: our account of counterfactuals cannot itself be cashed out in nonreductive causal terms. So not all counterfactual treatments of causation will be suitable candidates. For example, Woodward's (2005) nonreductive approach will not meet these standards (§3.1.1). One might think that there is not far to look—Lewis's oft-cited (1979) analysis aims to provide just what we need. But there are serious problems with Lewis's view.

Let's first recall what Lewis's analysis says about a simple counterfactual of the form "if event C had not occurred, then event E would not have occurred." The basic idea is, by this point, familiar. Assuming that C and E in fact occur, we evaluate this counterfactual by moving to a possible world with the following features: up until shortly before the time of C's occurrence, its history is perfectly qualitatively identical to the actual history. And then a "miracle" occurs—a violation of the actual fundamental laws of nature (though, obviously, not a violation of the laws that hold in the counterfactual world itself). Post-miracle history at the counterfactual world unfolds perfectly in accordance with the actual laws. The miracle should be as small and as inconspicuous as possible, subject to the requirement that it throws history off course enough to make it the case that C does not occur. The counterfactual is true, finally, just in case E also fails to occur.

We think that this is close to the account of the truth conditions for counterfactuals that a philosopher should endorse if she wants to give an ontological reduction of causation in terms of counterfactuals. But it's not quite right, and, more importantly, the motivations behind it strike us as deeply flawed. To clarify all this, let's look a bit more deeply into what Lewis took himself to be trying to accomplish in providing truth conditions for counterfactuals, and why he thought these truth conditions would take the form of the foregoing "small-miracles recipe" for the specific sorts of counterfactuals that appear in his analysis of causation.

Obviously, one of his aims was to meet the needs of his counterfactual analysis of causation, and to do so in a suitably reductive manner (so that the proffered truth conditions for counterfactuals did not themselves make use of any causal notions). But he also took on board, more or less explicitly, three additional constraints:

First, he took it for granted that his truth conditions should be general purpose, and not simply tailored to the kinds of counterfactuals needed in his analysis of causation. Thus, these truth conditions should be able to handle sentences such as "if kangaroos had no tails, then they would fall over" and even "if gravity worked by an inverse-cube law, planetary orbits would still sweep out equal areas in equal times."

Second, he took for granted that the proposed truth conditions should fit within a general framework of similarity semantics for counterfactuals. That is, we start with the assumption that the right form for the truth conditions for sentences of the form "if A were the case, then B would be the case" ("A $\rightarrow$ B" for short) is roughly as follows: among those possible worlds in which A is true, the one that is most similar to the actual world is one in which B is true.[19] The project then becomes to articulate the specific standards of similarity that our counterfactuals implicitly make use of.

Third—and rather too ambitiously—Lewis wanted an account of counterfactuals that would explain the asymmetry of time, in line with the idea that what distinguishes the future as such is that it counterfactually depends on the past, but not vice versa.

---

[19] We say "roughly" because there are complications if—as will often be the case—there is no uniquely most similar A-world.

Lewis managed to leverage these constraints into a specific standard for similarity; one that, no matter how much the cleverness of its construction may be admired, appears rather byzantine. Here it is: in selecting a most similar A-world, it is of first importance to avoid large, widespread miracles, of secondary importance to maximize the region of exact match of particular facts, of third importance to avoid small miracles, and of little importance to secure approximate match. So the general-purpose truth conditions are simply these: A → B is true just in case, among those possible worlds in which A is true, the one that is most similar to the actual world according to the foregoing standard is one in which B is true.

Let's consider how these truth conditions are supposed to yield the small-miracles recipe, for the specific case of conditionals of the form "if event *C* had not occurred, then event *E* would not have occurred." Suppose, for example, that at noon, Suzy throws a rock, which strikes a bottle a few seconds later, breaking it. Consider all those possible worlds in which Suzy does not throw a rock at noon. In some of them, the actual laws are not violated. But then—given that these laws are presumed to be two-way deterministic—these are worlds whose histories never exactly match the actual history. So, according to the official standard, they are too dissimilar to actuality to be relevant. Now, it is obvious that none of these no-throwing worlds can have histories that perfectly match the actual history, since what occurs in them at noon must differ from what actually occurs at noon. But they might match perfectly up until shortly before noon, or from shortly after noon onward, or both. Lewis claims, plausibly enough, that it would take only a small miracle to get a world of this sort: a few neurons in Suzy's brain misfire, so that she decides not to throw, etc. But it would take a massive miracle (or what comes to the same thing, a multitude of small miracles) to get a world of the sort that fails to match actual history only around the time of Suzy's throw. For while a small miracle might throw things off course just enough to get her not to throw, it would take a massive cover-up to erase all the traces of her not throwing, and make the world unfold exactly as if she had thrown. And that is because of what Lewis thinks are de facto features of the history and laws of our world, which guarantee that events in our world typically produce a multitude of traces of their occurrence towards the future, but not towards the past. It is these traces that would have to be mimicked, in order to get perfect match towards the future. Thus, we are supposed to have derived, as an extremely reliable heuristic, the small-miracles recipe for evaluating causal counterfactuals. Along the way, we get an argument for why, in worlds like ours, the future typically counterfactually depends on the past, but not vice versa.

But however influential, the account is wholly unsatisfactory. Here are three serious problems. First, Lewis has overlooked the possibility that some of the worlds in which Suzy does not throw at noon are ones that perfectly match actual history from a time shortly after noon and onward, but fail to match it beforehand. Adam Elga (2000) has argued decisively that given what we know about thermodynamics and statistical mechanics, there will almost certainly be such worlds. That result completely undercuts Lewis's claim to have shown where the asymmetry between past and future comes from. Second, the standard of similarity between worlds that is supposed to yield the small-miracles recipe seems far too convoluted not to be viewed as ad hoc and arbitrary. Among all the standards of similarity that we might have hit upon to govern our use of counterfactual conditionals, what could explain our choice of this one? (See Horwich 1993 for a forceful presentation of this objection.) Third, the small-miracles recipe almost always produces a gap between the time of occurrence of the miracle in the counterfactual world, and the time of the event in question. Lewis sees this "transition period" as unavoidable:

> We need the transition period, and should resist any temptation to replace [it with] . . . abrupt discontinuities. Right up to t the match was stationary and a foot away from the striking surface. If it had been struck at t, would it have traveled a foot in no time at all? No; we should sacrifice the independence of the immediate past to provide an orderly transition from actual past to counterfactual present and future. (Lewis 1979, pp. 39–40)

But that means that by his own lights there will be counterfactual dependence of the immediate past on the present. In that case, won't the small-miracles recipe, together with the principle that counterfactual dependence suffices for causation, guarantee that there is loads of backwards causation? Lewis is hopeful that the answer is "no," because the past-present dependence will be sufficiently indeterminate that we cannot say, of any event E in the recent past and any present event C, that if C had not occurred then E would not have occurred; rather the most that will be true is that if C had not occurred, then E might not have occurred (not a strong enough relationship to suffice for causation). But Woodward

(2005) argues persuasively that this response won't do. (As useful exercise, you might try to come up with examples that demonstrate Woodward's point.) Moreover having a transition period allows for the possibility of problematic "noise": all sorts of crazy things might happen during such a transition period, or might be caused by the changes wrought in the transition period prior to or simultaneous with the putative cause which would mess with the dependence facts we are trying to discover. So why have a transition period? Why should those of us whose reductive ambitions are focused on the causal, as opposed to a wholesale Lewisian reduction, endorse all the elements of the Lewisian pictures? (For example, one might accept primitive chances or suchlike, even if one wanted a perfectly reductive theory of causation.)

If our first interest is in the prospects for a counterfactual analysis of causation, then the right thing to do in response to these problems is not to try to fix Lewis's account, but rather to abandon it—and more to the point, to abandon the pretensions to providing truth conditions for counterfactuals that will simultaneously serve the needs of a theory of causation and meet Lewis's additional constraints. It should not be thought that abandoning these pretensions comes at any cost, or is any occasion for disappointment. Remember that what we are aiming at is ontological reduction. We are not trying to uncover the structure of our ordinary concept of causation (except insofar as doing so provides us clues as to where interesting ontological reductions might be found), nor are we trying to uncover the connections between this concept and our ordinary concept of counterfactual dependence. So we can, with a perfectly clear philosophical conscience, look for an account of the truth conditions of counterfactuals that tries to do nothing more than give us a useful tool in the construction of an account of causation, as long as it doesn't violate our rules, especially rule one. And once we limit our focus in this way, it seems to us that the needed account is not hard to find.

Here is the simple alternative to Lewis's account (adapted from Maudlin 2007a) that we have in mind. Suppose event C occurs at t, and event E occurs later. To evaluate "if C had not occurred, then E would not have occurred," we construct a counterfactual state of the world at time t as much like the actual state at time t as possible, save for the fact that C does not occur. Think of taking the actual time-t state of the world, and ringing carefully localized changes on it just sufficient to make it the case that

C does not occur. (An important refinement of this procedure will appear shortly.) We then evolve the resulting state forward in time, in accordance with the actual laws of nature. If the resulting history yields E, the conditional is false; otherwise it is true. That's the recipe—tailored, as you can see, to the kinds of counterfactuals needed in a theory of causation.[20] We don't try to display this recipe as an instance of some more general prescription for evaluating counterfactuals. Similarity enters in not as a relation between whole worlds, but as a relation between states of worlds at times. We don't try to get to the counterfactual state in which C fails to occur by way of some miracle that throws history off course—in fact, we don't care one whit where this state came from. (Note, however, that thinking in terms of such history-altering miracles might be a psychologically useful method for fixing attention on the appropriate counterfactual state; to this extent, the attractiveness of the small-miracles recipe makes sense.) And, finally, we don't try to squeeze out a story about the direction of time from our analysis of counterfactuals. (Nor even a story about the asymmetry of causation; more on this point in §4.2. Although we "evolve forward" we don't assume that this determines the direction of time or of causation.)

This alternative to the Lewis analysis is the one that we will make use of henceforth. Let's see it in action, applied to the example depicted in figure 1:

---

[20] Note that there is an issue here derived from statistical mechanics that we are overlooking. Consider a simple example. A gas is confined by a barrier to one half of a chamber, the other half of which contains a vacuum. Suppose we ask what would have happened if, at time t, the barrier had been removed. We would like to say that the gas would have diffused across to the other side of the chamber. And our recipe seems to guarantee this result: we construct a counterfactual state of the world at time t which is just like the actual state, save that the barrier is absent; evolving this state forward in time would seem to yield a future in which the gas diffuses. But that is not quite right. The more accurate picture is really this: There is not one single counterfactual t-state that meets our conditions, but rather a continuous infinity of such states, differing in minute and seemingly insignificant microphysical respects (in one, a certain gas molecule is moving with just this velocity; in another, it is moving with a slightly different velocity; etc.). But some of those states will be bizarre anti-entropic states, that yield forward evolutions in which the gas stays on one side of the partition. We know, on statistical mechanical grounds, that these bizarre states make up an astronomically tiny minority of all of the relevant counterfactual states. But we also know that they exist. So what we should really say is this: If the partition had been absent at time t, then, with a statistical probability vanishingly close to but not exactly equal to 1, the gas would have diffused across to the other side of the chamber. We will take it for granted henceforth that counterfactuals like this are good enough for the purposes of an ontological reduction of causation.

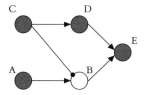

Figure 1

At time 0, neurons **C** and **A** both fire. To show that E does not depend on C, we simply change this time 0 state in a localized way, making neuron **C** dormant. The events that unfold are those depicted in figure 2:

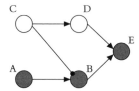

Figure 2

And to show that E in figure 1 does depend on D, we would simply construct a counterfactual state for time 1 in which neuron **D** is dormant, and everything else remains the same—so **B** is not firing, and the neurons are still connected together in the way depicted in figures 1 and 2. We don't need to worry about a transition state or other complications—since we simply don't care where this state came from. If you like, imagine that the counterfactual world just starts out in this state. It is then clear that the counterfactual state unfolds in such a way that **E** does not fire. What this result illustrates is that our simple alternative recipe for evaluating counter-factuals has the "non-backtracking" feature that, as we saw back in §2.2.1, it needs to have in order to have a chance of undergirding a successful account of causation.

3.3.3 Default and deviant states   We have one more serious issue to deal with, one that will likely arise for any account of counterfactuals. (It certainly arises both for Lewis's miracles-based recipe, and for our own "altered states" recipe.) Even the simplest of examples illustrates it. Let us reuse the example in which Suzy throws a rock at noon, breaking a bottle. It is utterly natural—and surely correct—to hold that if she had not thrown the rock, the bottle would not have broken (for remember that this is not one of those tricky cases in which some backup process aims to break the bottle as well). But then we must be supposing that, in the relevant counterfactual situation in which Suzy is not, at noon, throwing a rock at the bottle, she is not doing anything else that would lead to a bottle-breaking: she is not starting to run up towards the bottle to level a kick at it; she's not throwing some other object at it; she's not shooting her slingshot at it; etc.

Now, neither the small-miracles recipe that Lewis favors, nor the altered-states recipe we favor, automatically secures this result. Our own recipe instructs us to construct a counterfactual state of the world at noon by taking the actual state, and locally modifying it so that Suzy does not throw a rock. But—given the vast multitude of ways she could turn out to not be throwing a rock—these instructions simply underspecify what she is doing instead. And it would be foolish to appeal to similarity here, as if the right way to proceed is to have her do something very much like throwing a rock. The small-miracles recipe is, if anything, in even worse shape. Suppose that, shortly before noon, Suzy is deliberating about the best way to break the bottle. In fact, she settles on throwing a rock, rather than firing her slingshot (her second choice). If that is how things play out, then the smallest, most inconspicuous miracle that will throw history off course just enough to get her not to throw her rock will consist in a few subtle alterations of the neural underpinnings of her deliberations, alterations that lead her to fire her slingshot instead. So whereas our altered-states recipe wasn't fleshed out enough to yield a determinate result, Lewis's small-miracles recipe is sometimes guaranteed to yield the wrong result.

This problem has been noticed before—by Lewis himself. Here's a very pithy expression of it:

What is the closest way to actuality for C not to occur?—It is for C to be replaced by a very similar event, one which is almost but not quite C, one that is just barely over the border that divides versions of C itself from its nearest alternatives. But if C is taken to be fairly fragile [i.e., characterized by stringent conditions of occurrence], then if C had not occurred and almost-C had occurred instead, very likely the effects of almost-C would have been much the same as the actual effects of C. So our causal counterfactual will not mean what we thought it meant, and it may well not have the truth value we thought it had. When asked to suppose counterfactually that C does not occur, we don't really look for the very closest possible world where C's conditions of occurrence are not quite satisfied. Rather, we imagine that *C* is *completely and cleanly excised from history*, leaving behind no fragment or approximation of itself. (Lewis 2004*a*, p. 90; italics added)

We think Lewis's observations are right on target—up to the italicized portion, at which point they become mysterious. What exactly does such "complete and clean excision" consist in? Removal of the event by some sort of metaphysical scalpel? Leaving behind…what? The Void? (We should also note that it is unclear how Lewis's 2004*a* approach fits with his theory of event essences and causation in his 1986*a*.)

A much better view, if it can be had without violating rule one, is that for any given event, we work with an antecedently understood notion of a *default state* for the region in which the event occurs, or for the physical system or systems to which it pertains. Conceiving of the event as one among various possible *deviations* from that default state, we answer the question, "What would have happened, had that event not occurred?" by returning the relevant region or system to its default state, holding the state of everything else fixed. It is in this way—and not by metaphysical surgery—that we can fill in the altered-states recipe for evaluating counterfactuals. Thus, the counterfactual noon-state we have in mind in the world where Suzy does not throw her rock is one in which she is standing idle, doing nothing.

It may be the case that any ontological reduction of causation that makes use of counterfactuals will need to deploy some distinction between default states and deviations thereof. That seems obvious in the case of Lewis's original analysis, though perhaps less so in the case of his influence analysis, and de facto dependence approaches. The need is even clearer in the case of our minimal sufficiency account—which, remember, analyzed what it is for a set of occurring events S, all occurring at time t, to suffice for some later event *E* by means of the conditional, "if only the events in S had occurred at t, then *E* would still have occurred." Clearly, understanding this conditional requires an understanding of what it comes to for nothing else to be happening at the relevant time—which looks to be the same as saying: everything else is in its default state.

Once we begin the process of distinguishing default from deviant states, we might also consider a contrastive approach to causation. On this view, causation is more than a two place relation: a cause *C* doesn't cause its effect *E simpliciter*. Instead, roughly, the view is that *C*, in contrast to some relevant alternative event C^*, causes E in contrast to some relevant alternative event E^*. We are not sympathetic to some of the claims about the advantages of this sort of approach made by adherents of constrastivism, since we think that all too often such advantages accrue merely by eliding an important distinction between causation and causal explanation, or by embracing an overly extrinsic approach to events (see chapter 5, §1.2).

That said, if a contrastive approach can give an account that respects our reductionist constraints, then we can see it as a member of the same class of approaches to causation that rely on a default–deviant distinction. If we have the ontological means to distinguish between default and deviant states, we should have the ontological means to distinguish between relevant and irrelevant contrast events. But, a warning!—the need to respect reductionist constraints seems to be one place where the contrastive account has trouble, at least, if we are not to count an infinity of merely extrinsically distinguished events as "relevant" alternatives to every cause and to every effect. A challenge for the contrastive account is to define, without relying on pragmatic notions and conflating causation with causal explanation, and without flouting rule one, an appealing theory of objective relevance.

At any rate, we won't argue more for an objective default–deviant distinction or engage further with the contrastivist approach here (though at various points in the chapters ahead, we will discuss additional evidence for the importance of some sort of default–deviant distinction and we will also discuss contrastive approaches to omissions and transitivity). For now, we'll simply note that a supplementary account of this sort of distinction may be a major piece of unfinished business for ontological reductions of causation that make use of counterfactuals, given that such an account needs to respect the reductionist constraints laid out so far. This is an area in which, at present, matters are very much (though see Maudlin 2004, Hitchcock 2007a, and Hall 2007 for some discussion and attempts to apply a default/deviant distinction, and see Hitchcock 1996, Maslen 2004 and Schaffer 2005 for influential defenses of contrastive theories). We will return to a discussion of the difficulty of developing an adequately reductive account of default and deviant conditions in chapter 4.

One final note. It seems to us that the widespread use of neuron diagrams is partly to blame for the fact that philosophical discussions of causation typically overlook the centrality of the default/deviant distinction. And that is because, in the case of neurons, it is so obvious as to escape notice what counts as the relevant default state: it is just the dormant state, that is, the state describable as "not firing." Having said that, it is also precisely an advantage of neuron diagrams that their simple character obviates the need for some sophisticated story about the default/deviant distinction. They thereby make it much easier to foreground a host of other important problems that have a completely different source. It is these problems that will be our main focus in the chapters ahead.

3.3.4 De facto dependence counterfactuals   So far we have seen that—modulo some lingering and perfectly legitimate concerns about the status of the default/deviant distinction—we have been able to give suitably non-causal truth conditions for one important kind of counterfactual. That covers a lot of territory. But not all of it. What about the sorts of counterfactuals needed in de facto dependence accounts? Recall the general form of these accounts: what it is for event C to be a cause of another event E is for it to be the case that, for some suitably chosen fact F about the given situation, if C had not occurred but F had still obtained, then E would not have occurred. We will consider in the chapters ahead how challenging it is, given our reductive constraints, to specify how the fact F to be held fixed is to be selected. Let us set that issue aside for now, and focus on the question of how, once F has been selected, truth conditions are to be given for this counterfactual.

Everything depends on the form that F takes. If it takes the right form, then truth conditions come easily, by way of a natural extension of our altered-states recipe. But if it takes the wrong form, then it remains entirely too obscure what these truth conditions are. We will illustrate these two possibilities by a pair of examples.

Start with the case where things work well. Consider figure 1 again. Suppose, as part of your de facto dependence account, you have identified the fact F to be held fixed as the fact that neuron **B** does not fire at time 1. Then it is easy to extend our altered-states recipe in a way that allows for the clean evaluation of the conditional "if **C** had not fired at time 0, but **B** had still failed to fire at time 1, then **E** would not have fired." We do so as follows:

First, focus on the actual time-0 state of the world. Locally modify it so as to make it the case that **C** does not fire (i.e., return **C** to its default state). Evolve the resulting state forward until time 1. The result is a state in which **B** is firing. Now make local changes to this state, so as to make it the case that **B** is dormant at time 1 (i.e., in the same state as it is actually in that time). Evolve this resulting state forward until time 2. **E** does not fire. So the conditional is true.

More generally, if we have a conditional of the form "if *C* had not occurred, but the fact F had still obtained, then *E* would not have occurred," and there is a non-arbitrary way to make the fact F obtain by locally modifying the state of the world at one or more times, then we can follow the same procedure. Modify the state of the world at the time at which *C* in fact occurs so as to make it the case that *C* does not occur; update in accordance with the actual laws; and make localized modifications along the way, in a non-arbitrary fashion, so as to guarantee that fact F still obtains. If the fact F simply consists in the occurrence or nonoccurrence of specific, localized events, then this will in general be straightforward.

So far, so good. Unfortunately, not every case will be like this. Here's another example that resists such a clean treatment: Suzy and Billy both throw rocks at the same bottle, but Suzy's gets there first, shattering it. If she had not thrown, then Billy's rock would have shattered the bottle a moment later. It is a commonplace among fans of the de facto dependence approach to causation to point out that Billy's rock never in fact strikes the bottle, and to go on to claim that the conditional that grounds the fact that it is Suzy's throw that causes the bottle to break is therefore this one: if Suzy had not thrown, and Billy's rock had still somehow failed to strike the bottle, then the bottle would not have broken. But we immediately run into trouble if we try to analyze this counterfactual in the way just indicated. The fact F to be held fixed is too indeterminately specified for us to be able to tell just which state of the world to locally modify so as to guarantee that this fact still obtains in the relevant counterfactual situation. Worse: some local modifications that might seem to fit the specification will give exactly the wrong result—for example, the local modification that puts the bottle into a shattered state before Billy's rock can reach it.

Notice that if we could make free use of causal facts about the actual situation, then we could, plausibly, provide a different and successful recipe for constructing the relevant counterfactual situation. For we could proceed as follows: first, identify all the causes of the bottle-shattering; distinguish these from other factors that are non-causes. Next, construct a counterfactual situation in which Suzy does not throw, Billy throws, but in which other forces are introduced—let us provide them with the convenient label

"God"—that make it the case that Billy's rock never strikes the bottle, but without in any way interfering with the processes that are, in actual fact, causally involved in the bottle-shattering. The generalization would be something like this: to evaluate the conditional "if event C had not occurred, but the fact F had still obtained, then event E would not have occurred," we construct a counterfactual situation in which C does not occur, and in which fact F is made to obtain by means of processes that have no causal influence on whether E occurs; if, in this situation, E does not occur, the counterfactual is true, otherwise false.

Clearly that response won't do, given the kind of account of causation we are after. But it is useful to put it on the table, as it allows us to rebut a style of defensive quietism about the problem of explaining de facto dependence conditionals that we have sometimes encountered (or at least heard muttered in the back of the seminar room). According to this defense, we fluent speakers of English have a clear enough intuitive sense of what is required in order for a de facto dependence conditional to be true, so it is not really necessary to provide explicit truth conditions for these conditionals. But even if it is correct that we all have such a clear intuitive sense (has anyone checked?), it is all too plausible that it is founded on the application of something like the causally loaded truth conditions just sketched. Perhaps that's wrong. But to show it is wrong, you would presumably need to supply non-causal truth conditions—in other words, you would need to directly respond to the challenge we raise in this section.

3.3.5 Transference accounts   While we will treat transference accounts as live options, and will discuss advantages and disadvantages of them at various points throughout the remainder of this essay, we would like to register what we believe to be two very serious complaints. These problems are not tied to any particular example, but have much more to do with a failure to abide by the methodological precepts that we think should guide philosophical inquiry into causation; hence the reason for including this discussion in this chapter.

First, transference accounts seem to suffer from a surprising lack of ambition. (Cf. our rule, "thou shalt not be an ontological wimp.") Even if these views correctly describe the actual world, surely there could be worlds with laws that don't single out anything as a "conserved" quantity—more generally, that do not describe the transfer of anything physically fundamental.

Consider, for example, a world described in Maudlin (2004) that operates on principles akin to those at work in Conway's game of "Life": space is divided up into discrete cells, each of which can be either occupied or unoccupied; time is divided up into discrete moments; the pattern of occupation of the cells at one moment is lawfully and deterministically fixed by the pattern of occupation of the cells at the prior moment. There seem to be causal relations in such a world, and, importantly, we are perfectly capable of recognizing them. It is a mark against transference accounts that they can have nothing to say about why this is so.

But there is a more serious problem. Let us illustrate it by means of our example of Billy, Suzy, and the bottle. Suzy's throw is a cause of the bottle's shattering and Billy's is not. Can a transference account illuminate why this is so? You might think so. After all, it is Suzy's rock, and not Billy's, that transfers momentum or energy to the bottle, isn't it? To wit, consider what Ehring says about such cases:

Causal ancestry is determined by the origins of the energy/momentum manifested in the effect. A preempting cause is distinguishable from a preempted cause in virtue of the fact that the energy/momentum of the effect-event is traceable back to the preempting cause-event, but not to the preempted cause-event. (Ehring 1997, p. 45)

Is this the right way to analyze the problem? Unfortunately, no. Such an analysis relies on too soft a focus. Consider that Billy's rock, as it flies through the air, pushes air molecules ahead of it, and that some of these hit the bottle before Suzy's rock strikes it. We can, for that reason, credit Billy's throw with initiating a process that transfers energy, momentum, or indeed any other candidate quantity to the bottle. That is, whatever the stuff is whose transfer to the bottle makes it the case, according to a transference account, that Suzy's throw causes the bottle to break, it seems that we can find that stuff transferred to the bottle by Billy's throw as well. This creates trouble for the transference theorist, whose view seems to entail that "[i]f there is a transfer from both the main and the alternate lines, then there is simply no preemption, but only two lines of partial contributing causes" (Ehring 1997, 45).

Now, what one obviously wants to say is that whereas Billy's throw might transfer momentum (for example) to the bottle, it does not transfer enough to make the bottle shatter. So the limited amount of momentum Billy's throw transfers is not sufficient to render it causally relevant to the breaking. That is perfectly correct, but what transference accounts fail to do, as far as we can tell, is to provide any illumination about why it is correct. What's more, it is fairly obvious where such illumination should come from. We might, for example, focus on the fact that the breaking does not counterfactually depend on the transfer of such a small quantity of momentum (whereas, by contrast, it does depend on the transfer of the larger quantity of momentum that resulted from Suzy's throw); or we might focus on the fact that the transfer of the smaller quantity is not sufficient in the circumstances for the shattering (whereas the transfer of a larger quantity is). That is, we would focus precisely on the kinds of counterfactual and minimal sufficiency relations that counterfactual and updated regularity accounts place at center stage.

This sort of problem is going to be ubiquitous (unless, perhaps, we choose to restrict our attention to causation among the most microphysical events we can find). A certain confusion can make it difficult to spot. Suppose for example that you drink coffee, and a little while later become jittery as a result. It does not seem promising to try to illuminate this causal process by focusing merely on the transfer of energy, momentum, charge, or any other fundamental physical quantity from the drink to your body, or by searching for tropes that pass from the coffee to your body. And it won't help to, say, focus on the micro-constituents involved and the relations among them. Perhaps we can get a better scientific understanding of ordinary causal processes if we analyze their micro-constituents and the relations among them. But this fact alone wouldn't support a philosophical account of causation that tries to appeal directly to the transfer of some fundamental quantities, unless in giving a scientific analysis of the coffee-drinking episode in terms of its micro-constituents, we are somehow able to single out for attention only a small number of those constituents as being the relevant ones. (We ignore the tannins in the coffee, and focus on the caffeine; we ignore the fact that drinking the hot coffee increases body temperature slightly, and focus on the interaction of the caffeine with neurotransmitters; etc.) A good philosophically reductive account of caus-ation should help us understand the principles at work in making those judgments of relevance that direct us toward correct scientific reductions, and must do so, of course, without incorporating implicit causal assump-tions. (See for example Strevens 2009, which clearly and explicitly incorp-orates counterfactual elements.) It fails if, instead, it simply tacitly relies on unexamined judgments of relevance.

In summary, it seems to us very likely that transference accounts can have a chance of working only if they incorporate the analytical tools—maybe counterfactual dependence, maybe some notion of minimal sufficiency—that can be independently used to provide an equally good, and perhaps even better, account of causation. What will really be doing the work will be those notions of counterfactual dependence or minimal sufficiency we described earlier. If so, pure transference accounts inevitably violate rule three ("thou shalt not rely upon explanatorily idle notions").

4 Topics not addressed in detail

There are a number of interesting and important issues intersecting with the metaphysics of causation that we do not have the space to address in detail in this guide. We discuss them briefly in this section, with pointers to some of the relevant literature.

4.1 The causal relata

Most analyses of causation take the fundamental[21] causal relata to be events, and as noted we will follow suit. But some disagree, arguing that the causal relata are states of affairs, facts, tropes or aspects (property instances).[22] And even if the majority view is right, it is another question—and one with profound ramifications for one's account of causation—what the right philosophical theory of events is. A successful theory should provide answers to four sorts of questions:

First, how are events to be individuated? If Sandy walks as she talks, and walks and talks as she thinks, are there three events in this spatiotemporal region (the walking, the talking and the thinking) or only one? Say there is but one, and you may end up attributing what will seem to be too many causal powers to a single entity (e.g., it seems that her walking makes her legs tired but does not make her hoarse, whereas her talking makes her hoarse but does not make her legs tired, etc.). Say there are many, and you

---

[21] We need some such qualification as "fundamental," since, for example, particulars can be causes—as when *Suzy* causes a window to break by throwing a rock at it. We will assume, with the majority, that her status as cause is somehow parasitic on her *throw's* status as cause. And her throw is an event.

[22] See for example Bennett 1988, Goldman 1970, Ehring 1997, Paul 2000, Mellor 2004.

owe an account—in this context, what is ultimately a non-causal account—
of what distinguishes them.

Second, under what conditions do two events fail to be wholly distinct?
We need this notion, as witness the oft-cited requirement that in order to
stand in causal relations, events must be "wholly distinct." Ignoring this
requirement will make almost any analysis vulnerable to trivial counterexamples. For instance, as part of Sandy's walking she must take a single
step. The step and the walk are not the same event; what's more, had the
walk not occurred, then, plausibly, the step would not have occurred. But
the walk does not cause the step; rather, it has the step as a part. (See Kim
1973 for discussion of related examples, and Lewis 1986a for responses.) The
standard solution is to say that these events are disqualified from standing in
a causal relationship because they are not wholly distinct, in virtue of their
mereological overlap. A good theory of events should make clear how it is
that they stand in this relation of overlap, and whether there are any other
relations in virtue of which events can fail to be wholly distinct.

Third, how encompassing is the category of "event"? For example, when
a vase is resting on a table at a certain time, does there occur at that time
an "event" of the table's being present where it is, which causes another
"event" of the vase's being present where it is? Or must events correspond,
rather, to genuine changes? Certainly our ordinary understanding of the
category of "event" does not take it to cover such things as mere "presences." On the other hand, it seems that a systematic theory of causation (i)
needs to recognize that such uneventful things as mere presences can stand
in causal relations, even to paradigm events (as when the presence of oxygen
is one of the causes of the match's lighting); and (ii) can best do so by
stipulatively extending the category of "event" to include them. (See
Thomson 2003 for a contrary view.)

Some authors (see, e.g., Lewis 1986a and Yablo 1992a) hold that a theory of
events should answer this fourth question: Which features are essential, and
which accidental, to any given event? This question seems particularly urgent
for any counterfactual analysis that requires us to evaluate counterfactuals of
the form "If event C had not occurred, then. . . ." To do so, we apparently
need to find the "closest" world in which C does not occur. And to do that,
we need to be able to distinguish worlds in which C occurs from worlds in
which it does not, but in which some other similar event does. Suppose Sandy
had talked very softly, instead of loudly, as she did; would that have been a

numerically different talking? We must, so the thought goes, know how to answer such questions, if we are to evaluate these counterfactuals.[23]

For reasons that we have already discussed (see §3.3.3), we think that this viewpoint, though widespread, is probably mistaken. To evaluate some counterfactual circumstance in which a given actual event C does not occur, what matters is knowing how to change the region in which C occurs to an appropriate default state. The alleged need to distinguish essential from accidental properties of events is a red herring. Still, we certainly do have here a fourth desideratum on a theory of events, which is precisely that it include a theory of the default/deviant distinction.

Although the literature provides several different theories of events, each of which answers at least some of these questions, there is nothing like consensus about which theory is correct, or which set of answers most desirable. We will offer no developed view here. Instead, in our discussion of examples, we shall assume that we can pick out and distinguish events in some relatively commonsensical way, and (except where noted) that it is clear enough what would have happened in the absence of some event. We will not adopt controversial theses such as the view that all an event's properties are essential to it, or that events must be individuated solely by spatiotemporal region, or that events should be individuated when they differ extrinsically. Where a particular thesis about events is relevant to understanding or resolving the example, we will discuss the issue in more detail. For a suitably varied sampling of philosophical accounts of events, see Lewis (1986a), Yablo (1992a), Bennett (1988), Lombard (1986), Davidson (1969, 1970), and the articles in Casati and Varzi (1996).

4.2 Causal asymmetries

Why is causation asymmetric? Why is it invariably the case that if C is a cause of E, then E is not likewise a cause of C? That is the central metaphysical question about causal asymmetry.[24] Answering it successfully is, in our

---

[23] This issue, by the way, is a prime example of one that is obscured by the use of "neuron diagrams": for it is quite natural—so natural as to require perilously little thought—simply to equate a counterfactual situation in which C (the actual firing of neuron **C**) does not occur with a counterfactual situation in which **C** does not fire. But these are not obviously the same; at the very least, it requires serious argument to show that they are. See Bennett 1988 for excellent discussion.

[24] There is an epistemological question as well: Why is it that observed correlations are often good evidence for common causes, but not common effects? See for example Hausman 1998.

opinion, a wide-open problem. We won't have much to say about this problem in what follows, and in fact we will even allow any account of causation to guarantee causal asymmetry by piggybacking on the direction of time, stipulating that C is a cause of E only if C precedes E (and likewise stipulating that there are no closed time-like curves)—although more on this in §4.4.

Still, it is important to be clear on how little is accomplished by such a stipulation. Suppose, for example, that we adopted Lewis's original analysis: causation is the ancestral of counterfactual dependence. And suppose we analyze counterfactual dependence by using the altered-states recipe presented in §3.3.2—but with an additional stipulation concerning time order. Thus, C is a cause of E just in case there is a possibly empty set of events $\{D_1, \ldots, D_n\}$ such that D_1 temporally follows and counterfactually depends on C, D_2 temporally follows and counterfactually depends on $D_1, \ldots$ and E temporally follows and counterfactually depends on D_n.

This analysis guarantees the asymmetry of causation (provided there are no closed time-like curves), and thus, in some very minimal sense, answers the question why causation is asymmetric. But that question is, of course, really a request for understanding, and we can see that none has been provided by simply reframing it.

To set this up, observe first that the altered-states recipe doesn't have any time order built into it. Suppose that event E precedes event C. If we want to test for temporally backwards counterfactual dependence of E on C, then we can simply modify the altered-states recipe in the obvious way: construct a counterfactual state of the world at the time t at which C in fact occurs by locally modifying the actual t-state so as to make C not occur (perhaps replacing C by some default state); then run the laws backwards, so as to fix the pre-t history that lawfully follows from our counterfactual t-state. If this is a history in which E occurs, then the counterfactual is false; otherwise true.

Now we can define a relation causation* in the obvious way: C is a cause* of E just in case there is a possibly empty set of events $\{D_1, \ldots, D_n\}$ such that D_1 temporarily precedes and counterfactually depends on C, D_2 temporarily precedes and counterfactually depends on $D_1, \ldots$ and E temporarily precedes and counterfactually depends on D_n.

Returning to our original question: Why is causation asymmetric? We gave a feeble answer: because causes precede their effects, and the relation of temporal precedence is asymmetric. To see just how feeble this answer is, we simply replace our original question by this one: Why isn't the relation of causation* just as important and central a metaphysical relation, for just the same reasons, as the relation that we have called "causation"?

It is perfectly obvious that we have made no progress in answering *that* question—and it is also obvious it is that question whose answer we were really after, in the first place.

Still, we are at least in a position to appreciate two very different forms that an illuminating answer might take. First, we might give an account of causation that can work in either temporal direction, but then argue on independent grounds that the backwards-pointing "half" of it is somehow uninteresting or unimportant, or at any rate is to be sharply distinguished from the forwards-pointing half of it. The example just given will serve, presented slightly differently: start by saying that C is a cause† of E just in case there is a possibly empty set of events $\{D_1, \ldots, D_n\}$ such that D_1 lies temporally between C and D_2, and counterfactually depends on C; D_2 lies temporally between D_1 and D_3, and counterfactually depends on D_1; ... and E counterfactually depends on D_n. Causation† is thus just the disjunction of what we called "causation" and "causation*." Nothing about the account of causation† guarantees its asymmetry.[25] We then distinguish the two subspecies of causation†—causation and causation*—as before. Finally, we argue that causation* is substantially different from causation for such-and-such reasons, reasons that make this relation unsuitable for the work that we expect from any relation that deserves to be called "causation."

What might such reasons be? A very good question, which we will mostly dodge, offering up just one speculative suggestion.

Suppose that events C and E are macro-sized events. Suppose C occurs at time t. Since C is macro-sized, there will invariably be many ways—likely a continuous infinity of ways—to construct a counterfactual t-state in which C does not occur. (Set the velocity of a certain particle to be just this, or just that, etc.) Suppose it turns out, on statistical mechanical grounds, that the overwhelming majority of these counterfactual t-states, when evolved forward in accordance with the actual laws, yield near-futures that are extremely similar to each other in macroscopic respects. Then if event E

---

[25] Though, as the reader may care to confirm, nothing about the account guarantees its symmetry, either.

is in the near future of time t, they will likewise yield futures that almost all agree on whether E occurs. But suppose the same turns out not to be the case about the near-past of t: modify the actual t-state one way so as to make C not occur, and you get one sort of history that would have given rise to that state; modify it in a very slightly different way, and you get a history that, in recent macro-respects, is extremely different. If all this is true, then it is plausible that the causal relations between C and later events will be plentiful and systematic enough to be interesting, whereas the causal* relations between C and earlier events will be arrayed in a scattered and unsystematic fashion. That might be reason enough for us to care much more about causation than causation*—justifying us in reserving the term "causation" only for the former relation. See Loew (forthcoming) for an interesting related proposal.

There is, finally, a second way we might try to answer our metaphysical question about causal asymmetry in an illuminating fashion, and that is to construct an account of causation founded on some other relation that has the needed asymmetry built into it. The truth conditions for counterfactuals that Lewis proposed—the ones that led to his small-miracles recipe—would have provided an example, had they been successful. For more recent and quite interesting attempts along these lines, see Albert 2000, Loewer 2007, 2012.

4.3 Indeterminism and causation

We have assumed that the fundamental dynamical laws are deterministic. But in fact it seems likely that our world is not governed by such laws; rather, the state of the world at a time, plus the laws, makes later states of the world more or less (objectively) probable. We could conclude that if so, then there is no causation—a bad idea. Or we could conclude that causation is compatible with indeterminism at the level of the fundamental laws.

Pursuing this latter option raises a number of difficult problems that have no clear analogue for the case of causation under determinism. Let's start by assuming that our laws are not merely indeterministic, but probabilistic, in the sense that they prescribe, for each moment of time, a probability distribution over the set of nomologically possible futures. Then there is one key feature of causation in such a probabilistic setting that lies at the heart of all of the novel trouble cases. To bring this feature into focus, consider the simplest possible system of neurons, shown in figure 4:

Figure 4

Suppose neuron **E** is a chancy neuron: it will not fire unless stimulated by **C**, but even if stimulated, it has some chance less than one of firing—say, 50 per cent. Figure 4 depicts a situation in which **C** fires and sends a stimulatory signal to **E**, whereupon **E** fires. Notice that a case like this poses no new trouble for a counterfactual analysis, nor for a transference account. For if **C** had not fired, then **E** would not have fired; and if the transference account can deal with the deterministic version of figure 4 by tracking the transfer of some appropriate quantity from **C** to **E**, then presumably it can deal with this probabilistic variant in exactly the same way. But a regularity account will need some amendment, since the occurrence of C is not, in any obvious sense, sufficient for E.

Still, we haven't gotten to the really interesting issue yet. To see what that issue is, let's take figure 4 to describe a more complicated physical setup. Think of neuron **E**, now, as inherently unstable, with some default probability of firing per unit time. More specifically, we will suppose that unless and until it is stimulated by **C**, neuron **E** remains in a "ground state" with the following feature: while in this ground state, its objective probability, at any time t, of firing within the next hour is 0.01. But if **E** receives a stimulatory signal from **C**, it transitions into an "excited state," and its probability of firing within the next hour shoots up to 0.99.[26]

Now suppose what happens is this: **C** fires and sends a stimulatory signal to **E**, which enters its excited state. A minute later, **E** fires.

A plausible and attractive causal gloss on this little history immediately comes to mind: precisely because C raises the probability of E by such a substantial factor, C should be counted as a cause of E. Similarly, if C fails to do so—or more decisively, if C lowers the probability of E—then C should not be counted as a cause of E.[27] (Maybe you disagree; if so, hold tight until

[26] There is a technical subtlety that we're trampling on here. What we should really say is that if **E** is in its ground state at t, and if the physical state of the world is such that there is no probability of an exogenous influence on **E** changing this state within the next hour, then the probability that **E** fires in this time interval is 0.01.

[27] Of course this can't be quite right, as examples of preemption (like figure 1), adapted to the indeterministic case, demonstrate. But it's enough for present purposes to work with the rough idea that in simple probabilistic cases, where nothing like preemption is going on, probability raising is both necessary and sufficient for causation.

§4.5.) Suppose we accept this gloss. That's probably the right thing to do; still, we thereby open the door to some novel problems. Here are a few of the more interesting ones.

First, we have the problem of fizzling. Consider figure 5.

Figure 5

Here, the fat arrow between **C** and **E** indicates that stimulatory signals sent by **C** are themselves probabilistic, having some chance of dying out before they reach **E**. In the given case, that is exactly what happens (as indicated by the partial filling in of the arrow). Still, the probability of such fizzling out is, let us suppose, extraordinarily low. What's more, **E** manages to fire even though the signal never reaches it. The upshot is that, at the time at which **C** fires, the probability that **E** fires is much higher than it would have been, had **C** not fired. So *C* raises the probability of *E* by a substantial amount. But for all that, *C* is quite obviously not a cause of *E*.

Figure 6 illustrates the second problem, which we might call the problem of ambivalent causes.

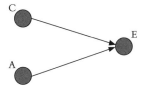

Figure 6

Here, **E** has no chance of firing unless it receives a stimulatory signal from either **A** or **C**. If it receives just one stimulatory signal, then it is certain to fire; but if, as in the events depicted in the figure, it receives two stimulatory signals, then its chance of firing is a mere 0.01. Nevertheless, in this case it does fire. Then we have an odd result: *A* and *C* are clearly symmetrically related to *E*; so if either is a cause of *E*, then surely both are. And, since *E* is clearly not *un*caused, and since *A* and *C* are the only candidate causes, it seems to follow that each is a cause of *E*. But each is also such that it substantially lowers the chance of *E*: if **C** had not fired, then the chance of

E would have been 1, and likewise for **A**. So we also have an argument that neither is a cause of *E*.

A lovely paper by Johann Frick (2009) introduces the third problem, which we will call the problem of aggregate effects. In figure 7, **C** is connected to 1 million other neurons, each of which has a default probability of firing of 0.9.

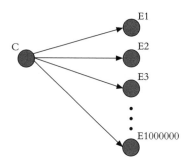

Figure 7

When **C** fires, it sends a weak stimulatory signal to each of these neurons, raising each one's probability of firing to 0.901. Suppose that what happens is that exactly 901,000 of the neurons fire. Here are some salient probabilistic facts: given that **C** fired, the probability that at least 901,000 of the neurons connected to it would fire was slightly greater than 0.5. If **C** had not fired, this probability would have been less than 0.0005. In fact, the probability would have been greater than 0.99 that not more than 900,700 of the neurons would fire. It seems clear, then, that **C** is causally responsible for at least some additional firings.[28] But, curiously, there is no firing such that *C* is causally responsible for *it*—since the probability raising that *C* creates is so slight.

These, and other fascinating problems, deserve much greater scrutiny. But we must bypass them, in part for obvious reasons of space, and in part because all of the issues we will discuss remain just as pressing when we shift our focus to indeterminism. But see Hitchcock (2004), Menzies (1996),

---

[28] As Frick notes, situations in which moral responsibility is involved evoke this judgment quite forcefully. Suppose that you are a polluter, recklessly dumping carcinogens into the environment. Suppose that as a result, each one of the million people living in a nearby city has a slightly increased probability of contracting a certain kind of cancer. Then you are morally responsible for at least some of the cancer cases that occur.

Kvart (2004), Ramachandran (2004), Schaffer (2000b), and Frick (2009) for sophisticated treatments.

4.4 Abnormal causation

In the normal case, a cause C will precede its effect E, and will be connected to E by a temporally or spatiotemporally continuous chain of intermediate causes. But perhaps abnormal causal relations are possible: perhaps causes can be simultaneous with their effects, or can come later than them; again, perhaps there can be "action at a temporal distance." We do not deny such possibilities, but we set them aside as special cases, likely needing special treatment.

It may not have escaped notice that our updated regularity account, i.e., our minimal sufficiency account, makes the asymmetry of causation parasitic on the asymmetry of temporal direction. As such, it provides no means for a causal analysis of temporal direction, and it appears to rule out backwards causation a priori. While that is certainly a problem, it is in fact not one that carries much dialectical weight. For accommodating backwards causation turns out to be difficult on any account of causation (or at least, any reductionist account; the non-reductionist who takes causation to be some kind of metaphysical primitive would, presumably, have no such problem). We omit a detailed discussion (but see Collins et al. 2004b). Very briefly, the problem for transference accounts is to explain, without resorting to causal notions, how it can be the case that the right stuff is transferred backwards in time; and the problem for counterfactual accounts is to give truth conditions for the counterfactual conditional that will apply in the right way to counterfactuals of the form "if C had not occurred, then (earlier) event E would not have occurred" (bearing in mind that only in exceptional cases will one want it to turn out to be the case that C and E both occur, that E precedes C, and that C is a cause of E—so the altered-states recipe discussed in §§3.3.2 and 4.2 won't do).

4.5 Anti-reductionism

The reductionist thesis that facts about what causes what are fixed, some-how, by the (non-causal) facts about what happens, together with the facts about the fundamental laws, has a great deal of intuitive appeal, and has served as a powerful guide for philosophical work on causation over the last

few decades. Predictably, it has also come under attack. Some anti-reductionists (e.g. Anscombe 1971) dispute the claim, familiar since Hume, that
causal relations are not observable, and take it that if they succeed in
establishing the observability of causal relations then they will have removed
one powerful motivation for reductionism.[29] Others (e.g. Tooley 1990)
argue on the basis of various thought experiments that causal facts do not
even supervene on facts about the laws plus what happens. Still others (e.g.
Cartwright 1983, 1999) launch a wholesale attack on the very concept of a
fundamental law.

The kinds of examples that draw forth anti-reductionist intuitions come
in many varieties, but here we will provide just one. We've seen it before, in
figure 4 in §4.3. This figure depicted a case in which events C and E occur,
and E had some non-zero chance of occurring without C. But C's occurrence significantly raised that chance. Cases like this strike many people
as simply underdescribed with respect to their causal features. They hold
that if events unfold as described, then, while it could be that C is a cause of
E—and while in fact this is the most likely state of affairs—it could also be
that C is not a cause of E. The idea seems to be that, since E had some
chance of occurring anyway, this might be just one of those cases—in which
case C gets no credit. Here for example is Armstrong:

A case that Lewis does not consider, but which brings out the strength of the
Singularist position here, is one where there are two possible probabilistic causes of
just one effect, and the chance of each possible cause being the actual cause is equal.
(Perhaps with a multiplication of the two chances giving the chance of an overdetermination.) Suppose that there are two bombardments of an atom, with the same
chance of the atom emitting a particle, which the atom duly does. Does there not
seem to be an objective question, which of the two bombardments actually did the
job? (Armstrong 2004, p. 450)

We think that Armstrong is confused (although the confusion is unques-
tionably seductive). Suppose the physical facts are as follows. Two sources
simultaneously bombard the atom. Given the fundamental physical laws, it

---

[29] The idea, we think, is that if causal relations are not observable, then there is a prima facie serious
problem about how we can come to know about them. The reductionist, at least, can hope to reduce this
problem to that of showing how we can come to know facts about what happens, and facts about what
the fundamental laws are. Some reductionists, of course, hope to make this second problem even easier
by reducing facts about the laws themselves to facts about what happens.

therefore has a 90 per cent chance of emitting a particle. It does so. If just one source had bombarded it, the chance of emission would have been the same; but if neither had, it would have been zero. If these physical facts are the only facts relevant to what causes what, then there can clearly be no distinction between a version of this case in which the first source causes the emission, and a version of the case—physically exactly the same!—in which the second source causes the emission.

Accordingly, the only way to make straightforward sense of Armstrong's reaction is to posit (as he is quite happy to do) a metaphysically primitive relation of causation, one that does not reduce to or supervene upon noncausal facts about what happens together with noncausal facts about the fundamental laws that govern what happens. While Armstrong is happy to accept this conclusion, we are not. Such metaphysical primitivism about causation carries no benefits beyond its ability to accommodate what strikes us as a naïve (even if intuitive) reaction to cases like figure 4. We emphasized in §3.2.5 that intuitions are important as guides or clues to where an interesting and fruitful ontological reduction might be found, but that in the end, they must be supported by the work done by one's overall theory. We think that, in that crucial respect, anti-reductionist intuitions about figure 4 and about other cases that populate the literature simply do not earn their keep.

At any rate, we will not delve further into these disputes, for the usual reasons of space—but also because we think that the reductionist position is really the one to beat. If a reductionist philosophical account of causation could be made to succeed—explaining our firm intuitive judgments in an elegant, theoretically well-motivated manner, and yielding a concept or concepts of causation with undeniable value—than the typical complaints of the anti-reductionists, inconclusive as they are, would seem to provide thin grounds for rejecting it. At the very least, even the most ardent anti-reductionist should agree that it is well worth investigating the prospects for such an account.

Let's start doing that now, in earnest.

3

Varieties of redundant causation

Take *redundant causation* to be a kind of causation where there is more than one event that is, in some sense, enough for the effect that occurs. In such cases, there can be, or can at least seem to be, competing candidates for the title of "cause." Problems involving redundant causation have been at the center of the most interesting and vigorous debates about how best to give a philosophical account of causation, since they bring out, in an especially pressing way, how difficult it can be to determine which events are the causes of an effect if the underlying causal structure of the case is not known.

In reviewing these debates, we will try to show how different kinds of redundant causation reveal deep tensions within many contemporary accounts of causation, and how inexorably the problem cases constrain the form of an account that can handle them. But even setting aside the aim of constructing such an account, we think the cases we will study are of enormous interest, since they highlight the ways in which we recognize and distinguish causal relations. Working through them with care is one of the most effective ways to become adept at drawing a range of careful causal distinctions.

1 Joint effects

Our first example concerns joint effects of a common cause. Though rarely mentioned as a variety of redundant causation, it fits our criteria well enough. While it poses no serious trouble for our candidate accounts, discussing it will allow us to undo a widespread misconception that counterfactual accounts can accommodate it much more easily than sufficiency accounts.

Consider figure 8:

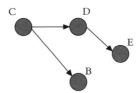

Figure 8

C fires, sending signals to **B** and **D**, both of which fire; **E** fires upon receiving the signal from **D**. *B* does not cause *E*. But in a sense, *B* is both necessary and sufficient for *E*: from a suitable specification of the circumstances, together with the relevant laws, it follows that **B** fires when it does iff **E** fires when it does (for **B** fires iff **C** fires, iff **D** fires, iff **E** fires). This observation has no special bearing on transference theories. (Perhaps *B* transfers some of the appropriate stuff to *E*, but if so this is just an instance of the more general problem for transference theories discussed in chapter 2, §3.3.5.) But the remaining accounts must find ways to accommodate it—ways, that is, to reveal how the admittedly tight ontological connection between *B* and *E* is nevertheless of the wrong type to count as causation.

Here is a red herring: in the events depicted in the diagram, *B* is not connected to *E* via any spatiotemporally continuous chain of events that runs solely from past to future. Altering that feature changes nothing of importance, as we can simply set things up so that neuron **B** is adjacent to neuron **E**, and fires immediately before it. So it cannot be the lack of spatiotemporal continuity that is making the difference here. Perhaps it is the lack of some other kind of physical connection; that, at any rate, is what transference theorists will say. But we think it is much more fruitful to look for a more abstract, structural feature of the relationship between *B* and *E* that goes missing. Counterfactual accounts and regularity accounts will give strikingly different diagnoses of this feature.

Counterfactual accounts will insist on a non-backtracking reading of the counterfactual that begins, "if *B* had not occurred . . . " (see chapter 2, §§2.2.1 and 3.3.2). In other words, we must not evaluate this conditional by working backwards and considering what, given the laws, would have to have been the case in order for **B** not to fire—for then we will reason that it would have to have been the case that **C** did not fire, hence that **D** did not fire, hence that **E** did not fire. Instead, we focus on the state of the world at the time of **B**'s firing, change it just enough to make it the case that **B** does not fire, and evolve the resulting state forward in accordance with the laws. As follows: the state evolves, and **E** fires. Hence E fails to depend on B; hence B does not come out (wrongly) as a cause of E. So the structural feature that goes missing is, quite simply, counterfactual dependence.

One might think that matters are not so happy for a regularity account. Isn't it a perfectly lawful regularity that if **B** fires at a certain time, then **E** fires shortly thereafter (cf. Davidson 1967)? Isn't it true that, for some suitably chosen fact F describing the circumstances of **B**'s firing, the fact that F obtains, and the fact that **B** fires, together with the laws, entail the claim that **E** fires—but F and the laws do not entail this claim by themselves (cf. Mackie 1965)? For some, these difficulties have long seemed decisive. (See for example Lewis 1973a.)

Thinking this way is mistaken. We can develop an account focused on lawful sufficiency that captures the spirit of a regularity account but has no difficulty distinguishing causes from joint effects of a common cause. Our minimal sufficiency account from chapter 2 (see §2.1) will serve our needs. Recall that on this account C is a cause of E iff C belongs to a set of contemporaneous events that is minimally sufficient for E; i.e., sufficient, but with no proper subset that is sufficient. And a set S of events occurring at some time t suffices for a (later) event E iff, were the events in S the only events occurring at t, E would (still) occur.

With this minimal sufficiency account in mind, let t be the time at which **B** and **D** fire, and consider the two relevant sets, $\{B\}$ and $\{D\}$. $\{D\}$ is clearly minimally sufficient for E, for if D alone had occurred at t, then E still would have occurred. $\{B\}$, equally clearly, is not: if B alone had occurred at t, then E would not have occurred. Where is the problem? Do not say: "The problem is that the counterfactual situations being considered violate the laws: for how (e.g.) could **B** fire at t without **D** also firing at that time?" There are two problems with this response. First, in the dialectical context—one in which regularity accounts are being considered as rivals to counterfactual accounts—the question applies equally well to the opposition (how could **B** fail to fire at t, without **D** also failing to fire?). Second, it applies poorly, since it is patently consistent with the fundamental dynamical laws at work here that, at t, (i) the four neurons be connected as shown, and (ii) only **D** (or only **B**) is firing. If you are having trouble seeing this, consider that the world could start out, at *t*, in just such a state.[1] And if it did, it would be perfectly obvious and determinate how it would evolve, in accordance with the dynamical "neuron" laws.

Why has the relatively trivial problem posed by cases of joint effects (sometimes called "the problem of epiphenomena") seemed so grave? We suspect the reason, as indicated in chapter 2, is that defenders and opponents of so-called regularity accounts have typically failed to distinguish the two quite distinct guiding ideas behind such accounts: one idea is that causation is somehow the instantiation of regularities; the other idea is that what is distinctive of the causes of some event is that they collectively suffice for it, without redundancy. Focus on the first idea, and you might—for good reason!—judge regularity accounts to be doomed:

It remains to be seen whether any regularity analysis can succeed in distinguishing genuine causes from effects, epiphenomena, and preempted potential causes—and whether it can succeed without falling victim to worse problems, without piling on the epicycles, and without departing from *the fundamental idea that causation is instantiation of regularities*. (Lewis 1973*a*, page 557; italics added)

But we need not burden a regularity account of causation with this "fundamental idea". If you jettison this requirement (as you should), and focus on the second idea, then, as we've seen, in short order you will have an account that handles the problem of joint effects just as easily as any decent counterfactual account. So we will focus on our minimal sufficiency account as the relevant version of a regularity account.

Let's summarize the key lessons that can be gleaned from cases like that depicted in figure 8. First, and most straightforwardly, they serve as a simple and vivid demonstration that correlation, no matter how robust and law-governed, is not the same as causation: firings of **B** may be ever so tightly correlated with slightly later firings of **E**, but no causal link connects the former to the latter. But, second, these cases leave it quite ambiguous what is the ultimate source of this difference between correlation and causation. For, while even modestly sophisticated counterfactual and regularity accounts can easily accommodate the distinction between causes and joint effects of a common cause on display in such cases, they do so in different

---

[1] Thanks here to Tim Maudlin.

ways. And nothing about the cases themselves suggests that one way is better, or less ad hoc, than the other.

This last point is all too commonly overlooked, especially in contemporary discussions of statistics and causation (see, for example, Pearl 2000). Consider a situation in which two "variables," A and B, are tightly correlated. Suppose there are two possibilities: A is a cause of B, or A and B are joint effects of a common cause. (We're being a bit loose here, assuming that there is some clean way to make sense of causal relations among variables.) What could the difference between these two possibilities consist in? A widespread suggestion is the following: if A is a cause of B, then "interventions" on A would lead to changes in B; if A and B are joint effects of a common cause, then this is not the case. The introduction of the technical notion of "intervention" notwithstanding, this is the counterfactual analyst's story about what distinguishes causes from joint effects. But there is a second option—one that, as far as this particular problem is concerned, is just as viable: if A is a cause of B, then A belongs to a collection of variables whose values non-redundantly suffice for the value of B, whereas if A and B are joint effects of a common cause, then this is not the case. As we have noted, while there is a counterfactual element embedded in this view in order to make the sufficiency notion suitably minimal, the addition of sufficiency may capture features of the causal relation that an analysis based only on counterfactuals cannot. (And it will need to do so if it is not to violate rule three; see chapter 2, §3.2.3.)

We will need subtler phenomena if we are to flesh out and properly assess the relative merits of counterfactual and minimal sufficiency approaches. On to more challenging cases.

2 Early preemption

There are several varieties of redundant causation where, intuitively, an actual cause C of some event E is accompanied by *backups*, poised to bring about E in C's absence. In the most well known sort of case—*early preemption*—a potential causal chain is interrupted by an alternative causal chain that brings about the effect. Figure 1 is our canonical example.

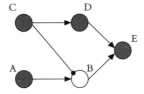

Figure 1

C is a cause of *E* and *A* is not. *C* is a *preempting* cause, *A* is a *preempted* backup.

As before, transference accounts confront no special difficulty in this kind of example. Not so, for regularity and counterfactual accounts. Although it is perfectly clear that *C* is a cause of *E* and *A* is not, simple versions of these accounts say otherwise. The simplest counterfactual analysis, which identifies causation with dependence, fails to count *C* as a cause of *E*: for if *C* had not occurred, *E* still would have occurred, caused by *A*. Simple regularity analyses, where *C* is a cause of *E* iff *C* (together with the laws) is sufficient (in the circumstances) for *E* are also inadequate: rightly counting *C* a cause, they also wrongly count *A* as a cause. Our minimal sufficiency account fares no better, at least when we focus on the time at which **A** and **C** both fire, since we find that {*A*} and {*C*} are both minimally sufficient for {*E*}.

Despite the superficial difference that the problem takes for counterfactual and for regularity accounts, at bottom it is really the same: these accounts fail to distinguish between genuine causes and idle backups, because their defining criteria treat them symmetrically.

What to do?

Let's start by quickly noting one thing *not* to do. A seemingly obvious solution is a non-starter in the context of an analysis of causation: individuate events in part by their causal origins. If the firing of **E** brought about by the preempting cause is numerically different from the firing of **E** that would have been caused by the preempted backup—because different in its causal origins—then the firing of **E** that actually (in the world of the example) occurs does in fact depend on the preempting cause, and the preempted backup does in fact fail to suffice for it. But such a strategy for addressing early preemption (and problems of redundant causation in general) is off the table in our reductive context of inquiry. If we are trying to construct an analysis of causation, we cannot assume that we can distinguish "ahead of time," as it were, the preempting cause of *E* (the *E* that actually occurs) from the preempted backup—yet that's exactly what we would need to do.[2]

2.1 Appealing to the transitivity of causation

A natural idea for handling early preemption comes from Lewis (1973*a*), and is built into the first of two candidate counterfactual analyses: insist that causation must be transitive, and secure this feature by identifying causation not with counterfactual dependence, but with the ancestral of counterfactual dependence. We then observe that in figure 1, E depends on D, and D on C. If it is not obvious that E depends on D, then remember the prohibition on backtracking: the counterfactual situation in which **D** does not fire is *not* one in which it fails to fire because **C** likewise fails to fire (hence: a situation in which **B** fires). It is, rather, one in which, inter alia, we hold fixed the non-firing of **B**.

Two quick observations. First, this approach makes transitivity a non-negotiable feature of the account—a fact which, as we discuss in detail in chapter 5, will lead to some grief. Second, it matters here that we have explicitly set aside cases involving action at a temporal distance. If such cases need to be covered, this revision to the counterfactual analysis will founder, for there may not be any events between the preempting cause and the effect for which stepwise dependence can be constructed: imagine, for example, that C somehow acts directly on E, across a temporal gap. Such cases can be thought of as far-fetched, though we will have occasion to reconsider them when we discuss more exotic types of preemption. (Note that if you think such cases are not far-fetched because you think that the history of physics has provided us with respectable examples of action at a distance (e.g., Newtonian gravity), then you might be failing to distinguish action at a spatial distance from action at a temporal distance.)

It might seem that the second candidate counterfactual analysis—the covariation account defended by Lewis (2000, 2004*a*) and Paul (2000,

---

[2] Well, perhaps this strategy is not completely off the table. One might try to provide, as a kind of philosophical package deal, an account both of events (and in particular, their individuation conditions) and of causation. And one might include as principles of this account both the claim that effects depend on their causes, and that events are individuated in part by their causal origins. One could then imagine going on to use this account in order to implicitly define both causation and the category of event (perhaps à la Lewis 1970). We know of no example of this kind of approach in the literature, although it is somewhat in the spirit of Menzies' 1996 approach. We will not consider it further here.

2004)—could handle figure 1 without amendment, and so would need to make no special appeal to transitivity. For it might seem that if **C** in figure 1 had fired slightly differently, **E** would have fired in a correspondingly different manner, whereas the same is not true of **A**. So it may be, in typical cases. But not always. Just tell a slightly more specific story about the events depicted in figure 1: stipulate that if **E** fires at all, it fires in a manner entirely insensitive to the signals stimulating it. Then if C had not occurred, or had occurred in even a slightly different manner than in fact it did, E would have occurred all the same, and in fact in exactly the same manner.

Okay, but what about the timing? If **C** had fired a little earlier, wouldn't **E** likewise have fired earlier? Not necessarily. Suppose the way **E** works is like this: it contains an internal clock and a switch; if the switch is flipped on, **E** will fire at precisely midnight; and any incoming signal, of any kind, flips this switch on. Suppose **C** and **A** both fire at noon. **E** fires twelve hours later. Then nothing about either the time or manner of E is sensitive to counterfactual variation in the time or manner of C. And that means that a covariation analysis has no special edge here. Lewis and Paul (see, e.g., Lewis 2004a, pp. 95–6), fully recognizing this point, build transitivity into the account, by taking causation to be the ancestral in a way similar to Lewis's original (1973a) counterfactual account.

2.2 The "gap" strategy

Another promising idea—albeit one we will end up rejecting as unworkable, for reasons that will emerge in §3.2—begins with the seeming insight that part of what makes the example tick is that the process initiated by A fails to go to completion: note how in figure 1 there is a "gap" where the stimulatory signal from **B** to **E** would have been. You might try to exploit this observation in a number of ways. For example, you might require that causes be connected to their effects by a spatiotemporally continuous sequence of events. More specifically: start by observing that while E depends on neither C nor A taken singly, it does depend on the two taken together; that is, if neither **A** nor **C** had fired, **E** would not have fired. Conclude that at least one of A and C must be a cause of E. Rule out A on the basis that it is not connected to E by a spatiotemporally continuous chain of events. Conclude that C is a cause of E.

Perhaps—but on inspection, this thought looks a bit clumsy. Sure, the diagram depicts no events that collectively carve out a region of spacetime joining A to E. But in realistic examples, there will be ever so many such events: little air currents, photons zooming by, etc. It's just that these events won't causally connect A to E. But, alas, if we could already account for the difference between causal and non-causal spatiotemporal connection, we'd be done.

In the context of the discussion of counterfactual analyses, much subtler approaches have been tried, for example Ramachandran 1997 and 1998, and Ganeri et al. 1996 and 1998. Ramachandran gives a nicely compact statement of the common idea behind them:

> It seems true in all cases of causal preemption . . . that the pre-empted processes do not run their full course, as we might put it. For any preempted cause, x, of an event, y, there will be at least one possible event . . . which fails to occur in the actual circumstances *but which would have to occur in order for x to be a genuine cause of y*. (Ramachandran 1997, p. 273; italics in the original)

Let's take a closer look at these approaches, using Ramachandran's "M-set" analysis as an illustration (1997 and 1998; the 1998 paper contains a slight revision to the original analysis). Say that a set of events S is a *minimal dependence set* (M-set) for E (where E is not a member of S) just in case, had none of the events in S occurred, E would not have occurred, whereas the same is not true of any proper subset of S. (Note that Ramachandran allows that some of the events in S could be non-actual events that merely could have occurred; more on this shortly.) Plausibly, if S is a minimal dependence set for E, then S contains at least one cause of E. That claim can be seen as a natural generalization of the claim that counterfactual dependence is sufficient for causation, as witness the case where S contains just one member. But if it contains more than one member, then we need some test to determine whether some of the members are playing the role of idle backups. For example, in figure 1 the set $\{A, C\}$ is an M-set for E. And there are others: letting B be the firing of **B** that would have occurred if the A-process had not been cut off, we can also see that the set $\{C, B\}$ is an M-set for E.

Ramachandran argues that what distinguishes A in the set $\{A, C\}$ as a non-cause of E is the fact that there is another M-set for E that differs from this set only in that A has been replaced by one or more non-actual events.

Thus, replace A by B, and we get just such an alternative M-set for E. Since, as it were, the work done by A in elevating the set $\{A, C\}$ to the status of M-set could have been done by something non-actual, A's candidacy as a cause of E gets undermined. By contrast, there is no way to replace C in the set $\{A, C\}$ by one or more non-actual events so as to reach another M-set for E: the only other events available to do the work of C are those in the C-D-E chain, which of course are all actual. For that reason, Ramachandran says, C, and not A, is a cause of E. In general, and a bit more exactly: C is a cause of E iff C belongs to at least one M-set for E, such that no other M-set for E differs from it by containing only non-actual events in place of C.[3]

An even simpler account along the same lines suggests itself. Observe that there is obviously no way to replace C in the M-set $\{C, B\}$ by one or more non-actual events and still be left with an M-set: for the resulting set would contain only non-actual events, and quite clearly no such set is an M-set for an actually occurring event. So we could also try this: C is a cause of E iff there is some M-set for E of which C is the sole actually occurring member.[4]

We can see how cleverly analyses like these exploit the idea that where there is preemption, there must be a gap in the preempted process: for if the effect E does not counterfactually depend on its cause C alone, surely, the thought goes, it will depend on the set that contains C, together with representative non-actual members of the preempted backup process or processes. That is the hope, anyway. Shortly, alas, we will see varieties of redundant causation in which the needed "gap" goes missing.

2.3 De facto dependence

Now let's consider yet another simple and attractive idea: that in cases of preemption like that depicted in figure 1, the effect will at least de facto depend on the cause, even if it does not depend on it outright. We will start by explaining what "de facto" dependence is.

---

[3] So, to establish that A in figure 1 is *not* a cause of E in fact requires showing that for *any* M-set containing A, there is another M-set which differs from the first only in that A has been replaced by one or more non-actual events. You should convince yourself that this stronger claim holds of the events depicted in figure 1.

[4] Observe that if C is a cause of E according to this simpler analysis, then it is a cause according to Ramachandran's; but the reverse implication does not hold. To see why, consider (as an exercise) cases of symmetric overdetermination (§4.5 of this chapter).

2.3.1 The two components of de facto dependence   The main idea, we may recall from chapter 2, is that E de facto depends on C just in case, for some suitably chosen fact F that obtains, the following counterfactual is true:

If C had not occurred, and F had still obtained, then E would not have occurred.

To reiterate some key points made in chapter 2 (in §2.2.3), a successful account along these lines needs two ingredients. First, it needs a story about which facts F can count as "suitably chosen." Second, it needs a story about how to evaluate the given counterfactual. For now, we are going to allow ourselves to get away with ignoring the second issue, by sticking to examples where it is clear enough how the evaluation should go; in particular, a sequential updating account will suffice. (We will come back to this issue in §4.2.6, however, where we will encounter cases that de facto dependence theorists try to handle by employing counterfactuals whose evaluation is far less obvious.)

Now, it is fairly clear what a de facto dependence theorist would like to say about figure 1: she would like to say that, in order to unmask C as a cause of E, we should hold fixed the fact that **B** does not fire (at, specifically, the time at which it would have fired, had **A** stimulated it). We then ask what would have happened had **C** not fired, but had it still been the case that **B** did not fire. And a sequential updating account provides an easy answer: we tweak the state of the world at the initial time just enough so that **C** does not fire (namely, by rendering **C** dormant at that time); we evolve forward to the time at which **B** is about to fire; we tweak *that* state of the world just enough so that **B** does not fire ("intervening" so as to render **B** dormant); we evolve forward again, observing that **E** does not fire. So the de facto dependence counterfactual comes out true, as needed. So far, so good.

However, it cannot be emphasized too strongly that, without some sort of reasonably sharp account of what makes a choice of fact "suitable," we have here nothing more than a suggestive idea, and not a solution to the problem posed by early preemption. Surveying the literature, one quickly sees that the range of possible accounts is vast, too vast for us to attempt a comprehensive overview. Instead, we will consider two illustrative examples, valuable not merely because they are philosophically interesting and significant but also because they are so strikingly different. The first is due to Christopher Hitchcock, and was briefly discussed in §2.2.3 of chapter 2. The second, also alluded to earlier, is due to Stephen Yablo.

To set the stage for our discussion of the illustrative examples, let's consider an extremely simple case that shows immediately that the easiest route is not available: one cannot hold that C is a cause of E just in case E de facto depends on C, for *at least some* choices of fact F:

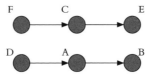

Figure 9

Let F_1 be the fact that either **C** fires or **A** does not (at the relevant time); let F_2 be the fact that both or neither of **C** and **A** fire. The de facto dependence counterfactuals are straightforward, and, unfortunately, B de facto depends on C for both of these choices of fact to hold fixed. So the simplest version of a de facto dependence account is really out of the question. And one useful question we can now ask of any de facto dependence account is this: how does it get around the rather trivial problem posed by figure 9? (If you are wondering why the overkill—why, that is, we distinguished F_1 from F_2—just wait for it: we will see that Yablo's account, rather surprisingly, needs to give a quite different treatment of the two versions of the problem posed by each of these facts. In showing why, we'll need to make use of the otherwise superfluous neurons **F** and **D** in figure 9.)

2.3.2 Hitchcock Let's start with Hitchcock's account. Recall that, in analyzing the causal structure of any given situation, he invites us first to construct a causal model for that situation, consisting of variables and functional relationships among them (again, see chapter 2, §2.2.3). We will take for granted that this can be done in a principled manner, noting that for neuron diagrams, at least, the appropriate causal model is obvious. With this model in hand, we can now straightforwardly pick out paths leading from one variable to another. The test for causation is then the following: where event C consists in some variable taking on a certain value, and E likewise consists of another variable taking on a certain value, C is a cause of E just in case there is at least one path from the C-variable to the

E-variable, such that, given some fact about the values of off-path variables, *E* de facto depends on *C*, holding that fact fixed.

These stipulations handle the problem posed by figure 9 twice over. First, there is no path from the *C*-variable to the *B*-variable. But, more importantly, even if there were, our two choices of fact to hold fixed cannot solely concern the values of off-path variables, since they are partly about the *C*-variable.

Turning now to figure 1, we can quickly see that Hitchcock's account secures the verdict that *C* is a cause of *E*: let the needed path be C–D–E, and let the true fact be the claim that **B** does not fire. It remains to check that the account does not likewise secure the verdict that *A* is a cause of *E*. And it does not: A–B–E is the only path from the *A*-variable to the *E*-variable, and no matter how we hold fixed facts about variables off this path, *E* still fails to depend on *A*.

Incidentally, it follows from Hitchcock's account that if *E* depends on *C* simpliciter—i.e., holding nothing fixed—then *C* must be a cause of *E*. For, given reasonable truth-conditions for causal models, *E* can depend on *C* only if there is at least one path from the *C*-variable to the *E*-variable. And given this path, we can simply let the needed fact about the off-path variables be a tautology.

2.3.3 Yablo   Yablo's approach is more complicated, and to see why we will start by motivating the account in much the same way that Yablo himself does. Consider figure 10, in which *C* initiates one process that threatens to prevent *E*, but also initiates a second process that counteracts this threat.

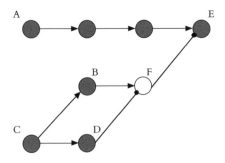

Figure 10

This example and others like it will come in for much more discussion in the next two chapters. For now, we use it simply to illustrate a serious problem for Hitchcock's account: for, quite implausibly, this account judges C to be a cause of E. Here is a path connecting the C-variable to the E-variable: C–B–F–E. And here is a fact about an off-path variable: **D** fires. Holding the latter fact fixed, E depends on C. And the point clearly generalizes: almost any time one event initiates a threat to a second event, but simultaneously initiates a process that counteracts that threat, the first will, according to Hitchcock's account, count as a cause of the second.

That's an intuitive cost, but let us set aside for now the question whether it is worth paying, noting simply that Yablo adamantly refuses to pay it. Instead, he seeks an account that draws a principled distinction between the treatment of figure 1 and the treatment of figure 10: in figure 1, it needs to come out appropriate to hold fixed the non-firing of **B** in order to unmask C as a cause of E, whereas in figure 10 it should be inappropriate to so hold fixed the firing of **D**. What could underlie this difference?

To answer this question, Yablo makes two key maneuvers. To bring the first into focus, observe that, in figure 10, the firing of **D** generates various "needs" that must be met, in order for E to occur: in particular, something needs to prevent **F** from firing. Various events count as taking care of this need: B does, as does C. But there is a distinction, for whereas B does indeed deserve credit for taking care of this need, C does not; after all, it is only thanks to C that the need exists in the first place. In other words, C takes care of a need that is strictly additional to the needs E would have had, had C not occurred. By contrast, C in figure 1 is guilty of no such offense: for E stands in need of a stimulatory signal regardless of whether C occurs.

Here (following Yablo) is a way to make this precise. Take some events C and E, and some fact F about the example. E will, holding F fixed, depend on various events, of which C may or may not be one. Examples: In figure 10, holding fixed the fact that **D** fires, E will depend on C, A and B (as well as other, unnamed events). In figure 1, holding fixed the fact that **B** does not fire, E will depend on C and D.

Now look at the set of events that E would have depended on, had C not occurred (depended on outright, i.e., holding nothing fixed). There are two possibilities. It could be that this latter set is identical to some (non-empty) subset of the events that E depends on, holding F fixed; if so, call F "bad." Or it could be that it is not identical to any such subset, in which case we call

F "good." Note that facts F are not good or bad simpliciter, but only relative to a choice of candidate cause C and effect E. Also, notice that if E depends on C outright, then the set of events that E would have depended on, had C not occurred, will be empty (since E, not occurring, wouldn't have been there to depend on anything); so any chosen fact will be good.

In figure 1, if we let F be the fact that neuron **B** does not fire, then we get the result that F is good: for if C had not occurred, E would have depended, inter alia, on A—an event it does not depend on, holding F fixed. By contrast, in figure 10, if we let F be the fact that **D** fires, then we get the result that F is bad: for if C had not occurred, E would have depended just on A, and the other events in the process it initiates—all of which it already depends on, holding F fixed. Note, by the way, that if we let F be a mere tautology, then we *also* get the result that F is bad: for in this case the events E would have depended on, had C not occurred, are *exactly the same* as the ones it depends on, holding F fixed.

Return now to figure 9, and as before let F_1 be the fact that either **C** fires or **A** does not. B depends on C, holding F_1 fixed. What else does B depend on, holding F_1 fixed? Well, among other things, all the events in the process initiated by D. But these are exactly the events B would have depended on, had C not occurred. So F_1 is bad (relative to C and B).

So far, all this is encouraging, and it might seem that Yablo's maneuver of distinguishing good from bad choices of F can yield a successful de facto dependence account along these lines: C is a cause of E just in case, for some good F, E F-depends on C (i.e., depends on C, holding F fixed). Alas, matters are not so simple. Look again at figure 9, and as before let F_2 be the fact that both or neither of **C** and **A** fire. Again, B depends on C, holding F_2 fixed. But now look at D, the event of the firing of **D**. Does B depend on this event, holding F_2 fixed? Arguably not. Let's consider how to evaluate the relevant counterfactual: had D not occurred, and had it still been the case that either both or neither of **A** and **C** fired, then B would not have occurred. We start at the initial time, making a localized change to the state of the world so that **D** does not fire. So it sends no signal to **A**. Evolving forward in time, then, we will—unless we make a further change to the state of the world—reach a state at the intermediate time in which **C** is firing and **A** is not. But, since we are holding fixed that either both or neither of **A** and **C** fire, we must make some localized change. There are two options: switch **C** off, or turn **A** on. Exercising the first option leads to a final state in which **B** does not fire, exercising the second leads to a state in which it does. We submit that, as nothing about the setup can make one option preferable to the other, we should conclude that, had D not occurred, and had it still been the case that either both or neither of **A** and **C** fired, then B might have occurred (and might not). But then it's not the case that it would not have occurred. So B does not depend on D, holding F_2 fixed. But B certainly does depend on D, in the counterfactual situation in which C does not occur. So F_2 is, alas, good.[5]

Here is where things stand. For any events C and E, there will always be a choice of fact F such that E F-depends on C: just let F be the claim that either C occurs or E does not. Many such choices of F will, of course, be bad. But the discussion of figure 9 shows that even when C is not a cause of E, it can be quite easy to find a good F such that E F-depends on C. So if C is not a cause of E, there will almost certainly be both good F's and bad F's such that E F-depends on C.

What if C is a cause of E? Here it looks like there are three cases:

First case. E depends on C outright. Then, as we have seen, every F is good, and so any F such that E F-depends on C is good. And there is at least one such F: just let it be a tautology.

Second case. E does not depend on C outright. In addition, there is, in the counterfactual situation in which C does not occur, at least one event X upon which E depends that is not identical to any actual event. It follows at once that every F is good (and so for any F such that E F-depends on C, this F must be good): for, since X does not actually occur, it cannot be included in the set of actual events such that E F-depends on them.

Third case. E does not depend on C outright. In addition, in the counterfactual situation in which C does not occur, E depends only on events that

---

[5] The argument of this paragraph closely follows Yablo 2004. But Yablo oversimplifies matters, by assuming—wrongly, in our judgment—that any nested counterfactual P → (Q → R) is equivalent to (P&Q) → R. That allows him to argue (adapting slightly) as follows: Begin by noting that if D had not occurred, C would, obviously, still have occurred. Render this claim as (¬D → C). Letting (A iff C) be the fact that both or neither of **A** and **C** fire, we observe that since (A iff C) is true, and (¬D → C) is likewise true, so must be the conditional (A iff C) → (¬D → C). By Yablo's assumption, it follows that [¬D & (A iff C)] → C. So, if **D** had not fired, but it had still been the case that both or neither of **A** and **C** fired, then **C**—and so likewise **A**—would have fired, hence **B** would have fired. That allows Yablo to derive the stronger claim that, holding F2 fixed, if D had not occurred B still would have occurred. We think the assumption needed for the derivation is false, but that it doesn't really matter—as the argument in the text shows well enough—namely because it's *not* the case that, holding F2 fixed, if D had not occurred B would not have occurred.

occur in the actual world. It follows that there will be at least one bad F such that E F-depends on C. To see this, let H be a fact consisting of the complete details of all of history up to the time of E's occurrence. Let F be the fact that either H obtains, or E does not occur. Taking for granted here that C precedes E, E will F-depend on C—and will likewise F-depend on every single other event that precedes it. Since every event upon which E depends, in the counterfactual situation in which C does not occur, is an actual event, it follows that this F is bad.

What all this means is that, even with the good/bad distinction in hand, we are still well short of a full account of causation. Hence Yablo's second maneuver, which is to introduce a different sort of distinction among the Fs. Some choices of F, it turns out, can be more "natural" than others. The idea is that some choices of F are more gerrymandered or ad hoc or disjunctive than others. For example, in figure 10 we can get E to F-depend on C by letting F be the fact that **D** fires, or by letting F be the fact that either both or neither of **A** and **C** fire. Yablo would insist that the second choice is less natural than the first.

With this way of ordering Fs in place, we have the official account: C is a cause of E just in case (i) there is some F such that E F-depends on C; and (ii) this F is more natural than any bad G. (It follows that this F must itself be good.)

Let's go through some examples with the official account in hand. In figure 1, matters are easy: since the set of events E would have depended on, had C not occurred, includes B—an event that does not actually occur—every F is good. So pick any F such that E F-depends on C: say, let F = the fact that either C occurs or E does not. This F is good. No more natural F is bad (since no F is bad). So C is a cause of E, as desired. (Note that the fact that E depends on C, holding fixed the fact that **B** does not fire, plays no special role in the account's demonstration that C is a cause of E. Apparently the account as developed has wandered some distance from the original animating intuition.)

Next, in figure 10, we have a fairly natural F such that E F-depends on C: F = the fact that **D** fires. But this F is bad. We also have a comparatively less natural F: F = the fact that either both or neither of **A** and **C** fire. This F is good—but there are bad Fs more natural than it. The F just mentioned will do as an example, as will the "null" choice, where we let F be a tautology. If we stipulate that this latter choice is the *most* natural one we can make, then we can conclude, without any further survey of all the possible Fs, that C is not a cause of E.

Finally, figure 9. We saw that B depends on C, holding fixed the fact that both or neither of **A** and **C** fire. What's more, this choice of F is good. But observe that the (more natural) null choice is bad: B in fact depends on D and A, and these are exactly the events it would have depended on, had C not occurred. So C is not a cause of B.

Something along these lines may work in the end. But as a solution to the problem posed by preemption, Yablo's account faces at least one serious technical obstacle. As a prelude to describing this obstacle, consider what might seem to be a mere logical possibility: E does not depend on C; but, had C not occurred, then even though E would still have occurred there would have been no event X such that E depended on X. So the set S of such events is just the empty set. Now, as we drew the good/bad distinction earlier, it follows that every F is good: for the only way F could fail to be good is if the set S was a non-empty subset of the set of events upon which E F-depends. And so it follows that C is a cause of E, provided only that there is at least one F such that E F-depends on C. But of course there will be— e.g., let F be the fact that either C occurs or E does not.

But this last consequence is unacceptable: it cannot be that C is automatically a cause of E, if the above conditions are met. For consider that one way for E to occur, but to fail to depend on any event, is for E to be symmetrically overdetermined, as in figure 11.

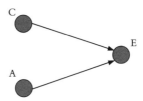

Figure 11

No single event (distinct from E itself, obviously) in the scenario depicted here is such that, had it not occurred, then E would not have occurred. So all we have to do to make good on the "mere logical possibility" just described is to construct a case of early preemption in which the backup causal pathway to E is a symmetrically overdetermined one, as in figure 12.

In figure 12, the left-hand diagram depicts what happens, the right what *would* have happened, had **C** not fired.

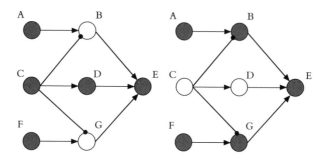

Figure 12

Now we have most of what we want: *E* does not depend on *C*, but had *C* not occurred, then even though *E* would still have occurred there would have been *no* event *X* such that *E* depended on *X*.—Most, but not all, since *C* in figure 12 is in fact a cause of *E*, which is what Yablo's account predicts. But it makes this prediction for the wrong reason: not because of the genuine connection between *C* and *E*, but merely because *C* keeps *E* from being symmetrically overdetermined. Figure 13 preserves the latter feature while dispensing with the former (imagine that something not shown stimulates **D** to fire, at the appropriate time).

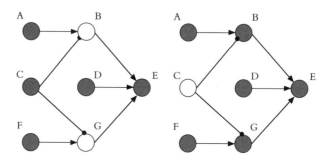

Figure 13

Figures 12 and 13 differ not at all with respect to the feature that, according to Yablo, guarantees that *C* is a cause of *E*. But they obviously differ with respect to whether *C* is a cause of *E*. This is a serious problem.

Notice that it won't help to amend the account by saying that a given choice of F is bad just in case the set of events that E would have depended on, had C not occurred, is a subset (non-empty or otherwise) of the set of events that E F-depends on. Then, in the kind of case we're imagining, we get the result that every F is bad, so C cannot be a cause of E. That gets figure 13 right but figure 12 wrong—no improvement. And no surprise. The problem, after all, is not in these details, but in the fact that the ingredients used to draw the good/bad distinction are blind to the difference between figures 12 and 13.

Let's summarize. Once the notion of de facto dependence is on the table, it can seem to be an ever so natural thought that this notion is tailor-made to handle cases of early preemption. The thought seems to be that, in cases like figure 1, what the effect in fact depends on (i.e., depends on, holding other relevant facts about the situation fixed) is precisely its causes. What we have seen in this section is that this thought can be developed in strikingly different ways, and also that examining these developments gives us fresh insight into the causal structure of preemption cases, but in the end it is not obvious that it can be developed in a way that produces a precise, successful account.

2.4 Minimal sufficiency

Can minimal sufficiency help with early preemption? If we were to focus exclusively on the kind of early preemption depicted in figure 1, we might think that the problem is this: there are, at the time at which **A** and **C** fire, too many sets that are minimally sufficient for E, and in particular there are sets containing non-causes that are nevertheless minimally sufficient for E (namely, the set $\{A\}$). We might take for granted that the account is at least correct to this extent: whenever C is a cause of E, C will belong to at least one set minimally sufficient for E. All that remains is to find some test to rule out certain minimally sufficient sets (in this case $\{A\}$) as containing spurious non-causes. A natural thought in the present context is to try to exploit the fact that there is a gap separating A from E. Still, we will not try to develop this strategy any further, for the key assumption behind it is incorrect: it can sometimes be the case that a cause fails to belong to any set of contemporaneous events minimally sufficient for its effect. Figure 14 provides an illustration:

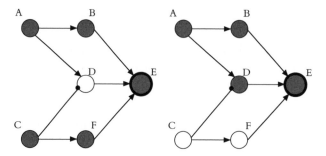

Figure 14

The left-hand diagram illustrates what happens if **C** fires, the right what happens if **C** does not fire. Here, **E** is a stubborn neuron, needing two stimulations in order to fire. It would have received both from **A**, but for the preempting action of **C**. So here we have a case of early preemption where a cause cuts off part (but not all) of an alternative causal pathway. Notice, finally, that at the time at which **A** and **C** fire there is a unique set minimally sufficient for E, namely $\{A\}$.

(We should pause to observe that figure 14 poses no trouble for any of the accounts considered in the last section. E depends on F, which depends on C; so we could take causation to be the ancestral of counterfactual dependence, and get this case right. If **C** had not fired and **D** had (still) not fired, then **E** would not have fired; so Ramachandran's M-set analysis gets this case right, as $\{C, D\}$ is a minimal dependence set for E of which C is the sole actual member. And, holding fixed the fact that **D** does not fire, E depends on C; so a de facto dependence account can get this case right, assuming, as usual, that it can provide a principled story for why it's appropriate to hold this particular fact fixed.)

So we'll need a different strategy for distinguishing C as a cause of E in figure 14, ideally one that will apply uniformly to figure 1 as well. A natural idea takes its cue from Lewis's original analysis: we assume that causation must be transitive, look for a relation that will at least yield a sufficient condition on causation, and take its ancestral. The obvious sufficient condition is this one: C is a cause of E if (but not only if) C belongs to a unique set of contemporaneous events minimally sufficient for E.[6]

---

[6] This will need some refinement. Suppose we are dealing with events that have spatial parts, and that C is composed of C_1 and C_2 (where, just to keep matters pristine, we stipulate that these parts take place over

That makes D in figure 1 a cause of E, and likewise C a cause of D. So now, as before, we simply take causation to be the ancestral of this relation, thereby securing C as a cause of E. Similarly, in figure 14 $\{B, F\}$ is a unique set minimally sufficient for E; $\{A\}$ is uniquely minimally sufficient for B; and $\{C\}$ is uniquely minimally sufficient for F. So the causal structure comes out exactly as it needs to. Again, this approach weds our minimal sufficiency account to transitivity. By the time we get to chapter 5, we will see that the trouble this causes is slightly less serious than the trouble caused for counterfactual accounts.

2.5 Summary

Let's review the main points to take away from this section. First, cases of early preemption serve as simple and vivid reminders that we must distinguish between causing and causally guaranteeing. In figure 1, for example, A causally guarantees E, even though it does not cause E. We think this distinction has widespread importance, quite irrespective of its role in constraining a philosophical account of causation. As an illustration, consider an important view in the philosophy of explanation that runs into trouble precisely because it overlooks this distinction: Kitcher's (1981, 1989) unificationist account of explanation. Without going into details, Kitcher's main idea is roughly this: given some explanandum E, a successful explanation of it will be a valid derivation of it from true premises, making use of a kind of argument that has a suitably widespread number of instances, in the sense that arguments of exactly the same form can be used to derive a very wide range of other explananda. That is supposed to capture the sense that a good explanation unifies the phenomenon to be explained with a wide range of other phenomena. But notice that mere derivation from true premises is blind to the causing/causally guaranteeing distinction. Imagine a world exhibiting an enormous variety of structures that all have the abstract form depicted in figure 1, and imagine furthermore that in every case where the equivalent of **E** "fires," the thing playing the role of **A** likewise "fires." Our explananda are the **E**-firings. We can give unified derivations of these

---

exactly the same duration as C). Then it may well be that if a set containing C is minimally sufficient for E, so is a set that results from this one by replacing C by one or both of C_1 and C_2. This strikes us as a fairly minor technical problem, to be circumvented by, for example, making the requirement of uniqueness relative to a choice of a non-redundant taxonomy of events. (So we could choose a taxonomy that contains C, or one that contains both C_1 and C_2; but not both.) We won't explore this issue further here.

explananda by correctly positing, for each case, a figure-1 structure, and correctly noting that **A** fires. But it doesn't follow that, in each case, we have thereby correctly explained the **E**-firing; for some of the time, the correct explanation is rather that **C** fires.

Second, we can now see that cases of early preemption come in a variety of flavors. Plain vanilla is this: we start with an ordinary situation where *A* causes *E* via a single process, and add an event *C* that both interrupts this process, and brings about *E* itself. But we could also start with a situation where multiple processes aim at bringing about *E*, and add an event that interrupts some or all of them; we could likewise start with a situation where *A* brings about *E* by way of several converging processes (as in figure 13), and add an event that interrupts just one of these. In short, the target cause *C* can preempt its "backups" in many different ways. It pays to remember this variety of early preemption when constructing your account of causation, since it obviously won't do to design the account to handle just some of the plainer varieties, leaving it to founder on more exotic others.

At this point it looks as though there are four main approaches one might take to handling early preemption: rely on a transference account; exploit the "gap" that the preempting cause opens up in the backup causal process; exploit the fact (assuming it *is* a fact!) that causation is transitive, and trace back to the cause *C* by way of intermediates; design a more subtle relation of de facto dependence to pick out *C* as a cause of *E*. The next section will add a wrinkle— one that shows, we think, that the "gap" strategy must be abandoned.

3 Tampering

3.1 *The structure of the case*

Consider the following curious variant on early preemption, which we call *tampering*.

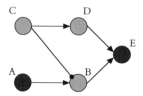

Figure 15

This diagram needs careful description. First, let us stipulate that neurons can fire with different intensities, emitting signals, stimulatory or inhibitory, with corresponding intensities, represented by darker or lighter shading. Second, let us stipulate that neuron **E** will fire iff it receives stimulatory signals of combined intensity 10 or greater (in some appropriate units). Third, **A** fires with intensity 10, and **C** with intensity 5. Finally, the inhibitory connection between **C** and **B** does not prevent **B** from firing, but just reduces the intensity of its firing: **B** would have fired with intensity 10, had it only received the stimulatory signal from **A**; but since it also receives the inhibitory signal from **C** it fires with intensity 5 (i.e., with an intensity reduced from 10 by the magnitude of the inhibitory signal). Since, as a result of the stimulatory signal from **C**, **D** likewise fires with intensity 5, **E** fires.

The case differs in certain respects from figure 1 (though it is rather similar to figure 14). In particular, *A* here is a cause of *E*; in fact, *C* and *A* are *joint* causes of *E*. But the similarities are more important. As in figure 1, *E* fails to depend on *C*, one of its causes. But this failure of dependence does not obtain because some backup process, sufficient to bring about *E* all by itself, is cut off; rather, it obtains because some backup process, sufficient to bring about *E* all by itself, is modified, so that it is no longer sufficient in this way. Observe that this modification does not, in any sense, prevent the process from going to completion. Consequently, any attempt to handle the kind of preemption exhibited in figure 1 by exploiting the fact that the *A*-process is cut short, or has, thanks to *C*, a "gap" in it, will fall apart when confronted with the variation exhibited by figure 15.

We have occasionally heard the claim in conversation that it is not really so clear that *C* in figure 15 is a cause of *E*—presumably because, after all, one of the things that *C* does is to partially inhibit a process aimed at bringing *E* about, and that is, supposedly, an inappropriate thing for a cause to be doing. This objection is misguided, and not merely because it would apply equally well to figure 1. Consider figure 16:

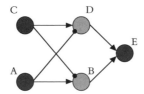

Figure 16

Here, **A** and **C** send strong stimulatory signals to **B** and **D**, respectively. In addition, **C** sends a weak inhibitory signal to **B** and **A** sends a weak inhibitory signal to **D**. Had **C** not fired, **B** would have fired with intensity 10; likewise, had **A** not fired, **D** would have fired with intensity 10. Instead, each fires with intensity 5. As before, **E** will fire iff it receives stimulatory signals with combined strength of 10 or greater. So **E** fires. It won't do to say that because one of the things that C does is to partially inhibit a process aimed at bringing E about, C cannot therefore be a cause of E. For given the symmetry of the situation, the same reasoning must apply to A, and the result is that E is left without any causes at all at the time at which **A** and **C** fire. Note finally that examples with essentially this structure are commonplace: Billy and Suzy need to move a piece of furniture. It is heavy, but not so heavy that either of them is incapable of moving it alone. However, they move it together. Because of Billy's help, Suzy does not exert as much effort as she would have, were she moving the furniture alone; Billy likewise scales back his efforts. Nevertheless, Billy and Suzy *jointly* cause the furniture to be moved.

3.2 The "gap" strategy reconsidered

Let us delve more deeply into why cases like figure 15 pose such trouble for the strategies for handling preemption that look for a "gap" in the preempted process. It will be instructive just to consider Ramachandran's "M-set" account (§2.2), and how it would apply to figure 15. Recall that a set of events S is an M-set for E just in case, had none of the events in S occurred, E would not have occurred, whereas the same is not true of any proper subset of S. The proposal on the table is that C is a cause of E iff C belongs to at least one M-set for E, such that no other M-set for E differs from it by containing only non-actual ("nonactual" relative to the example of course!) events in place of C.

Now, let's look at figure 15. Of course, we want to get the result that A is one of the causes of E, and that is no problem, as E clearly depends on A (so $\{A\}$ is an M-set for E). The difficulty arises in trying to get the result that C is likewise a cause of E. E does not depend on C, so the only way to get C into any M-set for E is to pair it up with at least one other event, so that E depends on the two taken together, but not on either taken singly. We can now simply inspect our diagram, to see whether we can find any such event.

Clearly, it cannot be an event in the chain that runs from C through D to E, nor one of the events that consists in the passage of the inhibitory signal from **C** to **B**. But since E depends on each of the events in the chain that begins with A and runs through B, the event with which to pair C cannot be one of these, either. And now we have run out of choices. (Observe that when, as in figure 1, the C-process severs all connections between the backup process and the effect, the problem we have unearthed will disappear: for severing this connection will remove any dependence of the effect on the backup process.)

The obvious response is to try to find an M-set to which C belongs that pairs it up with a non-actual event. Consider that if **C** had not fired, **B** would have fired with intensity 10. Suppose we insist that this firing of **B** that would have occurred is numerically different from the intensity-5 firing of **B** that in fact occurs. (A very similar situation with an interestingly different response will arise with our discussion of Yablo's de facto account in §3.3.) Let B^* be the former firing of **B**. We might hope that $\{C, B^*\}$ provides the M-set for E that will testify to C's status as a cause of E, the idea being that if **C** had not fired—and if it had still been the case that **B** did not fire with intensity 10—then **E** would not have fired.

But there are three problems with this response. The first is that it forces us into a controversial position about the individuation conditions of events; essentially, we must hold that any difference in the manner of occurrence of an event would make for a numerically different event. (It is relevant in this regard that **C** could have fired with, say, intensity 0.01, thus requiring us to distinguish, as numerically different events, an intensity-10 firing of **B** from an intensity-9.99 firing of **B**.) We will shortly see the sort of trouble that position leads to in the context of a counterfactual analysis of causation.

Second, the relevant counterfactual circumstance that will allegedly establish that $\{C, B^*\}$ is an M-set for E is specified as one in which **C** does not fire, but in which **B** nevertheless somehow fails to fire with intensity 10—not, observe, one in which it fails to fire at all. Absent some explicit instructions for how to evaluate the counterfactual, it is not at all determinate what would happen to **B** in such a circumstance. Arguably, one thing that might happen is that **B** fires with an intensity just a little bit greater than 10, in which case **E** fires all the same.

Now, it's not so hard to solve this problem. Here is one way to do so. Stipulate that the right way to evaluate the counterfactual is as follows: Start with the actual state of the world at time 0 (the time at which **C** and **A** fire). Modify this state by returning **C** to its "default" state—i.e., render it dormant. Evolve forward in accordance with the actual laws until time 1 (the time at which **D** and **B** fire). Make event B^* fail to occur by returning neuron **B** to its dormant state (instead of changing it just slightly to some other state in which it is not firing with intensity 10). Evolve forward in accordance with the actual laws. Then **E** does not fire—and so, on this way of evaluating the counterfactual, it comes out true.

But this maneuver simply accentuates the third problem, which is that however one tries to deal with figure 15, one had better not end up saying the wrong thing about figure 17.

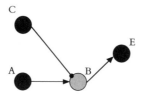

Figure 17

This time, **E** will fire if it receives a signal of any intensity. Had **C** not fired, the signal from **B** would have been of intensity 10. But thanks to C, it has intensity 5. By our lights, C is not a cause of E. But, if we use the recipe just sketched to get the counterfactual "if C had not occurred and B^* had not occurred, then E would not have occurred" to come out true of figure 15, then willy-nilly it will come out true of figure 17 as well. If so, $\{C, B^*\}$ will be an M-set for E of which C is the sole actual member, with the result, according to the M-set account, that C is a cause of E. So our brute force method of rescuing the M-set analysis fails, as it cannot distinguish the causal status of C in figure 15 from its status in figure 17.

At any rate, that's more than enough skirmishing. We conclude, partly on the reasonable assumption that we should look for a uniform treatment of tampering and early preemption, and partly because, as we will see in §4, there is another sort of preemption that the "gap" strategy has no hope of handling, that the strategy ought to be abandoned.

3.3 Tampering's other lessons

By contrast, cases of tampering pose no new trouble for accounts that assume that causation is transitive. Do they carry any lessons for de facto dependence accounts? Not for Hitchcock's: in figure 15, that **B** fires with intensity 5 is a fact about an off-path variable (the path in question being C–D–E). With this fact held fixed, E depends on C. So far, so good. But what about Yablo's account?

On the face of it, things don't look good. Consider the events that E in fact depends on: these are the events in the A–E chain, together with the events in the C–D–E chain not including C itself. That is, these are the events that E F-depends on, for the most natural choice of F (namely, F = a tautology). But now consider the events that E would have depended on, had C not occurred: these are the event in the A–E chain. So this most natural choice of F is bad. So C cannot be a cause of E.

But the objection isn't fatal—and, for quite different reasons, Yablo provides himself a way out.[7] In presenting the good/bad distinction in §2.3.3, we glossed over a subtlety. What Yablo in fact asks us to compare, in deciding whether a given F is bad, is the set of *needs* E has, holding F fixed, with the set of *needs* it would have had, had C not occurred. Badness is now a matter of F's simply adding needs:

Suppose that x is an event needed in the fallback scenario [= the counterfactual scenario in which C does not occur]; one finds in GAN [= the set of events upon which E F-depends], not perhaps that very event, but an event meeting the same need (henceforth, a counterpart of x). (Yablo 2004, p. 125)

So the test is now the following: Look at the set of events upon which E F-depends. Look at the set of events E would have depended on, had C not occurred. F is bad if and only if every event in the latter set "meets the same need" as some event in the former set.

Back to figure 15. The set of events upon which E depends (i.e., F-depends, for F = a tautology) includes the firing of **B**. The set of events upon which E would have depended, had **C** not fired, likewise includes the firing of **B**. But, in the actual scenario, the firing of **B** meets E's need for a stimulatory signal of at least strength 5, whereas in the counterfactual

---

[7] Which, in communication, he has indicated he would exploit.

scenario where C fails to occur, the firing of **B** meets E's need for a stimulatory signal of at least strength 10. Even granting that these are numerically the same event, they do not meet the same need.[8] So this choice of F is good, after all. This is Yablo's preferred response (personal communication).

And it might work. All we wish to emphasize here is that it adds a rather sizable chunk of unfinished business, because if Yablo wants to produce a suitably reductive account of causation, he will need a suitably reductive account of this crucial relation: *meets the same need as*. Yablo acknowledges this project with a brief comment:

> When do events speak in their respective scenarios to the same need? The idea is this. Needs that E would have had in C's absence can be paired off with actual needs in ways that preserve salient features of the case: energy expended, distance traveled, time taken, place in the larger structure of needs. One wants to preserve as many of these features as possible, while finding matches for the largest number of needs. (Yablo 2004, p. 126)

This is a start, but it needs a lot of finishing. The obvious worry is that what we deem "salient" will be largely a function of what we take the causal structure of the case to be. That is so in the case of figure 15: what it amounts to, to say that in the actual scenario, E "needs" from neuron **B** only a stimulatory signal of strength at least 5, seems exactly to be that E causally requires only this strong a signal. This problem should remind you of similar problems we raised in chapter 2 for other accounts that seem to rely on salience at crucial junctures, such as causal modeling accounts based on structural equations.

At any rate, we will set the problem aside now, resting content with the observation that cases of tampering show that a Yablo-style de facto dependence account will need to be quite subtle when it comes to drawing the crucial distinction between good and bad choices of fact-to-hold-fixed.

We also think that tampering holds a more general lesson for the literature, which is that too much of it has focused on what is, in fact, an inessential feature of figure 1: namely, that in addition to the process

---

[8] Recall our discussion in §3.2. Maybe these are not one and the same firing—e.g., maybe one is essentially a firing with intensity 5, the other essentially a firing with intensity 10. But nothing in the response we're advancing on behalf of Yablo requires such a controversial view. (Thanks are due to Stephen Yablo for clarifying this point.)

initiated by *C*, there is a backup process sufficient to bring about *E* that is cut off. We should relocate the focus: there is a backup process sufficient to bring about *E*, that also *happens* to be cut off. It does not matter one whit that this process *is* cut off; what matters is that it would suffice to bring about the effect in the absence of the target cause. It is this feature that makes the target cause so difficult for an analysis to discern as such.

And it is this feature that is preserved, in quite an elegant fashion, in the next sort of case we will consider—what to our minds is the single most important sort of case in the entire literature on causation.

4 Late preemption

Suzy and Billy both throw rocks at a bottle. Suzy is slightly quicker, and consequently it is her rock, and not Billy's, that breaks the bottle. But Billy, though not as fast, is just as accurate: had Suzy not thrown, or had her rock somehow been interrupted mid-flight, Billy's rock would have broken the bottle moments later. This case, like those reviewed in the last two sections, features a cause of an event that is accompanied by a backup, sufficient to bring about the effect in the cause's absence. But unlike those cases, the actual cause fails either to interrupt the backup process, or to modify it in such a way as to render it insufficient for the effect. Consequently—and this is the crucial feature that distinguishes these cases of so-called "late preemption" from the cases of early preemption and tampering just considered—*at no point in the sequence of events leading from cause to effect does there fail to be a backup process sufficient to bring about that effect.*

Consider figure 18:

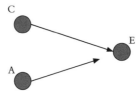

Figure 18

Here, the stimulatory signal from **C** reaches **E** just before the stimulatory signal from **A**; we represent this fact by drawing the arrow from **A** so that it does not quite extend to **E**.[9] Pick any point before **E** fires. Focus on the event occurring at that time which is a part of the causal process from *C* to *E*. If that event had not occurred, *E* would have occurred all the same. What's more, that event is not part of a unique set minimally sufficient for *E*. (It is, rather, a member of one of two sets each minimally sufficient for *E*.)

So the strategy of taking the ancestral is of no use to either the counter-factual or the minimal sufficiency analysis. (Transference accounts, on the other hand, once again appear to face no special trouble with this example.) That raises a question, to which we will need to return shortly: Was it really a good idea to try to handle cases of early preemption by what was, in effect, an appeal to the transitivity of causation? You might have doubts. For it might seem desirable to construct an account that can handle early and late preemption in a uniform manner, and for the latter kind of preemption, an appeal to transitivity is obviously of no use. But before taking up this question, as well as the question of what other strategies our accounts might use to handle late preemption, we need to clear up a possible confusion concerning what is and what is not essential to such cases.

4.1 Late preemption and "missing events"

To begin with, the name "late preemption," though enshrined in the literature, is unfortunate. It hearkens back to Lewis (1986*c*), in which the canonical example of late preemption was one in which the effect itself acted so as to interrupt the backup causal process, as in figure 19 (imagine here that **A** and **C** fire simultaneously).

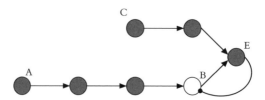

Figure 19

---

[9] Note that interpreting figure 18 in this way involves a slight change in the standard convention for reading the neuron diagram—it represents the causal story at a moment in time, rather than as a process over an extended time.

Here, the inhibitory signal from **E** prevents **B** from firing; if it had not done so, the signal from **A** would have caused **E** to fire. Take this example as paradigmatic, and you will think the term "preemption" is appropriate, since there is an obvious sense in which the backup process is cut short: neuron **B** is prevented from firing.

But as Paul 1998*b* shows, there need not be such missing events in cases of late preemption, or, for that matter, even modified events, as in cases of tampering. Understanding this will be central to what follows. Consider figure 18 again. First, we stipulate that the final effect will involve a firing of neuron **E** whose qualitative character in no way depends on the qualitative character, or timing, of the stimulatory signal. Next, **E** fires each time it is stimulated. In figure 18, **E** fires as a result of the signal from **C**—and then fires a second time as a result of the signal from **A**. There is thus no sense whatsoever in which the process initiated by *A* fails to "go to completion"; yet, quite obviously, *A* is not a cause of *E* (where *E* is understood to be the first of the two firings of **E**). Here is a real-world variant that shows how easy it is to generate the pattern we have in mind. Billy and Suzy throw rocks, this time not at a bottle, but at a bell. The bell rings twice in rapid succession: the first time as a result of Suzy's throw, the second time as a result of Billy's. Nothing deserving the name "preemption" is going on.

The focus on examples like figure 19 has done more than terminological damage. For observe that in the case depicted by figure 19, in the counter-factual circumstance in which **C** does not fire, there is an event in the *A*-process—namely *B*, the firing of **B**—that does not actually occur in the world of the example. That can make approaches like Ramachandran's M-set account seem very attractive (see also Ganeri et al. 1996): for observe that $\{B, C\}$ is an M-set for E, of which C is the only actual member. But cases of late preemption like that of figure 18, or the case of Billy, Suzy, and the bell, completely undermine such solutions. We thus recommend that attention focus on what we take to be the single crucial feature of cases of late preemption, which, once again, is this: at no point in the sequence of events leading from cause to effect does there fail to be a backup process sufficient to bring about that effect.

We should immediately flag one objection, most obvious in the case of Billy, Suzy, and the bell: "Look, the bell in fact rings twice. The target effect in question is the first ringing. But the 'backup process' is sufficient, not to bring about *that* ringing, but rather the *second* ringing." Fair enough, at least for the moment. We should rather have said: at no point in the sequence of events leading from cause to effect does there fail to be a backup process sufficient to bring about an event that, in its timing and manner, closely matches that effect. We thus do not beg the question against views that distinguish the effect brought about by the backup process *in the counter-factual situation* from the target effect *in the actual situation*. We are about to see, though, that such views have a high price to pay.

4.2 "Sensitivity" strategies

Return to our stock example of late preemption, where Suzy and Billy throw rocks at the bottle. A natural thought is that without Suzy's throw, the bottle would not have shattered just when it did. Likewise, in figure 19, without C, E would not have fired as early as it did. And in figure 18—which, recall, we can interpret so it involves two firings of E in rapid succession—E would likewise not have fired as early as it did. Perhaps these facts are somehow crucial to distinguishing Suzy's throw as the sole cause of the shattering, and C as the sole cause of E (taking, in figure 18, the event E to be the first firing of E).

4.2.1 Modally "fragile" events
It was long thought that the only way to exploit this observation was to build an extreme sensitivity to the time of occurrence into the individuation conditions for events (or, making use of what is a well-entrenched bit of terminology, to treat events as "modally fragile"; see Lewis 1986c). Thus, the shattering of the bottle that actually occurs—that very event—would not have occurred without Suzy's throw; rather, a qualitatively very similar but numerically distinct shattering would have occurred—numerically distinct, because it is essential to the actual shattering that it occur just when it does. Likewise, without C, only a numerically distinct firing of E would have occurred.

In a moment, we will review a quite different way to pursue this "sensitivity" strategy for handling late preemption, one that involves no claims about what is essential or accidental to an event. But first, we should look at two potential sources of confusion.

First, it is important not to confuse the descriptions with which we single out events with features of those events that are essential to their occurrence. Suppose many bottles are breaking, all over the place, in rapid succession. We might use the expression "the breaking that occurred at precisely noon" to pick out one of these events. But that we successfully pick out exactly one of the breakings in this way does not at all imply that the breaking so picked out has a nature so delicate (modally "fragile") that it—that very breaking—could not have occurred at a different time. It is a substantive metaphysical thesis concerning any given event that it has this or that characteristic essentially, and you do not endorse that thesis merely by helping yourself to some characteristic as a handle by which to identify the given event.

Second, it can be tempting to hold that, in the case where Suzy and Billy both throw rocks at the bottle, the shattering of the bottle that would have occurred (had Suzy not thrown) is a different event from the actual shattering, precisely because it has wholly different causal origins. In the case of figure 18, this temptation is even stronger: for notice that in the actual circumstances, A initiates a process that results in a firing of E (just not the first firing), and this process is duplicated wholesale in the counterfactual circumstance in which C does not fire (cf. the objection noted at the end of §4.1). It is therefore natural to think that the firing of E that occurs in this counterfactual circumstance must be numerically identical to the *second* firing of E that *actually* occurs: after all, its causal origins have been preserved intact. Therefore, one inevitably concludes, it cannot be identical to the first (actual) firing of E.[10]

But these principles for identifying and distinguishing events across possible worlds are not acceptable in the present context. As we mentioned earlier, the kind of reductive account of causation we are interested in needs to settle all such questions of event individuation antecedently to picking out the causal structure of any situation. So it must rather be that an account that insists that the actual shattering of the bottle does not occur in the counterfactual situation in which Suzy does not throw, and that the first actual firing of E does not occur in the counterfactual situation in which C does not fire, rests these claims on a theory of event individuation that makes the time at which an event occurs (and not its causal origins) essential to it.[11]

---

[10] Thanks to Stephen Yablo (in conversation) for pointing out this line of reasoning.

[11] Of course, one could try for a theory of event individuation much more complicated than this: time is essential to an event, if (but only if) it occurs in spatiotemporal proximity to another event qualitatively just like it, etc. We won't stop to explore these ad hoc corners of logical space.

4.2.2 Alterations   In fact, however, pursuing this strategy for handling late preemption does not really require such a controversial position about the individuation conditions of events, as Paul (1998*a*) shows. Instead, one can build the sensitivity to time into the kind of counterfactual dependence that one takes to suffice for causation. For example, we could take C to be a cause of E if, had C not occurred, E would not have occurred exactly when it did—leaving it open whether the consequent holds because E does not occur at all, or rather because it occurs at a different time.

Applied to the case of Suzy, Billy, and the bottle, that formula leaves it wide open whether, had Suzy not thrown, the shattering that would have occurred would be identical to the actual shattering. Lewis has fleshed out this approach in detail (in his 2000, 2004*a*), broadening it and arriving at the kind of covariation account sketched in chapter 2 (at §2.2.2); also see Paul 2000, 2004 for a slightly different way of fleshing it out. To get a grip on the main idea, imagine slight changes in the manner of Suzy's throw: either its timing, or its strength, or its angle, etc. The counterfactual situation thus produced might be one in which Suzy's throw still occurs, or it might be one in which a numerically different but qualitatively similar event occurs. Never mind. In either case, we can, following Lewis, say that an "alteration" of Suzy's throw occurs. We then check to see whether, in that counterfactual situation, some corresponding "alteration" of the bottle-shattering occurs. If it does—more generally, if there is a sufficiently pervasive pattern of counterfactual covariation between alterations of Suzy's throw and alterations of the shattering—then Suzy's throw counts as a cause of the shattering.

In our judgment, the studied ambivalence this approach displays about questions concerning the identity of events across different possible worlds is a significant virtue: after all, it's not as if our ordinary grasp of the category of "event" gives us much guidance concerning these questions. So it's much better if an account of causation doesn't need to presuppose answers to them. Lewis concurs, writing

Let an *alteration* of event E be either a very fragile version of E or else a very fragile alternative event which may be similar to E, but is numerically different from E. One alteration of E is the very fragile version that actually occurs: the *unaltered* alteration, so to speak. The rest are unactualized. If you think E is itself very fragile, you will think that all its unactualized alterations are alternatives, numerically different from E itself. If you think E is not at all fragile, you will think that all its alterations are different versions of one and the same event. Or you might think that some are alternatives and others are versions. Or you might refuse to have any opinion one way or the other, and that is the policy I favour. (Lewis 2004*a*, p. 88)

Still, there is a bit less of an advance here than it might appear. It is true that, in order to apply the influence analysis, we no longer have to settle whether, in one of the counterfactual situations under consideration (where some alteration of C occurs), E itself occurs. But we do have to settle what events (if any) in that situation count as alterations of E. Now, doing so will often be trivial. In a world like ours, if Billy and Suzy both throw rocks at a bottle and it breaks, then it breaks but once—and would have broken just once (at most), had either throw been different. And so, when we look to the counterfactual situations that feature alterations of one or both of Billy's and Suzy's throws, there is no difficulty in assigning the one breaking that occurs as an alteration of the actual breaking. But what about our bell-ringing variant? In fact, the bell rings twice in rapid succession: first under the impact of Suzy's rock, then under the impact of Billy's. Suppose we counterfactually alter Suzy's throw, so as to make it slower—by enough that the bell again rings twice in rapid succession, but, this time, first under the impact of Billy's rock. Presumably, we would like to say that it is the second of these counterfactual ringings that is an alteration of the first actual ringing. But why? Not because it has the same causes—that's cheating. On what grounds, then? The influence account needs an answer, and so has inherited an issue that—while perhaps not as troublesome as the issue of figuring out what's essential and accidental to an event—is certainly a close kin, since it still needs to figure out which properties need to be privileged when determining counterpart alterations.

4.2.3 Failure of the sensitivity strategy: the hardest cases of late preemption Setting this issue aside, we see serious problems of a quite different character with all the approaches (including Lewis's) that try to handle late preemption by assuming that the effect will be at least differentially counterfactually sensitive to the cause as compared to the backup. For such approaches threaten to erase the distinction between events that cause and events that merely make a difference to the manner of occurrence.

Consider that, e.g., thanks to the gravitational attraction between Billy's rock and Suzy's rock, Billy's throw will make some very slight difference to the time and manner of the bottle-shattering. But this does not qualify it as a cause of the event of the shattering (although it is, arguably, a cause of certain of the shattering's properties). But if, for instance, we took the bottle-shattering to be extremely modally fragile—so that any counterfactual difference in the manner or time of shattering would necessarily yield a numerically different event—then we get the unwelcome result that the shattering depends on Billy's throw, and hence is (according to counterfactual analyses) an effect of that throw.

According to the covariation account, the trouble is different: a wide range of alterations of the shattering manifestly will counterfactually covary with alterations of non-causes, for example, with alterations of Billy's throw. For example, just have Billy throw a little bit sooner, or a little bit faster, etc. (See Schaffer 2001 and Strevens 2003 for good critiques of Lewis's influence account along these lines.) The underlying moral is the same: for any candidate effect E, it is all too easy for an arbitrary earlier event C to become counterfactually implicated in the time and/or manner of E's occurrence; but to take that as automatic grounds for attributing a causal relationship would wreck the very sorts of distinctions that a philosophical account of causation is supposed to illuminate. (Further counterexamples to covariation accounts will emerge later.)

A possible reply asks us to imagine circumstances in which we might want to say that, in some sense, Billy's throw is a cause of the shattering. Imagine that we are scientists testing the minute gravitational effects created by moving objects. We set up a sensitive detector, and detect properties of the shattering that seem to be the result of Billy's action. Surely in such a situation we'd want to allow Billy's throw to be a cause of such properties of the shattering. Should we perhaps say that, in this context, Billy's throw does qualify as a cause of the shattering?

No. It's not just that the reply doesn't go far enough (since we would also like to be able to distinguish Billy's throw as a non-cause, simpliciter, in other contexts). It's also that the sensible move, at this point, is simply to become more sophisticated about the causal relata. One option, which we've already been a bit skeptical about, is to say that where (and when) the bottle shatters, there are in fact a multitude of perfectly coincident events. There is the plain-vanilla shattering, which is not at all modally fragile, and so could have occurred at different times and places. And there are other shatterings, distinguished only by the different ways in which they are modally fragile. One of these—an extremely modally fragile one—is indeed caused by Billy's throw (and also by Suzy's). We record, in ordinary language, our conviction that Billy's throw is not a cause of the plain-vanilla shattering simply by saying "Billy's throw isn't a cause of the shattering." But we register the fact that Billy's throw is a cause of a modally fragile shattering by saying (e.g.) "Billy's throw is a cause of the shattering happening in exactly the manner it does."

While some authors are quite comfortable enriching their ontologies of events in this way (see, e.g., Goldman 1970, Kim 1980, Yablo 1992a), we find a different approach more attractive. In short: take property instances to be the causal relata in the first instance, and particular events as the causal relata in the second instance, i.e., only insofar as they correspond to the right sort of property instances. If we make this move, then Billy's throw can be a cause of some property instances: for example, an instance of the property *being a shattering that happens at exactly noon*. But his throw will, by contrast, not be a cause of an instance of the property *being a shattering*. And for that reason, Billy's throw will not count as a cause of the event of the shattering.

Such a move requires additional metaphysical labor: most obviously, one must explain how property instances are related to one another and to events. Paul 2002 develops the basic underpinnings of an account of property instances and events, and Paul 2000 gives additional arguments in favor of taking property instances (in her terminology: "aspects") as the primary causal relata.

But as noted in chapter 2, a treatise on the causal relata goes too far afield from our main topic, so we will not pursue this point any further—save to point out that developing a theory of the relata that allows one to give Billy's throw some kind of causal status vis-à-vis the shattering doesn't by itself solve the problem we started with, which was to capture the clear sense in which his throw is not a cause of the shattering, while Suzy's is. If an account of causation cannot show how these two throws causally differ with respect to the shattering, then that account fails to draw a distinction that is, on the face of it, both obvious and important.

We will now argue that this problem is even more difficult than the examples so far discussed suggest. For it seems easy enough to construct late preemption examples in which, had the cause not occurred—or indeed, had any of the events connecting the cause to the effect not occurred—the effect would have occurred at exactly the same time, and in exactly the same manner. In figure 18, for example, suppose that the signal from **C** exerts a slight retarding force on the signal from **A**. Pick any point before this signal from **C** reaches **E**, and ask what would have happened if, at that time, the signal had been absent. Answer: the signal from **A** would have accelerated, and we can stipulate that it would have accelerated enough to reach **E** at exactly the time at which the signal from **C** in fact reaches **E**.

What we have in effect done by inserting this wrinkle is to turn our example into a kind of preemption case that was long ago dismissed by Lewis as having no probative value. The original case was due to Goosens (1979), who imagined a situation in which the main causal process successively cuts off an infinity of backups. (It also bears a strong similarity to Jonathan Schaffer's (2000c) case of *trumping*.) Here is Lewis, dismissing both Goosens' case and a case of early preemption involving action at a temporal distance:

> I do not worry about either of these far-fetched cases. They both go against what we take to be the ways of this world; they violate the presuppositions of our habits of thought; it would be no surprise if our common-sense judgments about them therefore went astray. . . . (Lewis 1986c, p. 203)

We disagree with this judgment of Goosens' example. (It is less clear what to say about cases of action at a temporal distance; see chapter 2, §4.4.) It is one thing to claim that a hypothetical situation is strange. It is quite another to claim that it fails to evoke clear, firm intuitions. Goosens' example, odd though it may be, does not at all fail in this respect. The stimulatory signal from **C** reaches **E**; no other stimulatory signal reaches **E**; **E** is the kind of neuron that will only fire if it receives such a signal; so how could there possibly be any doubt that *C* causes *E*? (See Maudlin 2004 for a forceful and more detailed defense of similar reasoning.) At any rate, the example is really not that odd. In all essential respects, it is just like our example of the delayed signal in figure 18: just collapse Goosens' infinity of distinct backup processes into one, and arrange things so that the main causal process is continuously interfering with this backup process.

So far, we have an example in which nothing about the effect counterfactually depends on any of its causes. But it might still seem to be open to a defender of a covariation account to claim that alterations of *C* would be followed by corresponding alterations of *E*. In fact, though, with a little bit of tinkering we can close this loophole as well. Let us now stipulate that in figure 18 the stimulatory signals from **C** and **A** are different. The one from **C** is a "special" signal, the one from **A** an "ordinary" signal. Neuron **E** can be stimulated to fire by a special signal only if that signal's physical characteristics are just right, and only if the signal reaches it at just the right time. (**E** is not so finicky when it comes to ordinary signals.[12]) And let us in addition stipulate that the power the signal from **C** has to delay the signal from **A** is exquisitely sensitive both to the physical characteristics of the **C**-signal, and to the time lag between the two signals. Piled on top of one another, these stipulations give the desired result: for we now see that if anything about *C* had been different—for that matter, if anything about *any* of the events leading from *C* to *E* had been different—then, in the first place, the **C**-signal would no longer have been capable of stimulating **E**, and, in the second place, the **A**-signal would no longer have been delayed, and so would have stimulated **E** to fire at exactly the time and in exactly the manner it does. So alterations in *C* would lead to no change whatsoever in *E*, and the same goes for alterations in any of the events causally intermediate between *C* and *E*.

Of course the case is convoluted. But what is important to appreciate is that the convolutions concern respects that are irrelevant to an evaluation of its causal structure. It will be instructive to see, in detail, why this is the case. Accordingly, consider figure 20:

Figure 20

What we have depicted here is a duplicate of part of what is depicted in figure 18; we have simply omitted **A**, and the signal traveling from it towards **E**. Otherwise, matters are exactly the same: **C** fires in just the same way; the signal traveling from it to **E** has exactly the same physical characteristics and reaches **E** at exactly the same time; **E** is finicky in just the same respects.

---

[12] This time sensitivity need not be due to some failure of time translation invariance in the fundamental laws. It can, instead, be due to the existence of some process internal to **E** that leaves open an extremely narrow window of opportunity for a special signal to stimulate it.

Now, forget about figure 18, and focus your intuitions firmly on figure 20, the pared-down example. Is there any doubt whatsoever that C causes E? Of course not. So return to figure 18, taking that firm intuitive judgment with you, and observe that, merely by adding to figure 20 a causally idle backup process starting with A, we arrive at figure 18. How could such an addition possibly make a difference to the fact that C causes E? And even supposing it did, should we then reason that E has no causes at all, or that it is somehow caused by A? Of course not. We conclude that there is no serious challenge to the intuitive verdict about figure 18 that C is a cause of E. But, since E does not counterfactually covary with C at all, the "sensitivity" strategies we are considering for handling late preemption fail.

4.2.4 Quasi-Newtonian laws   Perhaps the problem is with relying on counterfactuals to do the work of lawlike generalizations. Maudlin (2004) suspects that it is, and proposes a different way of thinking about the macrolevel causal structure of a situation. Roughly, the idea is that, by combining an assessment of the inertial states of a system with the appropriate "quasi-Newtonian" lawlike generalizations governing those states, we can determine causes of events in the system. Quasi-Newtonian lawlike generalizations have the form of generalizations that involve descriptions of how some entities behave when nothing acts on them, as well as generalizations that involve descriptions of the conditions under which these entities deviate from their "inertial" state. Maudlin seems to have in mind generalizations with the following form: "A system in state S will remain in state S, unless C happens, in which case it will change in such-and-such a way; or D happens, in which case it will change in such-and-such a way; etc." Causes bring about deviation from inertial states, and they are the sorts of things mentioned in the quasi-Newtonian generalizations about deviation.

In judging causes, we try to carve up the situation into systems that can be assigned inertial behavior (behavior that can be expected if nothing interferes) along with at least a partial specification of the sorts of things that can disturb the inertial behavior, analogous to the Newtonian forces that disturb inertial motion . . . we then think about how the situation will evolve by expecting inertial behavior unless there is an interaction with a threat, in which case we see how the threat will change the behavior. (Maudlin 2004, p. 436)

This suggests that a natural way to approach our case of late preemption is to determine the inertial and deviant states of the system in our example, and then use quasi-Newtonian laws to tell us which event is the cause of the effect in question. In our stock example, where Billy and Suzy each throw a rock at the bottle, take the quasi-Newtonian law to specify the inertial state as the state that unbroken bottles remain unbroken, and to describe the conditions of deviation by saying that unbroken bottles remain unbroken unless they are struck by rocks, or slammed down, etc. The bottle shatters after being hit by Suzy's rock, and so we read off from the laws that Suzy's rock is the cause of this "deviation".

The approach is appealing. Now, Maudlin does not propose this approach as an analysis of causation but rather as an explanation of some of our basic causal intuitions. But, given its simplicity and intuitive appeal, could it be dressed up into a reductive causal analysis? Unfortunately, no, for the account's simple and appealing approach to diagnosing the causal structure is too simple for reductivity. Our formulation embeds important assumptions—assumptions that reflect causal judgments. For consider an alternative formulation of the conditions of deviation that we used to diagnose the bottle-shattering: unbroken bottles remain unbroken unless they are struck by *accompanied rocks*, or struck by *unaccompanied rocks*, or slammed down, etc.

When we read off the causes from the laws this time, the most proximate condition that the laws count as "causing" the shattering is *the striking of the bottle by an accompanied rock*. To determine earlier causes, we must find *events responsible for this condition*. And so—tracing back—we find that both Suzy's throw and Billy's throw count as causes of the shattering. And this is exactly the sort of result we want to avoid. The trouble is, unless we have already somehow ruled out events such as *being struck by an accompanied rock* as ineligible for causal status, or have somehow already ruled out varieties of the quasi-Newtonian laws that "cover" these sorts of events, we will get the wrong causal diagnosis. And it is not at all clear how one could rule out this material without relying on the sorts of causal judgments that we are supposed to be using the account to discover.

4.2.5 De facto dependence once again   Let's consider next how a de facto dependence account might treat cases of late preemption. The literature expresses a great deal of optimism on this score. Here for example is Hitchcock (2001, p. 289):

Even without considering fine differences in the way Suzy throws her rock, or in the way the bottle shatters, it can be shown that there is an active route from Suzy's throw to the bottle's shattering. This is revealed by the following . . . counterfactual: *given* that Billy's rock did not hit the bottle, if Suzy had not thrown, the bottle would have remained intact throughout the incident.

Halpern and Pearl (2001, 2005), working within the same structural equations framework as Hitchcock but with a slightly different account, are likewise confident that their account can easily handle this case. Similarly, Yablo thinks his approach accommodates such cases straightforwardly. He writes (2004, p. 129),

Consider

DIRECT: Hit and Miss both roll balls down the lane. The balls do not come into contact. Hit's ball knocks the pin into the gutter. A moment later, Miss's ball reaches the spot where the pin formerly stood.

Once again, it is part of the circumstances that Miss's ball never gets close to the pin. That no other ball gets close puts the effect in need of Hit's throw.

In fact, however, the optimism on display here is unwarranted. A de facto dependence account may—just possibly—be able to provide an elegant solution to the problem posed by late preemption. But it must first surmount some serious obstacles.

Recall that when we introduced the de facto dependence treatment of early preemption in §2.3, we noted two general questions that this approach must answer: First, what principles determine the selection of the fact F to be held fixed? And second, how is the crucial counterfactual—"if event *C* had not occurred, but it had still been the case that F, then *E* would not have occurred"—to be evaluated? At the time, we waived the second question, as in the examples we were dealing with there was a ready answer, in the form of a sequential updating story. We will shortly see that matters are no longer so simple. But let's first examine the problems that arise in trying to answer, in a principled manner, the first general question, about the fact to be held fixed.

4.2.6 Finding the fact to be held fixed, part 1   It is usual, in constructing a case of late preemption, to introduce a pair of competing processes aimed at a given effect, where that effect is of a type that can (at least, in the circumstances) only occur once. A bottle or window shatters, or a bomb goes off, or a particular pin gets knocked over, etc. Take that kind of case as your paradigm, and you will naturally think that the fact to be held fixed should be some fact that bears witness to the backup process's failure to go to completion.

But we have already seen that there need be no such failure. Billy and Suzy throw rocks at the bell, which rings once as a result of her throw, and a second time as a result of his. Suppose you think that in the case where the two vandals throw rocks at a bottle, the fact to be held fixed is the fact that Billy's rock does not strike the bottle. Then what parallel fact to hold fixed will you find in the bell-ringing case? Not that Billy's rock does not strike the bell, for it does. What, then?

We think, in fact, that there is a subtle but serious dilemma here. But to bring it into focus, we first need to nip a certain temptation in the bud, which is to take it as too obvious to need argument that, in the counterfactual circumstance in which Suzy does not throw, the ringing that results (call it F) is identical to the second of the two ringings R_1 and R_2 that actually happen. (Cf. the discussion of this example at the end of §4.1, and the discussion in §4.2.1.) An argument for this judgment is absolutely essential, for, in the present dialectical context, it must be clear that the judgment holds—if in fact it does hold—for the right reasons. Or more to the point, we must be clear that it does not hold for this reason: $F = R_2$ (and $F \neq R_1$), because the causal origins of R_2 are preserved intact in the counterfactual situation.

Just to be clear, we have no particular objection to origin essentialism about events per se; its plausibility strikes us as on a par with Kripkean essentialism about objects. It's just that it cannot be appealed to in order to solve the problem posed by the bell-ringing case—else a noxious circularity infects the resulting account. (Not to mention that the whole apparatus of de facto dependence will have been rendered moot!) All of this, of course, is probably obvious. Still, it is worth emphasizing in order to guard against any tendency to simply accept the intuitive verdict that $R_1 \neq F = R_2$ and to make use of this verdict to handle the bell-ringing case without interrogating its source. No good: if you want to draw on this verdict, you need to show why you have a right to it.

And that leads to the aforementioned dilemma. The de facto dependence theorist needs to deal with the bell-ringing case by finding some fact F such that, had Suzy not thrown her rock, but had F still obtained, then R_1 would not have occurred. The problem is in securing this consequent. Now, in the usual kind of late preemption case—the kind where the target effect is, like a bottle-shattering, a kind of event that cannot easily recur—no such problem arises: the bottle in fact shatters just once, and so, had Suzy not thrown but had Billy's rock still failed to strike the bottle, it would not have shattered at all. (Later we'll discuss doubts about whether this counterfactual comes out true.) So there's no question of finding some event in the counterfactual situation that might turn out to be identical to the actual effect. But this easy guarantee that the actual effect goes missing, in the relevant counterfactual situation, is an artifact of perfectly idiosyncratic features of the bottle-shattering case, as the bell-ringing variant shows. So how will the de facto dependence theorist choose her F so that R_1 is, uncontroversially, absent in the counterfactual situation?

The first horn has her choosing an F so gerrymandered that, had Suzy not thrown but had F still obtained, the bell would not have rung at all, whence we can be sure that R_1 would not have occurred. That's easy enough to do: let F be the fact that either Suzy throws or the bell does not ring, or, for a touch more sophistication, let F be the fact that Billy's rock strikes the bell, if at all, only after it has already rung. But the trouble is in the gerrymandering. On an approach like Hitchcock's—where a candidate F needs to be a fact about the actual values of variables—it's not clear that we're entitled to either of the foregoing choices. On an approach like Yablo's—where we need to be sure that the fact F that bears witness to an event's status as cause is not "trumped" by a more natural F that undermines this status—the worry is just that the foregoing choices are quite unnatural.

The second horn has her choosing a less gerrymandered F, but with the cost that, had Suzy not thrown but had F still obtained, the bell would have rung anyway (thanks, presumably, to Billy's rock).[13] But then she needs to say why this ringing is not identical to R_1, its close similarity in time and manner notwithstanding. Now, she has answers available to her: e.g., make the exact time and manner of an event essential to it. But these answers carry costs of their own (see §4.2.1). And, as we already noted, with such an answer in place we render the de facto dependence account superfluous. For example, if she opts for an account according to which the exact time and manner of R_1 is essential to it, then R_1 will depend on Suzy's throw

---

[13] We note in passing that it's far from obvious what F would be, if not just a tautology.

outright, i.e., holding nothing fixed. In short, then, either she deals with the bell-ringing case by straining the apparatus of de facto dependence (first horn), or by not relying on it at all (second horn). Either way, it appears that the de facto dependence theory has no claim to be a new and improved method for dealing with late preemption.

4.2.7 Finding the fact to be held fixed, part 2   Let's set aside the bell-ringing variant for now and consider our standard Billy-Suzy rock-throwing case. The thought that many have is that the right way to handle this case is to note that Billy's rock does not, in fact, strike the bottle, and to choose this fact as the one to hold fixed. But problems arise: different ones for different accounts. In Hitchcock's case (at least, as we have understood him), the difficulty is that the fact to be held fixed is supposed to be a fact about the values of some variables (off-path variables, more specifically), and it is not clear to what values of what variables the preferred fact corresponds. Presumably, he will settle on some surrogate. Suppose, for example, that Billy's rock would have struck the bottle at precisely noon, had Suzy not thrown. We might then introduce a variable to characterize the state, at noon, of the region of space the bottle occupies (before it is shattered, that is!). We might then set the value of this variable to 1 iff this state consists of a rock striking the bottle, and 0 otherwise. So far, so good—except that as we will see later, the price of being clear and rigorous about the choice of variables is that the account's inability to produce an adequate and true counterfactual becomes easy to expose.

What about Yablo? He places no restrictions on what sorts of facts can be held fixed, so the problem that besets Hitchcock does not touch him. But another one does. For it is all too easy to find a choice of F that, by his lights, shows that Billy's throw is a cause of the shattering. This one will do: (F) at no time is Suzy's rock more than a few feet in front of Billy's.

Observe first that if Billy had not thrown, and if it had still been the case that Suzy's rock was never more than a few feet in front of Billy's, then, plausibly, the bottle would not have shattered. (For—plausibly!—Suzy's rock would have remained in the vicinity of Billy and his rock and never reached the bottle.[14]) Next, this choice of F is in fact good. To see this,

---

[14] The reason for the qualifier "plausibly" is that there are deviant ways of settling what happens in this counterfactual situation: e.g., have Billy fail to throw, but have his rock fly through the air anyway. But

observe that if Billy had not thrown, then one event the effect would have depended on is Suzy's throw. But, holding F fixed, the effect does not depend on her throw. So the set of events the shattering would have depended on, absent Billy's throw, is not a subset (non–empty or otherwise) of the set of events it does depend on, holding F fixed. So F is good.

Of course it does not yet follow that, on Yablo's account, Billy's throw is a cause of the shattering: after all, maybe there is some more natural choice of F that (by being bad) undermines its claim. But so far, there looks to be no salient difference between the way the account is supposed to secure Suzy's throw as a cause of the shattering and the way it appears to mistakenly secure Billy's throw as a cause. And that is, of course, bad news.

4.2.8 Evaluating the counterfactual, part 1   Time now to return to the second question: how are we to evaluate the needed counterfactual? Let's work with the case Hitchcock considers, where the target Billy and Suzy have selected is a bottle—precariously perched, let's suppose, on a post. Suppose we have somehow selected, on a principled basis, the fact F that Billy's rock never touches the bottle. We then need to consider the conditional, "If Suzy had not thrown her rock, and if Billy's rock never touches the bottle, then the bottle would not have broken." Is this conditional true? Remember that we are not to evaluate this conditional by, for example, supposing that Billy likewise fails to throw his rock—for that is not to find actual facts and hold them fixed, but rather to find actual facts and alter them; it would also presumably have the result that Billy's throw de facto depends on Suzy's throw. No, the counterfactual situation envisaged is one in which Suzy does not throw, but Billy does throw, and with just as deadly an aim.

It's unclear how exactly such a situation will play out, given that Billy's rock must somehow fail to touch the bottle. Note that we cannot simply apply, in some mechanical fashion, a sequential updating account. Such an account works well if the conditional's antecedent has a certain kind of content. For example, the sequential updating account can easily handle this one: "If Suzy had not thrown, and Billy's rock had vanished just before striking the bottle, then the bottle would not have broken." For we just proceed like this: First alter the state of the world at the time of Suzy's throw

---

to defend Yablo's account by claiming that such a deviant way is, in fact, the right way of treating the counterfactual simply exposes the account more fully to the criticism leveled in the next sub-section.

just enough to make her not throw (perhaps to engage in some default behavior instead). Evolve forward to the time just before Billy's rock would strike the bottle. Alter that state of the world by removing Billy's rock from it. Evolve forward. The bottle does not shatter.

But what makes that example work so smoothly is that each of the two parts of the antecedent specifies an "instruction," as it were, that can be followed by changing the total state of the world in a localized manner at a non-arbitrary place and time. In the case at hand, where we simply have an instruction like "Billy's rock never touches the bottle," what we are given is much more open-ended: we are to make some change to the world (in the counterfactual situation that begins with Suzy not throwing), so that Billy's rock fails to strike the bottle. But there are ever so many ways to do that, by making local modifications to the world at different times and places. So we seem to be left adrift.

Worse than adrift, really, since perfectly plausible ways of constructing the needed counterfactual scenario have the result that the bottle does shatter. Remember that the bottle is perched on a post. Then one way it could come about that Suzy does not throw, that Billy does throw, and that Billy's rock somehow fails to strike the bottle, is for a gust of wind to knock the ball off the post before Billy's rock arrives—in which case, fragile thing that it is, the bottle shatters upon hitting the ground.

Is the problem merely that we have been artless in our choice of fact to hold fixed? Well, if we could let this fact be the fact that Billy's rock vanishes at a certain time, then, as noted three paragraphs ago, all would be well. The antecedent of the counterfactual would have the kind of determinate character it needs to have, and the counterfactual would, very plausibly, come out true. But there is no such fact. On the other hand, we could observe that it is a fairly specific fact about the actual situation that, at a certain time (namely, the time at which Billy's rock would have struck the bottle, had Suzy not thrown), Billy's rock is flying through bottle-free air. But if we choose this fact to hold fixed, then an obvious way to make it obtain, in the counterfactual situation, is to have the bottle fall from its perch just before Billy's rock reaches it.[15]

---

[15] There are other ways, to be sure: you could have the bottle vanish (in which case, presumably, it does not break) before Billy's rock reaches it. Try, as an exercise, to find some grounds for preferring that way of constructing the counterfactual scenario that's more principled than just that doing so helps save the de facto dependence account.

Notice that if we could make free use of causal facts about our late preemption case, then we could plausibly provide a successful recipe for constructing the relevant counterfactual situation (a recipe quite different, we should note, from the sequential updating one). For we could proceed as follows. First, identify all the causes of the bottle-shattering; distinguish these from other events that are non-causes. Next, construct a counterfactual situation in which Suzy does not throw, Billy throws, but in which other forces are introduced—let us provide them with the convenient label "God"—that cause the events to be held fixed to occur, without in any way interfering with any of the processes that are, in actual fact, causally involved in the bottle-shattering. So we allow God to do whatever it takes to Billy's rock to make it the case that it does not hit the bottle, as long as these interventions do not causally interact with the bottle itself. Generalized, this approach might yield a recipe that gives the desired result, for any case of late preemption, that the target effect de facto depends on the actual cause. But even if so, it does so in a way that is, of course, unacceptable to the de facto dependence account, and unacceptable to any account that is suitably reductive.

By the way, one reason for mentioning this recipe for evaluating counter-factuals is to guard against the sort of mistake we discussed in §4.2.1. There, we noted that it might seem perfectly intuitively obvious that, in the bell-ringing case, the ringing that would have happened, had Suzy not thrown, is identical to the second (and not the first) of the two actual ringings. Maybe so. But, we said, given a reductive approach, you have no right to that intuitive verdict until you can show how to secure it without appeal to causal facts. Similarly, it may seem perfectly intuitively obvious that, in the bottle-shattering case, had Suzy not thrown, and had Billy's rock failed to strike the bottle, the bottle would not have shattered. But the same point applies: you have no right to this (allegedly) intuitive verdict until you can show how to secure it without appeal to causal facts—i.e., *not* by means of the account sketched in the last paragraph. Make sure that appeal to such an account is not what was operating in the back of your mind. Once you have done so, the verdict turns out to be surprisingly hard to secure.

A final temptation that is, we think, to be resisted is to try to handle these problems by building the sort of explicitly pragmatic component we discussed in chapter 2 into one's account, as some causal modeling theorists seem inclined to do. On such a move, a theory makes it merely a pragmatic matter, determined by certain evaluative contexts and interests, which "interventions" in the relevant counterfactual situation are allowed and which are not. In some contexts, the counterfactual "had Suzy not thrown, and had Billy's rock still failed to strike the bottle, the bottle would not have shattered" comes out false—because the contextually-relevant standards for constructing the counterfactual situation allow us to make the antecedent true by, in part, knocking the bottle off its perch. But in other contexts (so the story goes), the conditional comes out true.

We are not convinced by this response. You should say what the standards are—how, in detail, they function—in the contexts in which the conditional is true. But if you can do that, then you've got the ingredients for a non-pragmatic account, perhaps something close to a contrastivist theory of causation. Unless, of course, the standards function by paying attention to the causal structure of the situation, in which case the move departs significantly from the sort of reductive treatments of causation we are considering here. In that case, unless causal modeling theorists want to explicitly set aside reductivity, the appeal to pragmatics needs much more defense than we have seen in the literature.

4.2.9 Evaluating the counterfactual, part 2 At this point, you're no doubt wondering what advocates of de facto dependence accounts say about this problem of evaluating the counterfactual. Yablo doesn't address the problem. As for those who, like Hitchcock, pursue a de facto dependence account within the confines of a causal modeling approach to causation, there is more to say. For what one finds in this part of the literature is a widespread belief that a very simple set of structural equations can provide the tools for evaluating the given counterfactual (concerning, say, the bottle-shattering case). Let's take a look.

The model is quite elegant and simple, and judging from various personal conversations we have had, it is currently thought of as providing a canonical structural equations treatment of this case. It makes use of just five variables:

ST: has value 0 if Suzy does not throw; 1 if she does.
BT: has value 0 if Billy does not throw; 1 if he does.
SH: has value 0 if Suzy's rock does not hit the bottle; 1 if it does.
BH: has value 0 if Billy's rock does not hit the bottle; 1 if it does.
BS: has value 0 if the bottle does not shatter; 1 if it does.

We should understand each of these variables as making implicit reference to a particular time. More specifically, let's stipulate that Suzy throws at time 0, Billy throws at (slightly later) time 1, Suzy's rock strikes the bottle at time 2, Billy's rock would have struck the bottle at time 3 (i.e., if Suzy's had not already done so), and the bottle is in a shattered state at time 4. So ST characterizes what Suzy is doing at time 0; BT what Billy is doing at time 1; SH what Suzy's rock is doing at time 2; BH what Billy's rock is doing at time 3; and BS the state of the bottle at time 4. What we wish to write down are structural equations that show that it is Suzy's throw, and not Billy's, that causes the bottle to be in a shattered state at time 4.

This might seem easy. Many find the following equations satisfactory (e.g., see Halpern and Pearl 2005):

1. $BS \Leftarrow BH + SH - BH \bullet SH$
2. $BH \Leftarrow BT(1 - SH)$
3. $SH \Leftarrow ST$

(Here the arrow $\Leftarrow$, in place of an " = " sign, is just supposed to signal that we have an equality, but an equality in which the variable on the left depends on those on the right.)

Assuming these equations are correct, we can confirm that, for example, Hitchcock's account judges Suzy's throw to be a cause of the shattering. The equations themselves tell us what "paths" there are. Thus, there is a path from ST to BS by way of SH; the variable BH lies off this path. Since, in fact, $BH = 0$, we can establish the causal connection between Suzy's throw ($ST = 1$) and the shattering ($BS = 1$) by means of the conditional

if ($ST = 0$ & $BH = 0$), then $BS = 0$

To evaluate this conditional, all we have to do is make use of the foregoing equations. We start by setting ST to 0, and use the third equation to derive that $SH = 0$. Since the counterfactual's antecedent explicitly specifies the value of BH, we ignore the second equation. Finally, we fix the value of BS by means of the first equation. Since $SH = 0 = BH$, this value is likewise 0.

It's also not hard to confirm that Hitchcock's account will—again, given this set of structural equations—judge Billy's throw not to be a cause of the shattered state. But let's take a closer look at just what these equations mean. Here they are again:

1. BS $\Leftarrow$ BH + SH − BH•SH
2. BH $\Leftarrow$ BT(1 − SH)
3. SH $\Leftarrow$ ST

The third is unobjectionable: it says that Suzy's rock will hit the bottle iff she throws it. Given that we only mean to be considering four options for the temporally prior variables ST and BT—she throws/doesn't throw at just the time and with just the speed she does; he throws/doesn't throw at just the time and with just the speed he does—this equation is perfectly correct. The first equation might also seem correct: for it says merely that the bottle will be in a shattered state iff at least one of the rocks hits it. Likewise the second, which says that Billy's rock will hit the bottle iff he throws it, and Suzy's rock hasn't already hit it (for in that case, it won't be there for his rock to hit).

But now we should smell a rat. Look again, and closely, at the first two equations. The first strikes us as true in part because, when we envision a situation in which BH = 0 and SH = 0, we understand that BH = 0 because Billy's rock isn't thrown, and instead lies idle (we may suppose) in his hand. But the second strikes us as true in part for a different reason—when we envision a situation in which BT = 1 and SH = 1, we understand that BH = 0 because the bottle isn't there to be hit! But—this is the problem—this means the model is trading on this ambiguity in the content of the claim "BH = 0." Remove the ambiguity, and one or the other of the first two equations must be revised. But once revised, the causal model no longer delivers the conditionals it needs to. (See Hall 2007 for a more detailed presentation of this criticism.)

4.2.10 De facto dependence and reductionism about causation As we have already noted, we have found that defenders of a de facto dependence approach, whether in the guise of structural equations or something else, make selective use of causal information at various points, in order to defend their approach against the problem cases (late preemption being just one of the more prominent). Our discussion has developed some of the ways this can happen. Sometimes this deployment of causal information happens well below the surface; for example, we think this is going on when we are told that, in the bell-ringing case, it's just "obvious" that the one ringing that would have happened is identical to the second of the two ringings that do happen. Sometimes it's more overt, as when fans of causal modeling such as Pearl and Halpern tell us that we have quite a lot of freedom in writing down a (correct!) causal model for any given situation; that relative to some models, one of the situation's events might turn out to be a cause of another, whereas relative to other (equally correct!) models, it won't; and that this remarkable flexibility is actually a feature, not a bug. Now, this view may make sense, if we expect these causal models simply to provide the tools for compactly representing and explicating antecedently understood causal information. But we have argued that one needs to be very careful that this is all that is being claimed for such views. Do not misunderstand us— such representation and explication of antecedently understood causal structure is useful. It's just that we see a vexing lack of attention in the literature to the distinction between this sort of project and a reductive project which actually discovers antecendently unknown causal structure (recall our discussion of bad habits from chapter 2, §3.1.4).

Perhaps the defender of the de facto dependence approach can claim that she is within her rights to help herself to a certain amount of causal information when responding to varieties of preemption cases and other problems. Perhaps. But one must ensure that this response to our worries does not rely on an illegitimate shift of the terms of the debate. As we have emphasized, it is absolutely fine to defend one's right to explore the nature of causation from a partly nonreductive perspective. Such explorations often uncover surprising and deep insights about the nature of our causal concepts and the causal relation. Seen as this sort of enquiry, the de facto approach may be able to make important contributions to the discussion on causation, and at any rate we think it is well worth paying attention to.

But our task is different, and much harder: it is the attempt to analyze and understand causation from a reductive perspective. This is the task we are discussing, and this is what Lewis and many others who we have been engaging with have explicitly been trying to do.

Now, interestingly, in the service of a reductive approach, it can be perfectly acceptable to consider examples where various apparently causal stipulations about the nature of the case (such as the fact that a neuron will only fire if it is stimulated at intensity 10, or that some neurons prevent or reduce intensity) are in place. However, such examples are allowed to encode causal information because they are being examined to see how the analysis on offer treats them. They are not being offered up as situations described in causally-neutral vocabulary, where the point is to put to use a reliable analysis of causation to determine whether or not causation obtains in that instance.

But for any reductive analysis to have a prayer of being accepted, once developed, it must be able to do exactly that. So once we have developed and explored an analysis of causation using examples where causal information is relied upon to "get the example across," to complete the analysis we must be able to develop it so it can be used to handle cases where all we are given are patterns of dependence and other noncausal information. In the reductive end game, one must be able to throw off the yoke of requiring causal information.

As we have seen, the de facto approach, as it stands, does not seem to be able to accomplish this last step. And if it is insufficiently reductive, then it cannot be posed as a competitor to, say, Lewis's influence account, or indeed to any account that is constrained to rely only upon noncausal information when analyzing cases. If an account discussed in this context is not reductive, its success with cases of late preemption and the like is largely irrelevant, as it fails to engage with the goals and hence the problems of the reductive project.

We think this point has become obscured in the recent literature, and not just in the discussion of the de facto approach. There have been a host of attempts to solve problems with late preemption, overdetermination and the like using techniques such as causal modeling that—when one looks at the details—are being developed and deployed in a nonreductive manner.

Such attempts overreach if they present themselves as solving problems that earlier accounts like that of Lewis (1986b, 1986c, 2004a) do not. Nonreductive accounts are addressing a different, and frankly much easier problem than Lewis and other reductionists are trying to solve. We will return to this point when we discuss recent work by Hitchcock (2007a) in chapter 4 that exploits a distinction between default situations and deviant situations using what he calls "self-contained networks." Here the notion is of default and deviant values of variables used in structural equations describing causal models. Hitchcock conjoins the self-containment approach to the de facto approach in order to try to solve problems with late (and early) preemption. However, the self-containment approach (even when combined with the de facto approach) cannot explain why we make certain kinds of causal judgments in straightforward cases. And, since Hitchcock's self-containment account explicitly relies on a nonreductive distinction between default and deviant outcomes,[16] it is infected by the same problems.

It appears that we will need to look elsewhere for help with late preemption.

4.3 Causation and intrinsicness

Reflection on our intuitive verdict about figure 18, especially our verdict at the end of §4.2.3 after considering figure 20, points to the alternative and rather different strategy for dealing with late preemption that we have in mind. We noted in the opening paragraphs of this guide that we include the thesis that the causal structure of a process is intrinsic to it on the list of attractive general principles about causation. Arguably, some such principle is at work in guiding our intuitive judgments about figure 18, and about cases of late preemption quite generally. Surely, the thought goes, what singles out Suzy's throw, and not Billy's, as a cause of the bottle's shattering is that what happens to connect Suzy's throw to the shattering is just like what would have happened had Billy been absent (whereas the same cannot be said of Billy's throw). A little more carefully, if—in some yet-to-be-specified sense—the causal structure of a process is intrinsic to it, then perhaps the causal facts about the Billy-Suzy rock throwing case are grounded in the causal facts about a much simpler case (namely, the one that lacks Billy), together with facts about the intrinsic similarity between goings-on in the two cases. But to see whether a promising analysis can be distilled from these inchoate observations, we must first investigate in exactly what sense causal structure is intrinsic to processes that exhibit it. That turns out to be a subtle matter.

4.3.1 Statement of the intrinsicness thesis

How shall we capture, in a usefully precise form, the idea that causal structure is intrinsic? Start by taking "intrinsic" to mean something like "internal" or "metaphysically independent"; intuitively, the way something is intrinsically is the way it is independent of how anything else is. There are legitimate philosophical concerns about the best way to understand intrinsicness, but we'll set them aside and assume that the distinction is in good enough working order to be deployed

---

[16] See Hitchcock 2007a, p. 506.

in an account of causation. (For discussions of analyses of intrinsicness, see, e.g., Langton and Lewis 1998, Marshall and Parsons 2001, Sider 2001 and 2003 and Weatherson 2001.)

Assume that we can isolate the intrinsic character of a system from its extrinsic dependence on the laws of nature, either by adopting an account of lawful behavior as somehow internal to the system, or by keeping this extrinsic feature at bay by comparing systems governed by the same laws. Assume next that we have a clear method for individuating events and determining which of their properties are intrinsic.

Let's begin with this: the intrinsic character of a comprehensive structure of events S is determined by the intrinsic properties of the events in S and the spatiotemporal distances between those events. Another way to put the idea is this: two structures of events are alike in intrinsic character just in case there is some way to pair up the events in one structure with the events in the other, such that paired events share exactly the same intrinsic properties, and when C and D in one structure instantiate some spatiotemporal relation, their counterparts C' and D' in the other structure instantiate exactly the same spatiotemporal relation.

Even with this background in place, it is surprisingly difficult to state a defensible version of the desired "intrinsicness thesis." Here, for example, is a simple idea: whether C is a cause of E is determined by the intrinsic character of the C–E structure (i.e., the structure of events that consists just of C and E), together with the prevailing laws of nature. In other words, any nomologically possible structure that features the same intrinsic character as the C–E structure has the same causal structure. That is hopeless, as figure 21 shows.

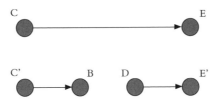

Figure 21

Here C causes E; the pair (C, E) perfectly intrinsically duplicates the pair (C', E'); yet C' does not cause E'.

Consulting the literature, we find a more sophisticated statement from Lewis (1986c, p. 205):

Suppose we have processes—courses of events, which may or may not be causally connected—going on in two distinct spatiotemporal regions, regions of the same or of different possible worlds. Disregarding the surroundings of the two regions, and disregarding any irrelevant events that may be occurring in either region without being part of the process in question, what goes on in the two regions is exactly alike. Suppose further that the laws of nature that govern the two regions are exactly the same. Then can it be that we have a causal process in one of the regions but not the other? It seems not. Intuitively, whether the process going on in a region is causal depends only on the intrinsic character of the process itself, and on the relevant laws. The surroundings, and even other events in the region, are irrelevant.

But if a "process" is any old structure of events, then this statement suffers the same refutation as the one just considered. And if Lewis means something more restrictive by "process," he does not tell us what that is.

Here, in the abstract, is our problem. Suppose we have two events, C and E, and some structure of events S to which they belong. If that structure is too impoverished—in the limit, if S just consists of C and E, and nothing else—then the chances are remote indeed that its intrinsic character will, together with the laws, settle whether C is a cause of E. Presumably, then, if we are to discern causal structure within intrinsic character, we must focus on the intrinsic character of a suitably comprehensive structure of events.

How comprehensive? To answer that question, let us separate our task into two parts. Take it that we are focusing on two events: C and, occurring later, E.

First, suppose that C is not a cause of E. How comprehensive would a structure of events containing C and E have to be, if its intrinsic character were (together with the laws) to settle that C is not a cause of E? Answer: very, very comprehensive. For it would have to tell the history between C and E in enough detail to rule out any way of adding stuff to that history that would secure a causal connection between C and E. That looks hopeless.

Second, suppose that C is a cause of E. How comprehensive would a structure of events containing C and E have to be, if its intrinsic character were (together with the laws) to settle that C is a cause of E? Answer: perhaps not so very comprehensive. More helpfully, it would, plausibly, only need to contain those events causally intermediate between C and E, along with those events with which C causally combines to bring about E. (For our reasons, see Hall 2004.) Don't be distracted by the reference to causation in our formulation: we will see in the next section how, for all that, the approach can aid a reductive approach to causation.

Here is another way to put the idea. Suppose we are given some event E. We focus on the causal processes that combine to bring it about, beginning at the time of one of its causes C. Then the thought is that if we hold fixed the character of these processes (together with E itself), but merely vary the environment within which they find themselves, we cannot undo the fact that every constituent event is a cause of E. And so we have a first pass at our intrinsicness thesis:

Intrinsicness Thesis: Let S be a structure of events consisting of event E, together with all of its causes back to some earlier time t. Let S' be a structure of events whose intrinsic character matches the intrinsic character of S and exists in a world with the same laws. Let E' be the event in S' that corresponds to E in S. Let C be some event in S distinct from E, and let C' be the event in S' that corresponds to C. Then C' is a cause of E'.

To introduce a handy bit of terminology, we might call the structure S a *blueprint*. We could then summarize the thesis: C' is a cause of E' if the two events belong to a structure of events that intrinsically matches a suitable blueprint. (Where "suitable" means: the blueprint consists of a counterpart E of E', together with all of its causes back to the time of a counterpart C of C'.)

We think this thesis is defensible, though not without some costs—the most dramatic of which is that it is, surprisingly, inconsistent with the claim that counterfactual dependence is sufficient for causation. (We'll see the reasons for this in the next chapter.) Moreover, as we shall see in chapter 5, §1.2, the thesis sharply contradicts the contrastivist's hope that extrinsic differences between structures of events can be employed to solve problems with transitivity arising from embedded double prevention.

But even though it creates trouble for counterfactual-based accounts, our thesis characterizes the heart of the deeply intuitive idea that we can match intrinsic character in order to determine causal structure. The central point we want to make here is that if the intrinsicness thesis or something like it is right, then it goes a long way towards explaining how our intuitive judgments about cases of late preemption work.

How so? By showing how we might use matching criteria to discover causal structure embedded within a complex system of events. If we have some determinately causal structure in a system S, and we can match this structure to a part of a complex system S', the intrinsicness thesis will ensure that the match will be a causal match.

To see the idea in action, consider a plausible claim about late preemption cases: we can arrive at a case of late preemption by beginning with a case of perfectly ordinary, garden variety causation involving a structure of events S, and then adding details to it that concern matters extrinsic to S. Thus, we can arrive at figure 18 by starting with figure 4, and adding extrinsic details. In this way, we can arrive at the case of Billy, Suzy, and the bottle by starting with a situation in which Suzy alone throws a rock at the bottle, and then adding extrinsic details (Billy and his throw), and so on. If, as our intrinsicness thesis states, such extrinsic changes make no difference to the causal structure of the process we begin with, then it is no surprise that cases of late preemption evoke such clear and firm intuitive judgments: we "see" embedded in them, as it were, perfectly ordinary cases of causation.

So far, so good: maybe we have, here, the right story about what makes our judgments concerning late preemption tick. The question that presses now is: Can we leverage this into a reductive account?

4.3.2 The blueprint strategy

Maybe. Our hope is that if we can come up with a partially reductive account in the form of a provisional analysis that succeeds for sufficiently simple cases of causation, we can let these simple cases serve as blueprints, and then bring in the intrinsicness thesis to do the rest of the reductive work.

Why does this strategy have such promise? Simply because we've identified one of the most—if not the most—important features of causation that obtains between events. Intrinsicness seems to capture a deep truth about causation, and we can exploit this in our approach towards constructing a reductive account.

We will start by breaking the task down into two parts. First, we find an account—a reductive account!—that, when applied to sufficiently simple cases, succeeds in identifying all the causes of a given event E back to some earlier time. Second, having used the account to identify such blueprints, we wheel in the intrinsicness thesis, thereby allowing the account to indirectly yield verdicts about a wider range of cases. (The hope, of course, is that its expanded range will be wide enough.) Note well that a provisional analysis must not get cases wrong—if it cannot correctly diagnose a case as a case of causation, it must simply fall silent about it.

As an illustration, consider figure 20 again:

Figure 20

Suppose we have come up with a provisional analysis that gets this case right: it successfully identifies C, together with the events constituting the passage of the stimulatory signal to **E**, as being all the causes of E. Further, let us suppose our provisional analysis simply falls silent about figure 18.

Still, figure 18 contains within it a perfect intrinsic duplicate of the structure of events depicted in figure 20. According to our intrinsicness thesis, then, C in figure 18 is a cause of E. More to the point: the combination of our provisional analysis and our intrinsicness thesis entails that C is a cause of E in figure 18.

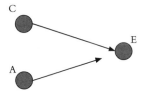

Figure 18

The advantage of this strategy is that it could considerably lower the bar for an analysis of causation to count as successful: all it really needs to do is get a range of simple cases right, and shut up about the rest! And that would be nice, since if we've shown anything in the preceding pages, we've shown that the bar for a complete, successful reductive analysis of causation is extremely high indeed.

4.3.3 Some challenges But even if the bar is lower, finding a provisional analysis that meets the new standard is still no easy task, since, in order to pick out a blueprint, it must at least sometimes be able to identify all the causes of E (back to some earlier time) as such. And that takes the bar back up a couple of notches.

Suppose, for example, your provisional analysis says that dependence suffices for causation, but does not say anything more. (Forget, for the

moment, that this would be a bad idea, since the intrinsicness thesis contradicts this sufficient condition.) Then it won't get late preemption cases
wrong; instead, it will just fall silent. But, arguably, it gets many simpler
cases—say, a case where Suzy is by herself, throwing a rock at a bottle—
exactly right. Still, it's not enough: for what it doesn't say, of such simpler
cases, is that the events it identifies as causes are all the causes. And it needs
to, if it is to single out a blueprint.

Let's try again. Suppose your provisional analysis says that, when a set S of
contemporaneous events is (i) minimally sufficient for E, and (ii) the only set
of events occurring at that time minimally sufficient for E, then it contains
all the causes of E occurring at that time. That looks better: the analysis still
knows when to fall silent (e.g., in cases of late preemption, which feature
multiple minimally sufficient sets), but can sometimes manage to identify
blueprints as such (e.g., in our simple Suzy-rock-throwing case). But the
problem is that it gets some cases flatly wrong, e.g., figure 15.

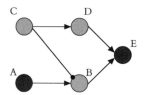

Figure 15

Here, at the time at which **C** and **A** fire, $\{A\}$ is the unique minimally
sufficient set for E (exercise). But C is one of E's causes. Oops.

So it remains to be seen whether the right sort of provisional analysis can
be produced. (One of us—Hall—is confident, though even he recognizes
that it will require delicate construction.) We won't pursue the matter
further, save to make two further points: first, it seems likely to us that a
successful provisional analysis would, like the example of the last paragraph,
need to be built along the lines of our minimal sufficiency account. And that
is because, again, the thesis that counterfactual dependence suffices for
causation—a thesis which is likely to feature in any attempt to build a
provisional analysis along the lines of counterfactual analyses—contradicts
the intrinsicness thesis. Second, even with a provisional analysis in hand that
seems to be of the right form—it identifies some blueprints successfully; it

doesn't get any case wrong—there will remain the question whether this analysis, when augmented by the intrinsicness thesis, will cover all cases.

A very different challenge concerns the very notion of intrinsic similarity and its use in the blueprint strategy. Some, of course, will balk at any appeal to a notion of intrinsicness, complaining about how difficult it is to provide a proper analysis of it. We see a deeper difficulty. Consider for example the contrast between the situation in which Billy and Suzy both throw rocks at the bottle, but Suzy's gets there first, and the situation which is just like this, except that Billy is absent, so the only rock thrown is Suzy's. Just like this? Well, no, of course not: because of Billy's absence, there will, of nomological necessity, be ever so slight intrinsic differences in the structure of events consisting of the flight of Suzy's rock towards the bottle. We have, in the case where Suzy is alone, a structure of events consisting of the shattering of the bottle together with all of its causes back to the time of Suzy's throw. We have, in the case where both Suzy and Billy throw, an intrinsic duplicate of this structure. But not a perfect intrinsic duplicate. Those who want to exploit the blueprint strategy will either need to come up with a structure of events that adequately minimizes the relevant intrinsic differences, or they need to explain, in a suitably reductive way, how these differences are irrelevant to the application of the intrinsicness thesis. Somehow, we need to be able to make out that the two structures are nevertheless intrinsically similar in all relevant respects.

So far, it may seem to the reader that we have done our best to make the blueprint strategy seem unattractive. (Still more trouble comes later when we examine an apparent counterexample to our intrinsicness thesis.) But in this domain, beauty is a highly relative matter, and the blueprint strategy deserves the attention we have lavished on it not merely because the intrinsicness thesis upon which it is based brings out, in an appealing way, some of the central content of our causal judgments, but more significantly because no alternative stands out as clearly superior to it. In addition, it is worth emphasizing that, given the conflict between the intrinsicness thesis and the claim that counterfactual dependence suffices for causation, we have here a quite dramatic fork in the road, a point at which counterfactual and regularity analyses must clearly diverge in the approach that they take to handling preemption, and diverge in a way that will have far-reaching ramifications for the picture of causation they ultimately settle on. We will see some of these ramifications emerge in more detail in chapter 4.

4.3.4 Virulent late preemption   It should be clear by now that cases of late preemption, such as the one depicted by figure 18,

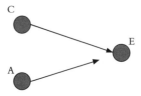

Figure 18

present an extremely serious challenge to any philosophically adequate reductive analysis of causation.

On the one hand, their structure is crystal clear, and the intuitions they evoke rock-solid—even when, as with Goosens' case, we consider unusual examples. It is obvious that *C* is a cause of *E*. There is thus little room—none, really—for arguing that our intuitive judgments about this sort of case should not be taken seriously, or can be explained away as resulting from misleading or overly unfamiliar features. On the other hand, once the dust settles it appears that only a very few strategies remain for handling late preemption, perhaps just two: the strategy based on the intrinsicness thesis, and the strategy based on the notion of de facto dependence. And we have seen that neither strategy, at least in its current state of development, is satisfactory.

But has the dust in fact settled? Could we think of some further refinement to our late preemption counterexample that creates new trouble—our most virulent example of late preemption yet? Perhaps. We will present a candidate for such an example, although we will see that the price for its greater intractability is a certain loss of intuitive clarity. So, although it is worth exploring, as it suggests that there is more to learn about late preemption, we don't want to rely too heavily on conclusions about its overall import.

The idea, in what follows, is to present an example that—if we can agree on the right interpretation of it—can be used as a sort of diagnostic test. The thought is that, by considering a particularly recalcitrant example of late preemption, we can identify some of the features of such cases that seem to be responsible for our causal judgments. In addition, we can evaluate the ways in which our various candidate analyses try to handle the example. Their successes or failures here may help us to determine effective ways to approach further analysis.

Let us begin to develop our diagnostic test by focusing on the concept of prevention, as realized, for example, by our familiar inhibitory signals.

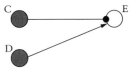

Figure 22

In figure 22, it is correct to say that the inhibitory signal from **C** prevents **E** from firing. It is also correct to say that the inhibitory signal from **C** prevents the stimulatory signal from **D** from causing **E** to fire by somehow interrupting the causal process from D to E. Notice that the latter sort of claim does not entail the former sort: in general, it does not follow from the claim that one process prevents another process from issuing in a certain effect that that effect does not occur. So it seems that we could add to figure 22 a second stimulatory signal from **A**—one that is immune from the inhibitory effects of the signal from **C**, and that therefore brings about E.

For example, in figure 23, the inhibitory signal from **C** prevents the signal from **D** from bringing about E; nevertheless, **E** fires as the result of the stimulus from **A**.

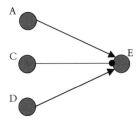

Figure 23

It may not be obvious that figure 23 supports the gloss we would like to give it: namely, that C and D interact such that C inhibits just the process from D to E, thus preventing D from bringing about E, while A, blissfully independent of the C–D tussle, succeeds in causing E. But why not? Why can't C neutralize D while A is left free to cause E? Something much like this happens all the time in the real world (if we allow some events to be prevented): Suzy aims her rock at the bottle, about to fire away with her usual deadly accuracy.

Billy, who has had some coffee, acts more quickly than usual, and blocks her throw. But to no avail, because Hillary throws her rock and shatters the bottle. So the basic thought that C can neutralize D while A is left free to cause E should not be an objection. The only objection that seems to remain is that somehow, we can't say C can neutralize D's causing of E just as (i.e., at the same moment as) A causes E. Again: why not?

One bad reason for balking at our interpretation of figure 23 would be to take the absence of prevented events between D and E to signal an absence of the interruption of the process between D and E. But our discussion earlier in this chapter shows that this is incorrect, since the case with figure 18,

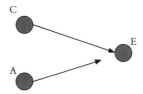

Figure 18

where **E** fires a second time when caused to do so by A, is an intuitively clear case of late preemption where a backup process is interrupted yet, given the standards of event individuation we have adopted, no events are prevented.

So we stipulate that we are to interpret figure 23 such that C interrupts the process from D to E, thus preventing D from bringing about E, while the signal from A succeeds in causing E.

A way to strengthen the interpretation we are suggesting is to stipulate that neurons **C** and **D** are of one type, producing one type of signal, whereas **A** is of another type, producing a correspondingly different type of signal. Further, we can stipulate that inhibitory signals only affect stimulatory signals of the same type.[17] Then we do not yet have our most virulent

---

[17] It is in fact not completely obvious that all of these stipulations are kosher, especially since the stipulation just given is stated in explicitly causal terms, whereas the content of the fundamental "neuron" laws ought to be given in purely non-causal terms. More specifically, it is worth asking why the following alternative gloss on figure 23 is inappropriate: When **A** and **C** both fire, the signal from **A** "neutralizes" the signal from **C**, thus allowing the signal from **D** to bring about E. To look to the patterns of counterfactual dependence displayed by our original interpretation of figure 23 (e.g., that E depends on A and not on D) for a reason to reject this gloss is idle, for as should by now be obvious, these patterns can always be erased or even reversed by suitable tinkering with the environment. A somewhat better

example of late preemption, but we do have a counterexample to the intrinsicness thesis, for notice that embedded within figure 23 is a perfect duplicate of the following sequence of events.

Figure 24

Since *D* in figure 24 is obviously a cause of *E*, the intrinsicness thesis has the consequence that *D* in figure 23 is likewise a cause of *E*.

We will consider in a moment how a fan of the intrinsicness thesis might respond. But let us first explore the way we want to convert what we want to say about figure 23 into a case of late preemption. The trick will be to "squeeze" the *A*-signal and the *C*-signal into one process. To that end, we will play around with the rules for our neuron world a bit more.

Forget the multiple neuron types just introduced, and suppose instead that neurons can be characterized by two distinct parameters: call them "shade" and "intensity." Figure 25 gives the basic structure of the neuron diagrams where neuron **C** can fire with various different shades and in various different intensities, as can **D**.

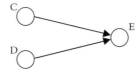

Figure 25

Here are the regularities that govern this particular arrangement (summarized in Table 1). First, if **C** does not fire and **D** does, then, regardless of the shade or

reason, which we will discuss shortly, is that if we assume that **C** and **D** are a different type of neuron from **A**, the structure of the case consisting of the converging signals from **C** and **D** is intrinsically just like the structure displayed in figure 22. This suggests that it could be assigned the same causal characteristics—in particular, one can argue that we could "project" from figure 22 to figure 23 (given our assumptions about neuron types) the fact that it is the signal from **C** that prevents the signal from **D** from causing **E** to fire.

intensity of the signal from **D**, **E** will fire when that signal reaches it. Second, if **C** fires but **D** does not, then **E** will fire iff **C** fires in the "triggering shade," a particular shade of grey. Third, if **C** fires with a particular intensity I—we'll sometimes call it the "inhibiting intensity"—and in some other shade than the triggering shade of grey, then **E** will not fire, regardless of whether and how **D** fires. Fourth, if **C** fires in in the triggering shade, then **E** will fire. Fifth, if **C** fires in some intensity other than the inhibiting intensity and **D** fires, then **E** fires. Sixth, if neither **C** nor **D** fires, **E** does not fire. Finally, the way that **E** fires is never sensitive to the character of the stimulatory signal that causes it to fire. This covers the options.

Table 1

	D fires	**D** doesn't fire
C doesn't fire	**E** fires	**E** doesn't fire
C fires in triggering shade	**E** fires	**E** fires
C fires with intensity I, not in triggering shade	**E** doesn't fire	**E** doesn't fire
C fires without intensity I and not in triggering shade	**E** fires	**E** doesn't fire

The permutation we are especially interested in is what we'll call our *test case*, figure 26: **C** fires in triggering grey with intensity I, and **D** fires. In this case, **E** fires:

Figure 26

Let us draw out a natural causal gloss to put on the various behaviors that this little system can exhibit. First, we shall stipulate that, of the various reasonable candidates for causal claims that support the regularities described earlier, the ones that attribute the simplest causal structure are true in this particular neuron world. (We shall discuss the reason for this stipulation later.)

Now on to the causal judgments the system and its laws can support. Clearly, if **D** alone fires, then the right thing to say is that *D* causes *E*. Likewise, if **C** alone fires, and fires in triggering grey, then the right thing to say is that *C* causes *E*. (We set aside, for the moment, questions such as whether *C* here is essentially a firing of **C** in grey.) If **D** fires, and **C** fires with intensity I (but not in triggering grey), then **E** will not fire, and the right thing to say is both that **C** prevents **E** from firing, and that *C* prevents the *D*-signal from causing *E*. If **C** fires neither in triggering grey nor with intensity I and **D** also fires, then the right thing to say is that *D* alone causes *E* (because we also know that if **C** fires neither in triggering grey nor with intensity I but **D** does not fire, then **E** does not fire). And if **C** fires in grey and **D** also fires, then it seems that the best thing to say is that *E* is symmetrically overdetermined by *C* and *D*. (We discuss overdetermination in detail in §5)

The upshot is that the labels "triggering shade of grey" for firing in the right shade of grey and "inhibiting intensity" for firing with intensity I seem entirely appropriate; that is, it seems that we can assert as causal generalizations that a signal from **C** with the inhibiting intensity I acts to prevent any *D*-signal from causing **E** to fire, and that a signal from **C** with the triggering shade of grey is capable by itself of stimulating **E** to fire.

Further, it seems both natural and plausible to extend these generalizations to our understanding of the deeper details of the causal structure of our test case, where **D** fires and **C** fires in grey with intensity I, as represented by figure 26 and covered by the second regularity listed in our table.

Figure 26

What would seem most natural, that is, is to project the causal structures appropriate for describing the cases in general onto the test case. If so, we should insist that the right interpretation of the test case tells us (i) that the *C*-signal prevents the *D*-signal from causing *E* (because the *C*-signal has the inhibiting intensity I); and (ii) that the *C*-signal itself causes *E* (because it is in the triggering shade of grey). Hence, in this neuron world, it is *C* and not *D* that causes *E*.

Let us take this as the correct gloss, while recognizing that there is certainly more room for dispute here than there was in our earlier cases of early and late preemption. In particular, we recognize that there might be other causal stories compatible with the regularities that obtain in our preferred neuron world (we are indebted to Caspar Hare for raising this point). Here is one such story. Consider an alternative neuron world which our regularities in Table 1 also describe. In this alternative world, the causal structure is as follows. When **C** fires in grey with intensity I, E is caused by C *unless* **D** also fires. (Perhaps because, in the singularly special case when **C**-type neurons fire in grey with intensity I and the **D**-type neurons fire as well, D-signals inhibit C-type causation, instead of the other way around.) This changes our diagnosis of our test case, for we must then evaluate the case where **C** fires in grey with intensity I and **D** fires as (i) the D-signal interrupts the C-signal and thus prevents it from causing E; and (ii) that the D-signal itself causes E. Hence, we should interpret the case such that it is D, not C, that causes E. Here is another story, with even more complex causal structure but still seemingly admissible: in the singularly special case when **C**-type neurons fire in grey with intensity I and the **D**-type neurons fire as well, C-signals simply fail to interrupt D-signals. In this third sort of neuron world, in the test case the D-signal and the C-signal overdetermine the firing of E.

Such alternative interpretations make intuitive sense given the assumptions one can make about different neuron worlds. However, it does not threaten our point. We merely want to show how, given the existence of one sort of suitably simple neuron world (one that is not too distant in relevant ways from the actual world), we can have a particularly virulent kind of late preemption.

So let's return to our preferred interpretation of our test case represented by figure 26, where C causes E and also interrupts the process from D to E. Then we have ourselves a particularly nasty example—a case of virulent late preemption. (Virulent late preemption, which is the interpretation we wish to impose on our test case, corresponds to the case of "trumping" preemption that Jonathan Schaffer 2000c discovered, although his diagnosis of its significance is quite different from ours.) Pick any event in the C–E chain, and ask what would have happened if it had not occurred: the answer is that **E** would have fired all the same. Similarly, focus on any time before the time at which **E** fires, and you will find at least two distinct minimally sufficient sets for E—one containing the appropriate event in the C–E process, the other containing the corresponding event in the D–E process. Try to fall back on the intrinsicness thesis, and you will certainly get the result that C is a cause of E, but you will also get the result that D is a cause of *E*. And appeal to de facto dependence seems equally futile: hold fixed whatever you like in the *D–E* process; **E** would have fired all the same.

We see two possible responses. First, a defender of a covariation account can be expected to pipe up at this point, observing that while *E* does not depend on *C*, it is the case that had **C** fired differently—specifically, with the same intensity but in a different shade—then **E** would not have fired. So there is some limited "influence" of *C* on *E*, here. *D*, by contrast, appears to exert no such influence on *E*.

But of course that cannot be the whole story: we already know how to construct late preemption cases that a covariation account cannot handle at all. In fact, we can simply tinker with the case before us: for example, add to the environment various "shade detectors" that check to see whether the *C*-signal is in the appropriate triggering shade of grey—and if not, quickly act to guarantee that **E** fires by other means. Such backup processes can obviously erase any influence that *C* has on *E*. Still, at this point a defender of a de facto dependence approach might try to appropriate elements of the covariation account, claiming that if we hold fixed not merely the facts about the *D*-process, but also the fact that none of the backup processes in the environment are ever engaged, then it will be the case that, if **C** had fired differently (i.e., with the same intensity but a different shade), then **E** would not have fired. There thus might be some hope for wedding the de facto dependence approach to the covariation approach.[18]

A second approach is to aim for more subtlety in both the statement and the application of the intrinsicness thesis. Recall that we stated that thesis solely as a constraint on causation that involves the production of events. But does not some such thesis also govern the way we think about causal prevention? Suppose we have a situation in which two processes intersect in such a way that the first prevents the second from bringing about some effect. Then if the original intrinsicness thesis was plausible, it should also be plausible that an intrinsic duplicate of this structure should share its causal characteristics, and so should likewise be a structure in which one process

---

[18] One could perhaps achieve the same effect by holding to the de facto dependence account in its original form—where the causes of *E* are those events whose occurrence *E* de facto depends upon—while distinguishing two numerically distinct though perfectly coincident firings of **C**: one that is essentially in the triggering shade but only accidentally of the inhibiting intensity, and one that is essentially of the inhibiting intensity but only accidentally in the triggering shade. The idea would be that *E* de facto depends on the first of these but not the second. We won't consider this variant further.

prevents the other process from bringing about some corresponding effect. That some such thesis guides our thinking about prevention would help explain why we arrive at the causal judgments we do about figures 22, 23 and 26 (cf. footnote 18).

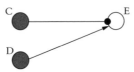

Figure 22

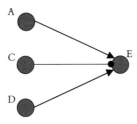

Figure 23

In figure 23, for example, where we take **A**-type neurons to be of a different type from **C**- and **D**-type neurons, we "see" embedded within figure 23 an intrinsic duplicate of figure 22, and so transfer the relevant causal characteristics of that situation—on our preferred interpretation, the fact that the C-process prevents the D-process from causing **E** to fire—over to the more complicated situation.

Likewise, in figure 27, where **C** fires with the inhibiting intensity but not in the triggering shade, we note that the intrinsic character of the two intersecting processes is relevantly similar to that displayed in figure 26 (where **C** fires in the triggering shade):

Figure 26

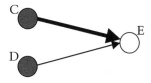

Figure 27

But even if this is right, we don't yet have a solution to our problem; rather, we just have an apparent conflict between an intrinsicness thesis that governs causation and an intrinsicness thesis that governs prevention. One outstanding issue concerns the account of a causal process: as we indicated earlier, it is unclear just what a causal process is supposed to involve. The way we think of causal processes ties very strongly into the way we want to interpret causal structures, and apparently, there are contradictory ways to "project" causal structures from simple situations into complex situations that feature intrinsic duplicates of those simple situations. For example, as we did earlier, we could appeal to similarity in intrinsic character (of processes, understood somehow) to project the causal structure exhibited in figure 24 into figure 23.

Figure 24

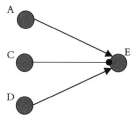

Figure 23

and thus arrive at the judgment that *D* causes *E*. Or, as we also did earlier, we could appeal to intrinsic similarity to project the causal structure of figure 22 into figure 23, thus arriving at the conflicting judgment that *C* prevents *D* from causing *E*:

Figure 22

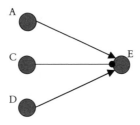

Figure 23

For a strategy using the idea that causal structure is intrinsic to the processes that exhibit it to succeed, it must handle a range of cases of late preemption including simple cases like figure 18 where the preempted process is slower to cause the effect, but also the more complex, virulent cases of late preemption such as that described by figure 26. On the assumption that our test case presents us with a type of late preemption that can occur in a world that is relevantly similar to the actual world (that is, that it presents us with causation that we, as reductionists, want our theory of causation to be able to explain), such a strategy must, it seems, appeal to some overarching principles to resolve conflicts such as these. (See Hall 2004 for related discussion.)

As we noted at the outset, there is room for debate about the proper interpretation of neuron diagrams and hence about whether virulent late preemption is even possible. But still, as we have laid it out, the example seems to us to be reasonably cogent and clear, and helps to bring forth a number of points. First, it strongly suggests that our causal understanding of a particular case can be usefully developed by the selective consideration of relevant causal patterns, viz., our embedding strategy discussed earlier. Second, it provides a methodological lesson with regard to developing neuron diagram examples for causal analysis (we will discuss this in more detail in §6 where we look at the problem of assigning causal structure in black-box cases). The preferred method, at least for cases where the interpretation is not obvious or is controversial, is to develop the example from the bottom up by starting with an assessment of the regularities true of the neuron world and recognizing the extent to which the consideration of other causal patterns and alternative assumptions about causal structure consistent with the regularities could affect the final assessment. Finally, it suggests that all of the most promising reductive treatments of causation to date have yet to adequately capture all of the features of the causal relation.

We have already remarked that late preemption has deservedly received a great deal of attention in the literature. For all that, it seems to us that it deserves a fair amount more. Of all the kinds of problem cases we will discuss, it appears to present the most stubborn obstacles to constructing an adequate philosophical account of causation.

5 Overdetermination

Consider a minor variation on our example of Billy, Suzy, and the broken bottle: this time, their two rocks strike the bottle simultaneously, each with sufficient force to shatter it. This minor variation converts our original case of asymmetric late preemption into a case of perfectly symmetric causal overdetermination, and this conversion brings trouble with it. The trouble comes in two flavors. First, we need to decide what the causal structure of the situation is. Second, a philosophical analysis of causation needs to accommodate this decision.

It will enhance the interest of the first problem if we stipulate at the outset that certain ways of dodging problems are to be avoided. For example, suppose that in the split second after the two rocks strike it, the bottle deforms in a certain way—in a way, let us add, distinctively different from the way it would have deformed had only one rock struck it. Let E be this event of deformation. Now, according to the laws of our example, the precise details of the properties of the deformation differ depending on whether two rocks strike the bottle or only one does, even though each deformation is counted as an instance of E. This means that, when the two throws overdetermine E, they do so by jointly causing properties of E, and in this sense both cause the shattering.

If so, the case loses interest, for there is nothing especially puzzling about overdetermination via joint causation, even if we don't always describe it as such. This sort of overdetermination is an especially boring sort—call it "impure overdetermination"—and occurs in the usual cases of multiple gunmen killing a victim or two golf balls shattering a window. It does not seem to pose any interesting questions for analyses of causation. What it does do, however, is bring out how the laws that "govern" causation can determine the causal structure of a situation. Given a set of laws such that there is a difference in the properties of the effect whether there is one cause (or two, or three . . .) because the properties of the effect depend in some way on how many of these causes it has, and our case of overdetermination is unmasked as a case of joint causation. This is so even with a very permissive theory of event individuation, for the diagnosis of joint causation is determined by facts about property dependence, not facts about which events, strictly speaking, occur.

Let us sidestep potential quibbles about impurities by sanitizing the example. Consider the far more interesting case depicted by figure 11:

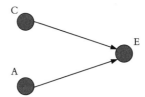

Figure 11

The stimulatory signals from **C** and **A** strike **E** simultaneously. Each signal is sufficient, all by itself, to cause **E** to fire. Furthermore, the way in which **E** fires differs not at all from the way in which it would have fired, had but one of **A** and **C** stimulated it. Cases like that represented by figure 11—cases with a structure that cannot be described as joint causation—are cases of *pure* overdetermination. (Often, where the difference doesn't matter or is stipulated away, we will just use "overdetermination.")

Let us now try to identify the causes of *E* in figure 11. What is clear, given the symmetry of the situation, is that either both or neither of *A* and *C* are among these causes; but many find it intuitively unclear how to make sense of either option. To say that neither is a cause of *E* runs the risk of leaving *E* wholly without causes, but to say that both are causes of *E* runs the risk of conflating the case in figure 11 with a case of joint causation and, worse, raises certain puzzles that we'll discuss in more detail later.

There is a prior question: What distinguishes cases of pure overdetermination as such? The most common response is that two events *A* and *C* purely overdetermine E just in case (i) E's intrinsic properties counter-factually depend on neither A nor C taken singly, but does depend on the two "taken together" (i.e., if neither A nor C had occurred, E would not have occurred with just the intrinsic properties it did); (ii) A and C are not part of the same causal process (instead, each initiates its own causal process); and (iii) the processes connecting A and C to E both go to completion. Even apart from problems with reductively specifying just what a causal process is, what it is to "go to completion," or what "initiating" a process amounts to, that response fails. Consider figure 16:

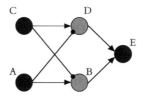

Figure 16

This is a straightforward example of joint causation that the definition above misclassifies as an instance of pure overdetermination.[19] (This example also shows that it won't help to add, as a further condition, a requirement that A and C be "causally on a par" with respect to E.)

Let us consider how our different accounts of causation might respond to these issues, starting with an approach that—because it relies squarely on the intrinsicness thesis—is most congenial to minimal sufficiency and perhaps transference accounts. To illustrate this approach, consider two ways that we could arrive at figure 11. First, we could begin with figure 20.

Figure 20

We could then add stuff to the environment: neuron **A**, its firing, the passage of its stimulatory signal to **E**. Second, we could begin with figure 28.

---

[19] We are assuming that in the case depicted by figure 16, the way in which **E** fires differs not at all from the way in which it would have fired, had but one of **A** or **C** fired.

Figure 28

We could then add stuff to the environment: neuron **C**, its firing, the passage of its stimulatory signal to **E**.

In each case, the extrinsic additions do not alter in any relevant respect the intrinsic characteristics of the event structures (including the intrinsic properties of the effect) we start with. For this reason, we could say that figure 11 contains within it two distinct potentially complete causal histories of *E*.

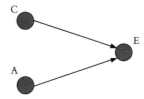

Figure 11

What marks an event structure as a potentially complete causal history of some event *E* as it intrinsically occurs (back to some time *t*) is that, when augmented by *E* itself, the resulting structure intrinsically matches some blueprint for *E* as it intrinsically occurs, for all of its suitably intrinsic properties. (Less accurately but more intuitively, a potentially complete causal history of *E* is some structure of events that could have been a complete causal history of *E* as it intrinsically occurs (back to the given time); the inaccuracy arises because what matters is not the identity of the structure, but its intrinsic character.) And saying this leads naturally to a simple account of pure overdetermination, according to which purely overdetermined events are exactly those with multiple potentially complete causal histories.

If we couple this account to the intrinsicness thesis to which it implicitly refers, then it follows at once that, as we have interpreted figure 11, *A* and *C* are purely overdetermining causes of *E*, and more generally that when some events purely overdetermine some other event, then they are all causes of that event. What's more, reflection on the intrinsicness thesis puts us in a position to explain why the causal structure of pure overdetermination is intuitively puzzling. Part of the explanation, no doubt, is that causes are typically thought to be necessary for their effects, in the way that counterfactual analyses place at center stage, but neither cause, given the occurrence of its companion, is necessary in overdetermination cases. But lack of necessity is obviously not the whole story—nor even a very significant chapter in it—for if it were, then we should presumably find the causal structure of cases of say, early preemption, just as puzzling as the symmetric cases of pure overdetermination.

We do not find the causal structure of such cases equally puzzling. It is obvious in simple cases of early preemption that the preempting cause is a cause and the preempted cause is not, even though the preempting cause is not necessary for the effect. We suggest that the more important ingredient in our puzzlement about pure overdetermination is that we tend, naïvely, to think of intrinsic match as making for complete similarity in causal structure, as follows: Suppose we are given a structure S consisting of an event E together with all of its causes back to some earlier time t. Now take S', a blueprint of S (as in §4.3.2 earlier in this chapter). Let E' be the event in S' that corresponds to E in S. It is natural to suppose that the match between these two structures shows not only that every event in S' distinct from E' is a cause of E', but that these are all the causes of E' back to the given time. Put another way, the supposition is that, just as adding extrinsic detail cannot remove any causes of E (by changing what was formerly a cause of E into a non-cause), so too it cannot introduce any new causes of E. Put yet another way, the supposition is that we cannot create or destroy causal processes (terminating in E) simply by adding detail that would be extrinsic to such processes. But, of course, that supposition is false if the addition of extrinsic detail to a region that includes a process from C to E can render E overdetermined.

So one source of our puzzlement about cases of pure overdetermination is precisely that they violate a natural presupposition of our thoughts about causation and intrinsicness. A second source of our puzzlement may be that—as we will discuss in more detail shortly—while cases of overdetermination seem to be conceptually and metaphysically possible, they may not be physically possible. Add to this that cases of pure overdetermination, if they were physically possible, would be quite rare (at least in our world and in nomically possible worlds, if we set aside varieties of nonreductionism between "ontological levels"), and it is no surprise that they engender the puzzlement that they do.

Let's discuss the second source of our puzzle about overdetermination. Look yet again at figure 11.

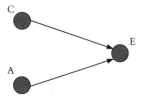

Figure 11

How, exactly, can *A* and *C* each cause *E* if they are not causing it jointly? We stipulated that the way in which **E** fires differs not at all from the way in which it would have fired, had but one of **A** and **C** stimulated it. What work is the much-needed stipulation doing when it holds that each cause brings about the effect just as it would if the other cause were absent?

The worry can perhaps be fleshed out in the following way. We stipulated that *A* and *C* each contribute, in precisely the same way and at precisely the same time, sufficient activation energy for *E* to fire at a certain intensity. If so, then, speaking roughly, why doesn't *E* fire twice or, alternatively, why doesn't *E* fire with twice the intensity? Or, again speaking roughly, why isn't it the case that only half of the activation energy provided by *A* and *C* is used when *E* fires? Of course, for the example to work, don't think of *A* and *C* as each contributing a part of the energy needed to cause *E*'s firing—that way lies joint causation, and by definition, we are considering pure overdetermination. In addition, don't think of *A* and *C* as each making its contribution to the activation energy where there is an activation threshold that is simply exceeded by the joint contributions of *A* and *C*. That case fails to distinguish joint or partial causation of *E*'s firing by the contributions of *A* and *C* from pure overdetermination of *E*'s firing by *A* and *C*.

The question is about how to understand the possibility that *A*'s activation energy causes *E*'s firing and *C*'s activation energy causes *E*'s firing, where the two causal contributions do not combine together in a way that makes the properties of the effect dependent upon the total activation energy contributed. Call this the *problem of additivity* (for discussion, see Paul 2007). An intuitive but possibly misleading way to put the worry is that it seems as though, in cases of pure overdetermination, there can be too much causation to go around.

Note that this worry does not hold water if we are considering worlds sufficiently unlike our own—since such worlds could have laws very different from ours. In such worlds, causation of one event by another need not involve transfers of conserved quantities or other kinds of causal contributions that are additive. But in a world physically like ours, there is room for puzzlement, for most of the sorts of overdetermination that philosophers worry about concern causal connections that normally involve transmissions of conserved quantities of some sort. When we stipulated that we would understand figure 11 as a case of pure overdetermination, this was unproblematic as long as said causation was not supposed to involve transfers of conserved quantities or other properties that combine in ways that entail, under the laws, additive property changes in the effect.

We will come back to how this puzzlement ties to philosophical debates about nonreductionism and ontological levels. For now, let us just note that in light of the problem of additivity, it seems that most if not all putative cases of pure overdetermination in the actual world (excluding cases involving omissions) will be nomically impossible. (This does not require us to assume that the laws are deterministic. It is consistent with indeterministic laws to hold that extremely improbable events are possible. But if the laws are indeterministic, we can ask why the presence of an additional, overdetermining cause would not change the probabilities of the outcome. How could it be consistent with the laws to claim that the probability of E occurring (just as it actually did) is exactly the same whether there are two causes, each of which is sufficient for E, or just one?)

We suggest that some sort of dim recognition of the possibility of nomic impossibility contributes to our puzzlement about pure overdetermination, since it can be difficult to determine whether we are implicitly (and perhaps mistakenly) applying a this-worldly understanding of the nomic possibilities to our sanitized version of overdetermination. Pure overdetermination seems to be conceivable and metaphysically possible. It is not obviously physically possible. These facts must not be conflated.

Setting this issue aside for now, it is a point in favor of minimal sufficiency analyses, as well as transference theories, that they can, quite obviously, endorse the rather natural treatment of pure overdetermination given earlier as involving events with multiple potentially complete causal histories. Counterfactual analyses, by contrast, run into a bit of trouble. One problem is that it is not clear how such accounts will distinguish this kind of causal structure from other varieties. For example, it won't do to say that we have a case of pure overdetermination if we have two processes—call them the *A*-process and the *C*-process—each of which suffices to bring about the target effect *E*. Such a definition would conflate the pure overdetermination of figure 11 with the kind of late preemption exhibited in figure 18.

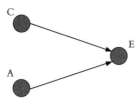

Figure 11

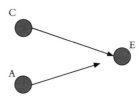

Figure 18

We could try to add the requirement that both the *A*-process and the *C*-process "go to completion," leaving us with the additional challenge of defining that notion in purely counterfactual terms. (Recall that some cases of late preemption do not require any events to go missing in the preempted chain even though that chain does not "go to completion.") We also need to say what "suffices to bring about" means here, and it won't do to test for such sufficiency by considering what would have happened if one of the processes had been present without the other. For it might be that had the *A*-process been absent, the character of the *C*-process would have changed in some way. Our figure 16 provided an example of just such a situation.

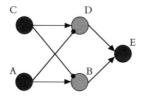

Figure 16

The *C–D–E* process does not, as it stands, suffice to bring about *E* (thanks to the diminishing strength of the stimulatory signal), but would have sufficed, had **A** not fired.

It seems that what we would really like to focus on is the character of the process as it actually plays out—perhaps by looking at the counterfactual structure of a process with just that character in circumstances where competing processes are absent. But to follow that suggestion is to travel most of the way toward an account of pure overdetermination that relies on some version of the intrinsicness thesis. At any rate, let us set this problem aside (although we will return to it briefly in §6).

There is a more serious problem, for it seems that counterfactual analyses threaten to leave overdetermined events without any causes at all. Consider figure 11 again. *E* depends on neither *A* nor *C*. It is connected to neither of these events by the ancestral of the dependence relation. We again stipulate that **E** fires in the same way, regardless of how it is stimulated, so that if either only **A** or only **C** had fired, **E** would have fired in exactly the same manner. Result: *E* does not counterfactually depend on *A* or on *C*, and neither *A* nor *C* exert any of Lewis's "influence" on *E*. (And observe that this lack of influence includes all the events in the processes initiated by *A* and *C*.) Finally, *E* does not seem to de facto depend on either *A* or *C*. For example, holding fixed the fact that **A** fires, it is still the case that **E** would have fired had **C** not fired, and likewise with **A** and **C** reversed. Are we to conclude that *E* has no causes at the time at which **A** and **C** fire (and, for that matter, at all intervening times as well)? Lewis 1986c seems to make just this claim when he denies that *A* is a cause and also that *C* is a cause.[20] (He tries to make this more palatable by holding that, even if *A* is not a cause, and *C* is not a cause, nevertheless, the mereological sum of *A* and *C* is a cause. We think this maneuver fails[21].)

---

[20] We are setting aside his 1986c "extended analysis" that relies on quasi-dependence to make overdeterminers count as causes (pp. 211–12), for Lewis later, in his 2004a, rejects quasi-dependence for good reasons (see Paul 1998b for discussion).

[21] Briefly: if we let sums such as *A* + *C* count as causes, then trouble seems quickly to ensue. Suppose *E* depends on *C*, and *F* depends on *A*—but *A* bears no connection to *E*, nor *C* to *F*. According to Lewis, *A* + *C* nevertheless causes both *E* and *F*. It also seems hard to escape the conclusion that any cause of *C* is thereby a cause of *A* + *C*; certainly, if it's true of some further event *D* that if it had not occurred, then *C* would not have occurred, then it seems likewise true that if *D* had not occurred, *A* + *C* would not have occurred. But then such a *D* is, by transitivity (which, remember, Lewis endorses), a cause of *F*. That's a reductio.

If the counterfactual analyst could come up with an adequate definition of pure overdetermination, she could avoid this problem by fiat: she could simply stipulate that when some events purely overdetermine some other event, they are causes of that event. That would answer our "no-causes" challenge, although perhaps at the cost of providing no insight into what makes cases of pure overdetermination so puzzling. However, we see no noncircular way for the counterfactual analyst to do this.

Lewis attempts to minimize the fallout from overdetermination cases in the following passage:

If one event is a redundant cause of another, then is it a cause simpliciter? Sometimes yes, it seems; sometimes no; and sometimes it is not clear one way or the other. When common sense delivers a firm and uncontroversial answer about a not-too-far-fetched case, theory had better agree. If an analysis of causation does not deliver the common-sense answer, that is bad trouble. *But when common sense falls into indecision or controversy, or when it is reasonable to suspect that far-fetched cases are being judged by false analogy to commonplace ones, then theory may safely say what it likes.* Such cases can be left as spoils to the victor, in D. M. Armstrong's phrase. We can reasonably accept as true whatever answer comes from the analysis that does best on the clearer cases. (Lewis 1986c, p. 194; italics added)

Lewis's subsequent discussion makes clear that he is happy to treat our cases of pure overdetermination[22] as "spoils to the victor."

We see problems with this response to overdetermination. First, why care so much about common sense? More on that later. Second, Lewis seems to have mislocated the place where common sense cannot give us a firm answer. It seems perfectly commonsensical to say that both over-determiners are causes, and perfectly puzzling to say that neither are. So it isn't right to simply say that common sense does not give us a clear answer about whether pure overdeterminers are causes—it does. What is puzzling to common sense is not whether both overdeterminers are causes, since they obviously are, but just how both overdeterminers could be causes without, speaking colloquially, there being too much causation to go around. (We addressed this earlier in our discussion of potentially complete causal histories and additivity.) This is not the worry that we don't think it is clear that A is a cause of E and that C is a cause of E. This is the worry that

---

[22] What we mean by "pure overdetermination" is not quite the same as what Lewis calls "symmetric overdetermination": he uses his term to cover cases like that depicted in figure 6 as well.

we don't understand the gory details of how to conceptually manage this in a world physically like our own. So Lewis's invocation of "spoils to the victor" doesn't absolve him from the need to have a plausible solution to pure overdetermination that allows both A and C to be causes.

Third, depending on one's account of conceivability and of the relationship between conceivability and possibility, one could claim that it is conceivable or epistemically possible that A and C are each causes of E. If such conceivability entails the metaphysical possibility that A and C are each causes of E, then on these terms alone Lewis's "spoils to the victor" argument should be rejected. Note that while the conceivability-possibility claim is extremely controversial, Lewis in his 2004a invoked just this reasoning to defend a much more controversial sort of case—trumping preemption—and has defended it in a number of philosophical discussions about the nature of mind. So, it seems as though he should be prepared to defend the metaphysical possibility that A and C are each causes of E.

But even if we set these concerns to one side, if we assume that Lewis's analysis of causation is—at least, officially—really only intended to explain the workings of our ordinary concept, it becomes mysterious why the "spoils to the victor" response could ever be appropriate. Lewis notes, immediately after the passage quoted earlier, that

It would be still better, however, if theory itself went indecisive about hard cases. If an analysis says that the answer for some hard case depends on underdescribed details, or on the resolution of some sort of vagueness, that would explain nicely why common sense comes out indecisive.

Why merely "better"—as opposed to crucial?

Perhaps because the counterfactual analyst is not interested merely in analyzing our ordinary concept of causation, but in partially reforming it. She could take herself to be in the business of constructing a new and better concept, using our common sense as a rough guide—but exhibiting a willingness to deviate from it when necessary. The perfectly determinate verdict she gives about cases of overdetermination would simply be an example of such deviation. This won't help Lewis, though, since even if we take ourselves to be in the business of constructing a new and better concept of causation, we do not want it to turn out that overdetermined events lack causes altogether. That would hardly be the sort of "improvement" we are looking for from a revisionary analysis of causation.

Let us therefore look elsewhere, considering whether advocates of the de facto dependence approach have the resources to provide a better treatment. Both Hitchcock (2001) and Pearl (2000) give roughly the following account: focusing on some path (sequence of connected variables) from C to E, if we can find some off-path variables, and some non-actual values for those variables, such that E depends on C when we hold those off-path variables fixed at those values, then C is an overdetermining cause of E.[23] Thus, in figure 11, if **A** had not fired, then E would have depended on C, and vice versa.

That's a very permissive standard: it comes close to saying that C is (at least) an overdetermining cause of E just in case E could have depended on C. And indeed, trouble is not hard to find. Consider figure 29, an example of *double prevention*: given that **B** fires, E depends on C.

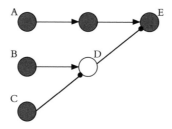

Figure 29

Does it therefore follow, in a case where **B** does not fire, that C is an overdetermining cause of E (together, presumably, with the failure of **B** to fire)? A "yes" answer might at first glance seem not wholly unattractive, but we will see in chapters 4 and 5 that endorsing it appears to make overdetermination ubiquitous: it is far too easy to concoct ways in which an event C completely unconnected to some later event E nevertheless could, if circumstances had been suitably different, have counteracted a threat to E. And interestingly, if we choose to count such overdeterminers as causes simpliciter, then disaster results: every event C turns out to be a cause of every later event E. Hitchcock (2007a) tackles causal overdetermination using the notion of a self-contained causal network and achieves some success in

---

[23] Hitchcock and Pearl both add restrictions on how the off-path variables and non-actual values can be chosen; they will not be relevant here.

modeling the problem, but as we show in chapter 4, §3.4.2, his account does not succeed for internal reasons (and in addition falls afoul of our reductionist standards).

It is an unfortunate feature of the literature that the serious problems with the causal analysis of pure overdetermination, especially for counterfactual-based accounts, have received so little attention in the literature. (Schaffer 2003, Hitchcock 2007a, and of course Hitchcock 2001 and Pearl 2000 are exceptions.)

With one exception: a worry about causal overdetermination that has generated a lot of interest is a worry about whether nonreductionism about entities like mental states or composite objects implies pure overdetermination in the actual world. In the rest of this section, we will discuss the way that such nonreductionism connects to analyses of the causal relation. Those who are uninterested in debates over whether certain varieties of nonreductionism involve objectionable overdetermination may wish to skip to the next section, §6, where we return to our focus on analyses of causation with the discussion of black-box cases. Those who want know more about the ways that debates about nonreductionist theories of mind, constitution and mereology, among others, connect to our metaphysics of the causal relation and its relata, should read on.

Before we discuss these issues further, we need to do some ground-clearing. First, there are two general ways to be a nonreductionist. One might be an epistemic, linguistic or explanatory nonreductionist, holding that conceptual or linguistic facts or explanations from one realm of theory cannot be reduced to the other. For example, one might hold that biological concepts or terms cannot be defined in terms of the concepts or terms of fundamental physics.

Or one might be an ontological nonreductionist, holding that objects, events, property instances or states from one realm cannot be reduced to the other. For example, one might hold that genes are not reducible to more fundamental physical entities, since genes have different essential properties from the collections of molecules that constitute them. Or one might hold that mental states are not reducible to the physical states that realize them. And so on. One could also accept ontological reductionism while accepting epistemic and linguistic nonreductionism: for example, one might hold that, ontologically speaking, everything reduces to states explicitly recognized by fundamental physics which occupy spacetime regions, yet wish to preserve a special place for higher-level concepts, terms and explanations.

We shall set mere epistemic, linguistic and explanatory nonreductionisms aside. Our concern here is solely with ontological nonreductionism. Whether nonreductionism involves puzzles with pure overdetermination is an issue for those who think—in some important sense they need to specify—that the catalogue of what exists includes more than just fundamental physical states occupying regions. Places where the puzzles crop up include the much-discussed problem of mental causation, where advocates of the ontological reduction of the mental to the physical argue that certain nonreductive views imply the pure overdetermination of physical events, states or property instances (depending on one's preferred account of the causal relata involved). Overdetermination also needs to be addressed in discussions of material constitution, where nonreductionists deny that constitution is identity, and discussions of mereological composition, where reductionists about composition argue that the relation of composition that holds between parts and their sum is strict identity, eliminativists about composition deny the existence of mereological sums, and compositional nonreductionists of various sorts argue for claims like "composition as identity," according to which composition is not identity but is somehow analogous.

Advocates of reductive ontologies in each of these debates argue that the nonreductionist view is threatened by the causal overdetermination it seems to imply. For example, her pain causes Suzy to choose to take an aspirin, but surely the physical state that realizes the mental state of this pain is also a cause of Suzy's choice (Kim 1998). Those who would argue that Suzy's pain state has different contents, essences or phenomenal properties from the neural state that realizes it need to explain what the ontological relationship is between these states along with how the causation is supposed to work. (The dualist must do this along with explaining what extra properties and laws his dualist ontology involves and whether pure overdetermination of Suzy's choice is possible.)

Those who argue that material constitution is not identity must make sense of how the oversized statue and the piece of bronze that constitutes it seem to overdetermine the cracking of the pedestal on which it stands (Paul 2007). Nonreductionists about composition must make sense of how the throwing of the baseball in addition to the throwing of a bunch of particles arranged baseball-wise seem to overdetermine the shattering of the window (Merricks 2001). Other debates beckon: nonreductive views about agent causation where an agent along with the fundamental entities it supervenes upon seem to overdetermine effects such as a throwing of a baseball or the raising of an arm.

Note that the causal overdetermination in these cases is not impure overdetermination. Nonreductionists are not arguing that, say, when Suzy decides to take her aspirin, Suzy's decision partly causes her act and the physical realizer of Suzy's decision partly causes her act. No: the idea is that, somehow, both Suzy and her body purely causally overdetermine her aspirin-taking behavior.

The idea is that if, *per impossibile*, the physical state could occur in just the same way but without realizing its mental state, Suzy would take her aspirin in just the same way. If the piece of bronze were to exist in just the same way but without constituting the statue, it would shatter the base in just the same way. And so on. Although each possible case of overdetermination needs to be analyzed in terms of the particular relations between the putative over-determiners (supervenience, constitution, composition, etc.) involved, in no case is there a commitment to impure overdetermination.

So now the problem of additivity comes into its own. If we are concerned about making sense of the possibility of the sort of pure overdetermination that nonreductionist views suggest, we must make sense of such cases as physically possible cases.

In our sanitized case of figure 11, we stipulated that we had multiple potentially complete causal processes, without regard to whether such cases were physically possible. This was a perfectly fine way to proceed, since we were only interested in demonstrating the coherence of causal overdetermination, hence, whether it was conceptually or metaphysically possible. But in the cases involving mental and physical states, persons and bodies, proteins and molecules, and so on, we need to have an account of how it could be physically possible that each purely overdetermining cause is part of a numerically distinct, perfectly sufficient and complete causal history of the effect.

So now we see the problem. If pieces of clay and their statues, agents and their bodies, and mental events and physical events are all causes, and if they cause by contributing conserved quantities like momentum (or whatever) to their effects, then these physical quantities should be additive. But, apparently, they are not. When the pedestal cracks under the statue, we don't think the crack was caused in part by the weight of the statue and in part by the weight of its constituting bronze. The weight of the statue caused the crack, and was perfectly sufficient to cause the crack that actually occurred, yet the weight of the bronze also caused the crack, and was perfectly sufficient to cause the crack that actually occurred. But, if each object caused the crack, and if such causation involves an object's imparting a certain amount of downwards pressure, why wasn't the crack twice as big? If nonreductive overdetermination violates the laws in our world, or violates the usual relationship between laws and causes in our world, then nonreductionist theses about our world that imply such overdetermination are in trouble.

One option the ontological nonreductionist has is to replace her ontological views with a reductionist thesis, perhaps while continuing to endorse epistemic and linguistic nonreductionism. Few ontological nonreductionists choose this route, for obvious reasons (but see Merricks 2001). Another route some try to take is to refuse to give any account of how the overdetermination in question works. This move is as unconvincing as one would expect it to be. The ontological nonreductionist is arguing for a controversial metaphysical hypothesis, and providing the ontological details is precisely what she needs to do in order to defend her account.

A slightly different way of trying to dodge the overdetermination bullet also involves the postulation of special, ontologically tight relations between the causes of the effect that somehow make causal overdetermination physically possible. Some claim that this removes the problems (Yablo 1992b, Wilson 2011). Some argue that the causal powers of the tightly related overdeterminers are somehow shared (Shoemaker 2001, Pereboom 2002). Some argue that there is no problem with overdetermination because of the truth of certain counterfactuals (Bennett 2003, LePore and Loewer 1987, 1989). The trouble with all of these proposals is that to varying extents they fail to give a sufficiently explicit treatment of just how the special, ontologically tight relations remove the problems with overdetermination. Why should the reductionist feel moved to accept the assertion that the mere existence of sufficiently strong ontological relations between, say, the physical state and the mental state, removes the problems with pure overdetermination?

An example will help to press the point. Yablo (1992b) argues that it is plausible to assume that property instances related by the determinate-determinable relation do not overdetermine their effects. But for many the intuitive plausibility of this claim derives solely from the implicit acceptance of the reductive thesis that property instances of determinates are just instances of their determinables—cold comfort for a nonreductionist who wishes to apply this to the case of the mental that is not reducible to the physical. We think that Yablo needs to develop a more explicit argument for how the presence of a determinate-determinable relation between property instances, where the instance of the determinable does not simply reduce to the instance of the determinate, mitigates worries about pure overdetermination.[24]

Our point about the need for metaphysical explicitness in the handling of overdetermination applies to both sides of the debate over reduction. On the one hand, reductionists need to be clear about the fact that one does not refute a particular nonreductionist theory merely by showing that it implies causal overdetermination of some sort, for we have seen that even pure overdetermination is at least conceptually possible. On the other hand, nonreductionists cannot dismiss reductionist objections to overdetermination by simply claiming that there is nothing to worry about. They need to explain—in brutal metaphysical detail—why their view avoids the problem of additivity. (And not by simply stipulating that there isn't additivity because of the existence of special strong ontological relations that, while not the identity relation, are still somehow special!)

Our point here is really just that we should use lessons drawn from our exploration of the metaphysics of causation to clarify what is potentially objectionable about the sorts of overdetermination that nonreductive ontologies imply. We can also use these lessons to suggest what is needed: an understanding of the causal structure of such cases that avoids the problem of additivity.

We see two possible ways around the problem for the nonreductionist. The first way focuses on the fact that it is the actual laws that entail, however indirectly, that certain sorts of properties or quantities associated with having such properties are additive. Perhaps we should hold that the laws do not entail additivity in such cases. This is an intriguing possibility, but

---

[24] Yablo 1992b develops an account of how mental and physical events are related as determinable to determinate, but then, using his "proportionality" criterion, argues that in many cases it is just the mental event that causes the effect. This avoids problems with pure overdetermination by denying that both events are causes, that is, by denying that there is overdetermination.

much more work on the metaphysics of nomic subsumption would need to be done to make this intriguing possibility into a viable theory.[25]

The second way around the problem gives an explicit account of how, according to nonreductionist lights, the special relation between overdetermining causes can make overdetermination physically possible. The idea is that the intimate, material relation between nonreductive overdeterminers entails that token causal properties are shared, hence there is no problem of additivity. (See Paul 2007 for development of this view.) Nonreductive causes share their material and any fundamental physical parts, and in virtue of this, perhaps they share the token properties that cause the overdetermined effect. When the statue and the clay both crack the base, and when the mental state and its realizer both cause the act, perhaps the causation involves a shared, token property that brings about the effect.

There are other versions of this solution (see especially Shoemaker 2007, Wilson 2011), although they seem to require functionalism in order to be successful. Each in effect argues that an effect can have multiple numerically distinct (but not metaphysically distinct) sufficient causes at time t as long as the events share the property instance that causes the effect. (Arguably, this approach could be made consistent with those of Bennett, Pereboom and Yablo, although more would need to be said in order to make them so.) If the causally efficacious property instance(s) of each sufficient cause at t are literally shared (so the causes overlap with respect to the instance(s)), the overdetermination is benign and we avoid the problems with additivity and its attendant mysteries.

Much of the discussion of overdetermination in the debate about reduction has proceeded in blissful ignorance of the problems with and characteristics of overdetermination developed in the literature on the metaphysics of causation and the causal relata. (There are important exceptions, such as Bennett 2007 and Yablo 1992b.) This is unfortunate, for, especially for those who wish to rely on counterfactuals in their understanding and treatment of pure overdetermination, they need to be clear about how they prefer to interpret the relevant causal conditionals. Claims about grounding, multiple realization and the overall relations between multilevel phenomena

---

[25] We are indebted to conversation with Terence Horgan and Timothy Williamson here.

will be greatly affected by the semantics for the causal conditionals under consideration.[26]

It should be clear at this point how general issues about the nature of causation and pure overdetermination affect the reductionist-nonreductionist debate. A truly rigorous and well-developed philosophical account about the causation of objects, events or property instances of any kind, especially when that view involves issues of pure overdetermination, cannot avoid paying attention to the gritty details of the metaphysics of causation.

For example, those who endorse a counterfactual analysis of causation, have, as we have seen, especially difficult problems with pure overdetermination. In contrast, those who endorse a minimal sufficiency account, transference theory or intrinsicness account are endorsing a kind of theory which gives the right result for overdetermination (that multiple events or property instances are causes), and may be able to explain particularly clearly why pure overdetermination, at least in worlds with the right sort of laws, is unobjectionable. Those who are moved by the problem of additivity should pay particular attention to the fact that causation of any sort works via the nomic subsumption of property instances, even if events are the causal relata, since this may solve the problem. In any case, we hope that the discussion in this section has helped to illustrate some of the ways that future work on overdetermination should proceed.

6 Black-box cases

In §4.3.4, we suggested that variations on how we could interpret our test case of virulent late preemption held methodological lessons for analyses of causation. In particular, the range of interpretations brings out just how important it is to remember that, in "black-box" cases, that is, cases where we do not already know all of the causal structure involved, we must

---

[26] For an example of the importance of the last point, note how Yablo's 1992*b* (p. 278) theory of when mental events are causes depends in part on the claim that we must evaluate the antecedents of certain causal conditionals where P realizes a mental event M so that in the closest possible world where P does not occur it is replaced by a similar event that also realizes M. (P is not entirely absent in the sense of being replaced by vacuum or empty space.) Yablo also relies on intuitions directly orthogonal to Lewis's influence theory to defend his views on mental causation. "When an effect depends not simply on an event's occurring, but on its occurring in some specific manner, one rightly hesitates to attribute causation." Yablo 1992*b*, p. 278. Yablo's skepticism here undergirds his defense of proportionality, which in turn is essential to the way he resolves the problem of pure overdetermination for mental (event) causation. Clearly, one's theory of causation can have an important role to play in the debate over mental causation. For related discussion, but from a different perspective, see Campbell 2010.

proceed with extreme caution. For we must be exceedingly careful not to overlook the possibility of structures internal to the systems of events that could change our causal judgments quite radically. As should be obvious, black-box cases are of special interest to those who would like to use causal models to discover antecedently unknown causal structure, such as those working in branches of the natural or social sciences.

In this section, we will develop some examples to show how important it is to accurately capture all of the deep level structure of a causal system before making a causal judgment. To begin, consider figure 30:

Figure 30

Here, **C** and **D** both fire, in the same color but in different shades: **C** fires in black while **D** fires in grey. As it happens, **D** is a neuron that can only fire weakly, while **C** only fires strongly (the difference in strength is represented by the darkness of the shade of the firing neuron). A short while later, **E** fires in black, that is, with the same strength as **C**. The empty space between neurons **C**, **D** and **E** represents the black box—the portion of the causal structure that is unknown to us.

The events in figure 30 display the following pattern of counterfactual dependence, which we will henceforth call the "test pattern:" if **C** had fired in any different color, such as green or red, and **D** had still fired in grey, then **E** would have fired in the same color as **C**; but if **D** had fired in any different color, and **C** had still fired in black, **E** would have still fired in black. If **C** does not fire but **D** does, **E** fires in black, and if neither **C** or **D** fire, **E** does not fire. In the test pattern, **E** counterfactually covaries with **C**, and not with **D** (at least when both neurons fire we restrict such variation to color).

What should we say about this situation? In particular, should we say that *C*, and not *D*, is a cause of *E*? It depends. Specifically, it depends on what the explanation of the test pattern is. Here is a mistake that some might be inclined to make: assert that (i) the test pattern is constitutive of (virulent) late preemption; and (ii) in any case that has such a pattern, the event that corresponds to *C* is the (sole) cause of the target effect. It will pay to take some care in showing why such an assertion is confused.

To begin, one simple explanation of the test pattern—and one that vindicates the judgment that *C* and not *D* causes *E*—could be that, first, it might turn out that **E** can fire in different colors, but not in different intensities. But within the black box, matters are different, and the process initiated by the more intense firing somehow cuts off the process initiated by the weaker firing. Figure 31 depicts one way that might go:

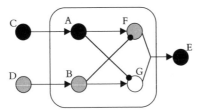

Figure 31

When a signal travels along one of the inhibitory channels from **A** to **G** or from **B** to **F**, it reduces the strength of any incoming stimulatory signal by an amount equal to the strength (represented by the darkness of the color of the firing neuron) with which the neuron sending the inhibitory signal fired. (Darker shades fire stronger, and signals can't go "negative": they can be reduced to zero, but not below.) So the strong inhibitory signal from **A** more than cancels out the weak stimulatory signal from **B**, so **G** does not fire; but the weak inhibitory signal from **B** does not cancel the strong stimulatory signal from **A**, so **F** does fire (though a bit weakly); this in turn is enough to get **E** (which, as we noted, only fires in different colors, not in different shades) to fire in black. A transparent explanation of the test pattern—a "backup process" is interrupted—results. It is also transparent that it offers up no novel lessons about causation.

Such "cutting off" of a process isn't necessary to achieve an explanation: other mechanisms could do the job as well. In figure 32 for example, neuron **A** with the funky checkerboard pattern acts as a kind of "shunt," deflecting the weaker signal into the downward path (the arrow to **B**), where neuron **B** absorbs it, and sending the stronger signal along the main path to **E**. We can further suppose that if only one signal is received, **A**'s shunt short circuits, such that **A** merely sends the sole incoming signal along the main path.

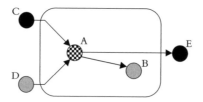

Figure 32

But there are still other structures that would explain the test pattern in a way that gives us the verdict that, when **C** fires in black and **D** fires in grey, D and not C is the cause of E. Consider for example figure 33:

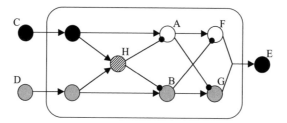

Figure 33

Here, the striped neuron **H** acts as follows: if there is just one incoming signal (or none), it does nothing. If there are two incoming signals of different colors, **H** emits an inhibitory signal along the "lower" channel to neuron **B**. But, if there are two incoming signals of the same color but different strengths, **H** emits an inhibitory signal along exactly one of the exit channels, equal in strength to the stronger of the two incoming signals. If the stronger incoming signal came from the "upper" channel, then the inhibitory signal likewise exits to the upper channel; if it came from the lower, then to the lower.

Given the way the black-box portion of figure 33 works, in the case where **C** fires in black and **D** fires in grey, it is the weaker firing from **D** that causes **E** to fire—and this, despite the fact that the test pattern characterizes the relationship between C, D, and E just as accurately as it does in figures 31 and 32.

The point of going through all these examples is to emphasize that the presence of the test pattern does not by itself guarantee that there is an event occupying the C-role that is the sole cause, or even one of the causes, of the effect under consideration. That fact appears immediately to refute accounts such as Lewis's "influence" account, since its central feature is the claim that *E* is caused by every event with which it counterfactually covaries.[27] It also helps to highlight how careful we must be when drawing conclusions about cases that exhibit our test pattern, and in general, when we consider cases that seem to exhibit a single regularity. Moreover, it brings out just how easy it can be to make false assumptions about the deep level causal structure of a case, which should encourage the causal modeler who is unconcerned about such assumptions to pause and reflect on her methodology.

For one more lesson, recall the alternative interpretations of our test case of figure 26, in §4.3.4:

Figure 26

The different ways of filling in the causal structure of figure 30 bring out the very same lesson we learned from the availability of the different interpretations of figure 26. In a black-box case, even where we have quite a bit of information about the overall regularities, absence of complete detail must constrain robust intuition-mongering about what causes what.

Let's close by examining one more sort of move we might make when diagnosing the causal structure of a case. Consider figure 34.

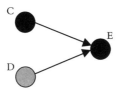

Figure 34

Suppose that in figure 34, **C, D,** and **E** exhibit a particular firing pattern, but that there is no explanation for this pattern in terms of facts about how the

---

[27] Lewis requires variation to a sufficient degree. This qualification is clearly met by figure 33.

neurons work or are connected up to each other. It is just a fundamental law that when **C** and **D** both fire, **E** fires in the color matching whichever of **C** and **D** fired more strongly. Note here a special feature claimed for the case: the claim is that a causal process is initiated by C and a causal process is initiated by D, and neither process is interrupted along the way to E. (This interpretation corresponds with Schaffer 2000*c*'s interpretation of the causal processes of "trumping" preemption.)

When, as here, **C** and **D** both fire in the same color but with different strengths, do we think that C but not D causes E? (We stipulate, as before, that the intensity with which **E** fires is insensitive to how it is stimulated.) Before deciding, observe that in figure 35—a situation which is just like that in figure 34 except that the events leading from D to E are absent—C is a cause of E:

Figure 35

Likewise, in figure 36—again, a situation just like figure 34 except that this time the events leading from C to E are absent—D is a cause of E.

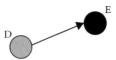

Figure 36

Figure 34 contains intrinsic duplicates of both of these "blueprints," so, on the account of overdetermination that appealed to the intrinsicness thesis, E in figure 34 has two distinct potentially complete causal histories, and is therefore (symmetrically) overdetermined. If this is right, then cases like that of figure 34, when both neurons fire in the same color, are best understood as cases of overdetermination.[28]

---

[28] Halpern and Pearl 2005 and Hitchcock 2007*a* suspect that trumping is best understood as overdetermination.

But this is not the only way to read them. One claim you might try to make is that neither causal process is interrupted, yet only one causal process generates the effect. This claim is puzzling: if neither causal process is interrupted, this seems to imply that a causal signal moves from each prospective cause to the effect. But if so, it is most natural to hold that the effect is overdetermined by both causal processes. Indeed, whatever we might mean by claiming that a causal process is "not interrupted" or "goes to completion," such a claim seems to entail that the events in the chain are causally connected to the effect.

For those who want to insist that it is C alone in figure 34 that causes E, it would seem far better to say that the process initiated by C does interrupt the D-process: namely, by preventing it from bringing about E. And the best way to enforce such a judgment is to observe that that is exactly what we would say, should it transpire that when **C** fires in a different way, **E** also fires in that way, as in figure 37.

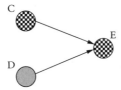

Figure 37

Recall, of course, that there are no further "black boxes" embedded in Figure 37 that would disrupt this judgment, because there is no deeper explanation for this pattern in terms of facts about how the neurons work or are connected up to each other.

In this situation, it seems right to say both that C causes E, and that C prevents the D-process from itself causing E—and so, in that sense, interrupts the D-process (perhaps without preventing any events). And it also seems right to say that figure 37 and figure 34 are structurally similar in key respects. Perhaps, in light of that similarity, the most natural way to interpret what occurs when **C** fires is that it is better after all to say that the process initiated by C interrupts the process initiated by D. If so, then the right verdict about figure 34 is that C alone causes E, even when **C** and **D** fire in the same color.

On the other hand, if we wish to deny that the process initiated by C interrupts the process initiated by D, perhaps what figure 34 shows us is that it may be possible, at least in some conceptual sense, to have cases of asymmetric causal overdetermination. Such cases would be cases where we have multiple overdetermining causes such that each cause produces the effect independently of the other, but intuitively, one cause is somehow more dominant than the other.

7 The lessons of redundant causation

Let us close this chapter by trying to summarize the main lessons that cases of redundant causation appear to teach us. A good way to begin is by noticing a very general strategy for constructing counterexamples to an analysis of causation that emerges from the foregoing discussion. Suppose you have proposed some necessary and sufficient conditions for causation, and that those conditions successfully identify all the causes of some event E for some reasonably simple example. The strategy for constructing a counterexample to your position is to try to come up with a situation that is just like the situation your analysis gets right—except for respects extrinsic to the causal processes leading to the event E—and where these extrinsic respects either introduce non-causes that meet your conditions, or make it the case that some of the genuine causes don't. Let's focus on the latter option in particular. Pick some candidate cause C of E, that is, and tinker with the environment so as to make it the case that C no longer bears what you take to be the definitive relation to E. If one can eliminate this relation—and do so merely by means of suitably extrinsic modifications to the environment of the processes connecting C to E—then one will almost certainly have a counterexample to the necessity of your analysis, since such extrinsic modifications will not undermine the intuitive verdict that C remains a cause of E.

Perhaps the best way to effect such modifications is to introduce some alternative causal process or processes aimed at the effect, processes sufficient to bring it about in C's absence. For the fact that the alternative processes have this causal capacity will very likely guarantee either that (i) their constitutive events will also bear the definitive relation to E (this is what happens to a simple regularity account, where we end up with more than one set of events minimally sufficient for the effect), or that (ii) C no longer bears the definitive relation to E (this is what happens in the case of the simple counterfactual account, where the presence of the backup processes destroys the dependence of E on C). Do not be distracted by the fact that (i) yields a counterexample to the sufficiency of the analysis, whereas (ii) yields a counterexample to its necessity; for it will almost always be possible to convert the former kind of counterexample into the latter, by making the analysis more restrictive in some obvious way. For example, if our analysis says that a cause of E is any member of a set of contemporaneous events minimally sufficient for E, then any standard case of pre-emption will show that our analysis fails to provide a sufficient condition for causation. We can easily "fix" this problem by making the analysis more demanding in the obvious way: let it say that a cause of E is any member of a unique set of contemporaneous events minimally sufficient for E. Now the very same cases will undermine the necessity of our analysis. In fact, we think it is most illuminating to take it for granted that we have started with an analysis restrictive enough to be relatively immune from counterexamples to its sufficiency; the strategy for refuting it is thus to start with a case where it works, and wring intuitively irrelevant changes on the environment in such a way as to erase the conditions that the analysis identifies with causation.

Some easy ways of making this kind of modification can leave it open that the targeted analysis succeeds at least for the late stages of the process or processes leading to the effect; this is exactly what happens when we introduce alternative causes of E, and also introduce mechanisms by which the genuine causes cut them off. Again, the counterexample may leave it open whether or not the idle backup processes are distinguished by the presence of "gaps"—events that did not happen, but would have to have happened if those backups were to have brought about E. Finally, it may be that very subtle relations—in particular, of counterfactual dependence—still distinguish C from the events in the backup processes. The most typical cases of late pre-emption are like this, featuring backup processes that would have brought about E a little bit later, or in a slightly different manner, than do its actual causes. But we have seen that all of these loopholes can easily be closed if one simply takes enough care in the construction of the example. It is therefore unfortunate, if understandable, that so much of the literature has been devoted to developing "solutions" to the problem posed by redundant causation that take advantage of one or another of these loopholes.

It seems that a far better strategy is to try to find some relation between C and E that is guaranteed to be stable under modifications of the environment of the processes connecting C to E. Assuming we can work out an acceptable account of causal processes, some evidence that this is indeed a better strategy comes from considering that the two approaches that appear to have any promise of being able to handle redundant causation—the approach based on the intrinsicness thesis, and the approach based on the concept of de facto dependence—both fix on relations that have this feature. It is pretty much obvious why the first of these approaches has the feature: for if C and E belong to a structure of events that intrinsically matches, in relevant respects, some E-blueprint, then of course this fact will remain stable under modifications of the environment that leave the intrinsic character of this event structure unchanged (or unchanged in relevant respects). It is perhaps less clear that de facto dependence accounts delineate a relationship that remains stable under perturbations of the environment of the processes that exhibit it, and that is in part because it remains insufficiently clear how we are to evaluate the counterfactuals that feature in such accounts. But bracketing that problem, it seems that relations of de facto dependence can remain stable in at least a wide range of cases. That is, it seems that in at least typical cases, if E de facto depends on C, then, making modifications to the environment of the processes connecting C to E, it will remain the case that E de facto depends on C.

As partial vindication of this point, imagine an arbitrary neuron diagram in which C is connected to E via a series of stimulatory signals and intervening neurons, and in which C is in fact a cause of E. On a de facto dependence account, this causal status is likely to be exhibited by the fact that if we hold fixed the pattern of neuron-firings off the path connecting C to E, we will find that if C had not fired, then E would not have fired. But if this counterfactual is true then it will presumably remain true if we reconfigure the relationships and patterns of firings among these off-path neurons.

But we must highlight two caveats. In the first place, this result will not extend to examples in which C is straightforwardly connected to E, but in which the facts that need to be held fixed cannot simply take the form of facts about firings of neurons. Late preemption of the kind exhibited in figure 18 is a prime example. In the second place, there are situations in which reconfiguring the off-path neurons can introduce or erase relations of de facto dependence. Notice, for example, that in cases of symmetric overdetermination, we can tinker with the environment in a way that completely erases de facto dependence. It should be somewhat troubling to those who still favor such accounts that they must turn to such strikingly different dependence relations in order to try (unsuccessfully, in our view) to accommodate symmetric overdetermination.

If we had to issue a summary judgment, we would say that on balance, a minimal sufficiency account that makes use of the intrinsicness thesis does a better job of handling redundant causation than does a de facto dependence account. Granted that there are important details of the minimal sufficiency account that need to be worked out, and there are apparent counterexamples to the intrinsicness thesis that need to be dealt with in a principled way; still, the challenges facing a de facto dependence account—the only decent rival on the table—seem even more daunting. The foundations of these accounts remain obscure, their ability to provide reasonably precise truth conditions for the counterfactuals upon which they rely uncertain, and the counterexamples to them—both in the form of examples that exhibit spurious de facto dependence, and in the form of cases of symmetric overdetermination—seem serious and may be resistant to any principled treatment.

Still, it would be hasty to issue a firm judgment, for while we take ourselves to have covered in this chapter the most important class of examples that drive debates about causation, there are other examples that a comprehensive treatment would need to explore—most especially, examples that highlight issues involving the causal status of omissions. (And, as we shall see in chapter 4, the inability of transference accounts to handle causation involving omissions, in addition to our suspicion from chapter 2 that they involve explanatorily idle notions (see rule three in chapter 2, §3.2.3), keeps them off the table.) The most significant of these feature relations of apparent causation by double prevention, in which an omission plays the role of an intermediate. This kind of relation is too ubiquitous to be ignored, and there is a good case to be made that it would be a disaster to deny that it is any kind of causal relation (see for example Schaffer 2000a). But while it is clear that a counterfactual account can easily accommodate causation by double prevention, it is also clear that the sort of minimal sufficiency account that is wedded to the intrinsicness thesis cannot (for further discussion, see Hall and Paul 2003). So at the end of the day, the balance sheet may look rather different: it may turn out that de facto dependence accounts, despite their struggles with cases of redundant causation, provide the most attractive analysis of causation on offer. Then again, it may also turn out that the best approach is to "divide and conquer," seeking distinct analyses of what are distinct kinds of causal relation (see for example Hall 2004).

At any rate, there is an issue here that strikes even deeper than the question which of the various extant accounts of causation is best: there appears to be a deep tension in our thinking about causation, which can be brought out by contrasting cases of late preemption and cases of causation by double prevention. We will explore this contrast in more detail in chapter 4.

4

Causation involving omissions

This chapter focuses on examples that, in one way or another, involve omissions—which for now, we will loosely understand to be failures of events to occur. We begin by surveying a variety of ways in which causal structures can involve omissions. We then examine a number of reasons for thinking that a philosophical account of causation ought to treat omission-involving causation differently from causation between events. We intend for the reasons we introduce here to be as theory neutral as possible, in the sense that they do not suppose any particular analysis of causation, as this way of getting them on the table will put us in a much better position to evaluate the kinds of trouble different accounts have in accommodating omission-involving causation. After laying them all out for examination, we will discuss how our different candidate approaches try to handle causation involving omissions. We will close with a discussion of some recent and sophisticated attempts to connect the treatment of omission-involving causation with a distinction between default states and their deviations (for an introductory discussion of default and deviant states, see chapter 2, §3.3.3).

1 Three kinds of cases

Three canonical ways in which omissions appear to enter into causal relations will give us a baseline to work from.

1.1 Causation by omission

For the first, consider figure 3.

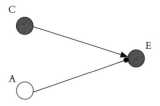

Figure 3

C causes *E*. In addition, if **A** had fired, **E** would not have fired. What is perhaps less clear—but certainly defensible, and at any rate is widely although not universally assumed in the literature—is that this latter fact makes for an additional cause of *E*: namely, the omission that is **A**'s failure to fire (at the relevant time) is also a cause of *E*.

For a closer-to-real-life version, imagine a case where David wants some coffee (*C*), and so takes a sip from his cup (*E*). If Steffi, who was standing next to him, had gestured wildly, she would have knocked the cup over, preventing *E* from occurring. (Steffi's wild gesturing would be *A*, and *A*'s not occurring is represented by the unfilled circle, the non-firing of neuron **A**.) David's desire for coffee is a cause of his taking a sip. And, if we allow for omission-involving causation, Steffi's calm, cool and collected behavior is also a cause of his sip.

1.2 Causation by prevention

Next, consider figure 22.

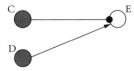

Figure 22

D fires, stimulating **E**. But **C**, by firing, prevents **E** from firing. Should we take the further step of counting *C* a cause of the omission that is **E**'s failure to fire? Again, many (but not all) think the answer is "yes."

James the cat lashes his tail wildly (*C*), knocking away Matilda's coffee cup as she tries to sip. Matilda's desire for coffee (*D*) would have been a cause of her sipping (*E*). Is James's lashing of his tail a cause of the omission of Matilda's sipping? Many find it quite reasonable to say it is.

1.3 Causation by double-prevention

Finally, figure 29 depicts a case of double prevention, which is a different, and very important way in which omissions can be involved in causal relations between ordinary events.

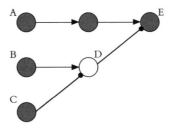

Figure 29

E depends on C: for if **C** had not fired, then **D** would have fired, thereby preventing **E** from firing. Again, for many theorists this relation of dependence decisively qualifies C as a cause of E. Our (sort of) real-life case: David makes the coffee (A), and fills his cup (E). Meanwhile, Steffi scoops up James the cat (C) as he lashes his tail wildly (B); her quick action prevents a disastrous spilling (D). Most of us want to say that Steffi saved the coffee— that is, C was among the causes of E. Schaffer (2000a) gives a number of real-life cases of double prevention, including the firing of a gun whose internal trigger works by double prevention.

Observe, in the case of double prevention, that while there is an obvious sense in which **D**'s failure to fire serves as a kind of causal intermediate between C and E, it is not necessary to formally admit omissions into one's ontology in order to recognize a causal relation here. One can simply say the following: E counterfactually depends on C, and that is enough to make C a cause (by double prevention, as we put it) of E. This observation will be important below when we consider the trouble that causation involving omissions makes for both sufficiency and transference accounts, as well as for the idea that intrinsicness intuitions govern our causal judgments, and should also be kept in mind when considering the issues involving transitivity in chapter 5.

2 The question of uniform treatment

In what follows, we will mostly take for granted that omission-involving causation is, indeed, causation—or at any rate, a kind of causation. So we reject eliminativism about causation by omission, or about causation by prevention, or about causation by double-prevention. (We will sketch our reasons, briefly, in §2.3.) Given that we are making room for causation by omission in our ontology, a main topic of investigation is whether a philosophical account of causation should provide a uniform treatment of omission-involving causation and ordinary causation between events. Are omission-involving causation and ordinary causation just apples and apples, mixed together without incident? Or is omission-involving causation like apples, while ordinary causation is like oranges, where mixing can cause trouble?

We think the balance of considerations favors a "yes" answer to the latter question, even if not decisively. One reason why we need some sort of uniformity is that we want our theory of causation to be able to handle cases where omissions are embedded in longer chains of causally related events. If an account is not uniform, then in cases with such embedding, not only would we need to apply different analyses to different parts of the chain, but we would have to have an exhaustive knowledge of every portion of the chain—else the wrong analysis could be applied. But with many, indeed most, causal chains, we lack exhaustive knowledge of the sequence. This problem, of course, is particularly obvious when we confront black-box cases, like those discussed in chapter 3, §6. So either an analysis must be uniform, or it must provide some way of generating enough uniformity to handle a wide range of "mixed" cases where omissions are embedded in causal sequences of events.

The next section begins a more explicit, case-based weighing. But first, some clarifications. We will speak of "garden-variety" causation below. When we do so, you should take us to have in mind cases of ordinary causation where (i) both cause C and effect E are ordinary events, with well-defined intrinsic features, mereological structure, and locations in space and time; and (ii) C is connected to E solely via a spatiotemporally continuous sequence or via sequences of intermediate ordinary events, each an effect of C and a cause of E. For short, in garden-variety causation one ordinary event brings about another by way of some continuous process or processes. Note that if a case is not garden-variety, it does not follow that it involves omissions; cases of action at a distance are counterexamples. But it won't serve any useful purpose to refine our definition of garden-variety to cover such cases; it is enough that this definition renders omission-involving causation distinct from garden-variety causation.

Second: we are largely setting aside the distinction between allowing versus causing, since for our purposes there are more productive ways to address the intuitions this distinction involves (for example, we prefer to focus on the distinction between default and deviant causal processes discussed in §3.4.2 and §3.5). In any case, given our focus on uniformity, it does not seem that the distinction will be helpful in developing a reductive metaphysical theory of causation (although it may be exceedingly useful when giving an account of causal explanation).

Now, if you are already wedded to a particular account of causation, then your fidelity to it will likely provide you with reasons for or against a uniform treatment of omission-involving and garden-variety causation. We will see examples in due course. But first, it would be a good idea to canvass some reasons for rejecting uniformity that are not at all tied to a particular account.

2.1 The ontology of omissions

In considering causation involving omissions, one might balk at the apparent ontological extravagance of admitting this sort of causation into one's ontology. The worry seems to be that, in recognizing causation involving omissions, we will be committed to recognizing a deviant species of event in addition to ordinary events, instances of which somehow consist in the failures of ordinary events to occur. We will go on to look at this in more detail: as we will see, simply rejecting causation involving omissions for this reason is misguided, for no such commitment is required. Instead of rejecting causation involving omissions, we need to see how to accommodate it: with this in mind, excellent reasons remain for holding that causation involving omissions merits some kind of special treatment. The trick is in seeing what sort of treatment that is.

Let's start with perhaps the simplest reason. Consider a case of garden-variety causation: Suzy throws a rock, which flies through the air and strikes a window, breaking it. Here is one event: Suzy's throw. Here is another: the breaking of the window. To say that the first is a cause of the second would, it seems, be to assert that a certain relation obtains between the first event and the second event. And a philosophical account of causation just is an account of the nature of this relation.

But if, in garden-variety cases, causation is just a relation between events, then we would seem to have a quick argument that causation involving omissions should not be assimilated to garden-variety cases. When Suzy breaks the window, Billy is standing by doing nothing, although he could have prevented her act. Let's grant that his failure to block her throw is also a cause of the window's breaking. But, says the quick argument, this failure is not itself an event. It is, rather, the absence of an event (of a certain type). Since garden-variety causation is a two-place relation between events, and since in this case, there is no event to slot in as the first relatum, causation by omission has been revealed to be a metaphysically distinct species from garden-variety causation. (See Lewis 2004b for discussion.)

So too, perhaps, prevention. Suppose, this time, that Billy blocks Suzy's throw, thereby preventing the window from breaking. Again it seems that when we say, perfectly correctly, that his action caused the window not to break, we are not asserting that the two-place relation of garden variety causation obtains between his action and some other event.

Now, this argument, just as stated, strikes us as very far from decisive, and it may well strike you the reader as suspiciously quick. All the same, it will prove highly instructive to go through worse and better reasons for resisting it.

2.1.1 Against "negative events"   One not very good reason for resisting this argument rests on an insistence that omissions are events—just events of a metaphysically distinctive, negative variety. We think this position raises just the sorts of questions that are often (and rightly) taken to be symptomatic of an unwelcome ontological commitment. One of us (Hall) didn't go into the office this morning. Where was that omission located? How long did it last? Did it have other omissions as parts? What particulars were involved in it? Any precise answer to these questions will smack of stipulation. Not so, where ordinary events are in question.

That ordinary events have (within the usual, and unsurprising, vague boundaries) parts, and well-defined locations in space and time, serves as a reminder that they should be thought of as more concrete-object-like than proposition-like. Here is the contrast we have in mind. When it comes to propositions, Boolean principles reign: given the proposition that Suzy smiled and the proposition that Billy scowled, there is the proposition that Suzy smiled and Billy scowled; and there is the proposition that Suzy smiled or Billy scowled; and there is the proposition that Suzy did not smile. But given Suzy and Billy themselves, the only sense in which their "conjunction" exists is the mereological sense, which reads "conjunction" as "fusion." And there is no intelligibility to the claim that some special entity that is their disjunction exists, or that there could is some special object that is the negation (or absence, or omission, for that matter) of one or the other. Philosophers who want to subscribe to negative events or omissions must not run roughshod over this basic distinction in ontology: one cannot simply hold that there "are" nonexistent objects that somehow "exist." (Perhaps a better treatment of omissions existing in a special way can be fashioned out of recent work on the metaphysics of different ways of being (e.g., Turner 2010, McDaniel 2009): further work along these lines is merited.)

There is another option, which involves tacitly treating causation as a relation between true propositions. That's a worthy view, which we will come back to in §2.1.3. But it's also a response to our argument that should be distinguished from the ontologically muddled view where absences or negations of objects are simply assumed to somehow exist.

2.1.2 *Against omissions as ordinary events, oddly described*   A different response insists that omissions are just ordinary events. There are two bad reasons for adopting this response, which we should quickly set aside. First, one might be taken in by ordinary language, which can occasionally mislead—as when we note the occurrence of an ordinary event by saying that Billy "failed to leave the lights on" (i.e., he turned them off). Second, one might take note of two incompatible events—events that cannot both occur, such as Billy's death at a certain time and place, and his survival at that time and place—and mistakenly think that (i) one of them must be an omission, the failure of the other to occur; but that (ii) there is no non-arbitrary way to decide which is the omission and which the genuine event; therefore (iii) there can't really be a distinction between omissions and genuine events. The right answer is that neither incompatible event is an omission. We have an omission just in case no ordinary event of some specified type occurs. Deaths are ordinary events. Survivals are ordinary events. In a region of spacetime where Billy is simply absent, it would be correct to say both that he fails to die, there, and that he fails to survive, there. In a region where he dies, it would be correct to say that he fails to survive—but quite wrong to equate the token event of his particular death with this omission.

A rather more sophisticated, and often explicitly theory-driven response is to say that omissions are perfectly ordinary events, albeit referred to in a non-ordinary way, in statements describing causation by omission or prevention. Return to our example of vandal Suzy and idle Billy, for an illustration of the guiding idea: when we say that Billy's failure to block Suzy's throw was a cause of the window's breaking, that claim is true in virtue of a causal relation between a perfectly ordinary event and the event of the breaking. Which perfectly ordinary event? Why, whatever Billy was doing instead. So if, for example, Billy was digging in the sandbox, then it is that event—his digging, there and then—that stands in the causal relation to the window's breaking.

Now, viewed as a response to the claim that causation involving omissions needs a different treatment from causation that does not involve omissions, this move faces a problem: if, in speaking of Billy's failure to block Suzy's throw, we are really talking about the event that consists in his digging in the sandbox, then we should be happy to say that his digging in the sandbox was a cause of the breaking—which we surely are not, since such a claim would be highly misleading at best.[1] But this worry is far from decisive. And at any rate the idea that omissions are really just ordinary events, oddly described seems to have a fair bit of currency in the literature. Here for example is Lewis (1986c, p. 192, italics in the original; note that he changed his view in his 2004b):

The third . . . strategy accepts events of omission as causes; but this time, the events of omission are not essentially specified as such. Fred omits the precautions, sleeping through the time when he was supposed to attend to them. His nap was

---

[1] Interestingly, this particular problem does not seem to have much bite when directed at a treatment of prevention of the same kind. That is, suppose you think that, in the case where Billy blocks Suzy's throw, and so prevents the window-breaking, the event that his action stands in the causal relation to is not a spookily negative "non-breaking," but rather the boring-but-ordinary event of the window's being present in an unbroken state. That sounds fine: isn't it clearly true that Billy's action was a cause of the window's being in that state?

a genuine event; it is not objectionably disjunctive. There are many and varied ways in which he could have omitted the precautions, but there is just one way that he did omit them. We could plausibly say, then, that his nap *was* his omission of precautions.

Here, in a similar vein, is Schaffer, applying his view that causal claims are essentially contrastive to the case of causation by omission:

> The reconciliation strategy is as follows: (i) *treat negative nominals as denoting actual events*, and (ii) treat absence-talk as tending to set the associated contrast to the possible event said to be absent. For instance, given that the gardener napped and my flowers wilted, 'The gardener's not watering my flowers caused my flowers not to blossom', is to be interpreted as: the gardener's napping rather than watering my flowers caused my flowers to wilt rather than blossom. (Schaffer 2005, p. 331; italics added)

But the idea that negative nominals can, whenever needed, be treated as denoting actual events fails to capture the full range of cases that can exhibit causation by omission. Return to our case of vandal Suzy. Suppose that this time, tragically, Billy died a week ago. So, at the time of Suzy's throw, he is not doing anything, as he no longer exists. For all that, it remains true that Billy's absence, and consequent failure to block Suzy's throw, is a cause of the window's breaking.[2] Or suppose that overpopulation of rabbits in a certain region, at a certain time, is caused in part by a lack of predators. Are we really to suppose that there are some (potential) predators in that region at that time, doing something else other than preying on these rabbits—and that it is that something else we are referring to by the expression "a lack of predators"? At best, we might claim that the region of the rabbits, just as it is, counts as the event described by "the lack of predators," but this again is unsatisfactory. (See §3.2 for our preferred rendering of the contrastive treatment of absences in terms of counterfactual dependence.)

A final cost of taking omissions to be vaguely specified ordinary events that are described in some ontologically obscure fashion is that we then adopt many, many more events as causes than we are commonsensically inclined to accept, since many of these "causes" will simply be vast regions

---

[2] If you need more convincing of the propriety of this judgment, here's a helpful back story: Billy has trained, from childhood, to be Suzy's Keeper, charged with preventing her from committing the random acts of vandalism toward which she is so prone. This charge he has faithfully and unerringly kept, up until last week's tragedy. Notice, now, how natural it is to cite his absence as partly responsible for the window's breaking.

of the world at a time where we specify that an "omission" is "occurring" (viz., our "lack of predators" example above). Such trivialization of causation involving omissions should be avoided if at all possible.

2.1.3 Must causation be a relation between events?

We conclude that there is little hope for defending the "uniform treatment" position by insisting that omission are events, whether ordinary or metaphysically novel. But the argument in §2.1 against assimilating causation involving omissions to garden-variety causation made an additional assumption, which is that causation is a relation between events. A more interesting way to resist that argument denies this assumption. (See also our discussion in chapter 2, §4.1.)

Sometimes the denial takes a form that won't obviously help the defender of uniformity, as in this remark by Lewis: " . . . when an absence is a cause or an effect, there is strictly speaking nothing at all that is a cause or effect. Sometimes causation is not a relation, because a relation needs relata and sometimes the causal relata go missing." (2004a, p. 100) The remark begs for clarification. Compare: *being taller than* is a relation. Now suppose that Billy, being quite short, is taller than no one. "Then there is, strictly speaking, no one than whom he is taller. Sometimes *being taller than* is not a relation, because a relation needs relata and sometimes the tallness relata go missing." No: the logical form of "Billy is taller than no one" is simply different from that of, e.g., "Billy is taller than Suzy." Lewis needs to give us some reason for thinking that he isn't making an analogous mistake here. At any rate, even supposing he is right—so causation is sometimes a relation and sometimes not—why think that the correct account of causation should give the two sorts of cases a uniform treatment?

It would be more sensible, we think, to adopt a suggestion of Hugh Mellor (2004), and maintain that causation is a relation, but between true propositions (or "facta") rather than events. (Or better still: the causal relation that ought to be the target of analysis is a relation between true propositions. Then events can still be causes and effects—just as, for that matter, things or ordinary objects can—by being suitably related to such true propositions.) Then your defense of uniformity is safe from the simple argument with which we began: "Suzy's throw caused the window to break" becomes, more perspicuously, "the true proposition that Suzy threw caused it to be the case that the window broke"; and likewise, "Billy's failure to block Suzy's throw caused the window to break" becomes, more perspicuously, "the true proposition that Billy failed to block Suzy's throw caused it to be the case that the window broke." Although we won't pursue it further here, this strategy looks fairly promising to us. See Lewis 2004*b* for related discussion.

2.2 Infection by the normative

The next reason for being suspicious that causation involving omissions ought to be treated uniformly with garden-variety causation is that our judgments concerning it are remarkably sensitive to, broadly speaking, normative considerations, in a way that our judgments concerning ordinary causation are not (although see Hitchcock and Knobe 2009). Here are some examples that serve to illustrate the remarkable heterogeneity of these normative considerations.

Suzy goes away on vacation. Billy promises to water her plants. He does not water them, and they die. If he had watered them, they would not have died. It is also true that if Vladimir Putin had watered them, they would not have died. But we count Billy's failure to water the plants a cause of their death, and do not count Vladimir Putin's failure to water them a cause of their death. Here, it seems that the relevant normative consideration is that Billy promised to water the plants, and Putin did not.[3]

Billy and Suzy are playing soccer with each other, but on rival teams. One of Suzy's teammates successfully kicks a goal. Both Billy and Suzy were nearby, and either one of them could easily have blocked the goal. But we credit the goal in part, at least, to Billy's failure to block it, and not to Suzy's failure to block it. Here, it seems that the relevant normative consideration is that, in virtue of his role in the game, Billy was supposed to block the goal, whereas Suzy was not supposed to.[4]

In the rainforest, where it rains almost every day, on one particular day, the ground is dry. In the desert, where it almost never rains, the ground is also dry on that day. It strikes us as appropriate, in first case, to cite the absence of rain as one of the causes of the ground's being dry; not so in the second case. Here, what we think of as the relevant normative consideration is perhaps not so readily flagged as such, but it seems to be something like this: given what is normal for the rainforest, it was supposed to rain in the

---

[3] Thanks to Sarah McGrath, for the example.
[4] This example is adapted from Beebee 2004.

last 24 hours; given what is normal for the desert, it was not supposed to rain in the last 24 hours.[5]

It remains an open question how best to give a precise characterization of the phenomenon these examples illustrate. (But see McGrath 2005 for a sophisticated proposal, Sartorio 2005 for a different way of thinking of these cases, and Swanson 2010 for an excellent discussion about the context-sensitivity of causal claims involving omissions.) But assuming it is correct, as we think it is, that broadly speaking normative considerations play a role in informing our judgments of when a given claim of causation involving omission is appropriate (and perhaps even true), we can reasonably ask for an explanation of why this is so. Now, there is certainly no guarantee that an adequate answer must appeal to some difference in the metaphysics of causation involving omissions and ordinary causation. All the same, we will see below that some have found it to be an attractive strategy.

2.3 The metaphysical primacy of garden-variety causation

Dowe (2000) provides an additional argument against uniformity (also defended by others: e.g., see Armstrong 2004). He observes that facts about omission-involving causation are parasitic on what, following Armstrong, we will call "active" causation. The idea is transparent in our neuron diagrams: the patterns of counterfactual dependence that undergird our judgments about causation by omission, prevention, and causation by double prevention quite evidently supervene on the facts about what neurons there are, what sorts of stimulatory and inhibitory connections link them, and which of them fire. One might therefore think it appropriate for a philosophical account of causation to give one sort of treatment for the more ontologically fundamental "active" causal facts, and another for the ontologically dependent facts about causation involving omissions, etc.

But while we are somewhat sympathetic to this line of reasoning, ultimately it is inconclusive. Dowe's argument would be more persuasive if we could rest it on the following supervenience claim: no two worlds differ with respect to their omission-involving causal facts without differing with respect to their garden-variety causal facts. But, for a reason pointed out by McGrath, this supervenience thesis is incorrect. Consider figure 3 again.

---

[5] Thanks again to Sarah McGrath, both for the example and for the point that the relevant normative consideration can include facts about what typically or normally happens.

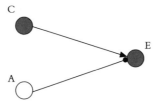

Figure 3

Let us imagine the events depicted in this figure unfolding in just the same way, in two different worlds (w1 and w2). These worlds agree exactly, let us suppose, with respect to what happens in them; but they disagree in their neuron laws. According to the laws of w1, a firing of neuron **A** will, in the depicted circumstances, prevent **E** from firing only if it has a very specific character—say, intensity 17. In w2, the laws are not so fussy: according to them, any firing of **A** at the right time would have prevented **E** from firing. Then these worlds differ with respect to their omission-involving causal facts: for example, in w2 but not w1 it is the case that **A**'s failure to fire with intensity 10 is a cause of *E*. But they do not differ at all with respect to their "active" causal facts.

There is an obvious way to amend the supervenience thesis: let it state that any two worlds that differ with respect to their omission-involving causal facts likewise differ with respect either to their garden-variety causal facts, or with respect to their fundamental laws. But the problem now is that, arguably, this amended version of the supervenience thesis is too trivial to support the claim that omission-involving causation needs a different kind of analysis from garden-variety causation. For suppose two worlds are exactly alike with respect to their fundamental laws, and exactly alike with respect to their garden-variety causal facts. Then—unless, implausibly, one of them includes events that enter into no garden-variety causal relations with any other events—the two worlds will be exactly alike with respect to what ordinary events they contain. Arguably, then, they will be exactly like with respect to their total histories. But we have been taking for granted that every fact about the world supervenes on the facts about its total history, together with the facts about the fundamental laws governing that history. So of course facts about omission-involving causation will supervene as well. Why take that obvious result as grounds for thinking they need a different kind of analysis from garden-variety causal facts?

An even less acceptable way to deny uniformity is simple eliminativism: i.e., to reject causation by omission by fiat. The reason this is unacceptable is that there are clear-cut cases where omissions cause things. If Billy fails to take his medicine and falls ill, his omission causes his illness. To deny causal efficacy in such cases is to give up any hope of a reasonable model of causation. If you are skeptical, consider Schaffer's 2000*a* discussion showing how guns work by chains of causes that include omissions. Deny that there can be causation involving omissions and you deny that guns cause gunshot wounds (and that guns kill people...). Apart from becoming the poster child for the National Rifle Association, this means that you are rejecting intuitions that even non-experts accept. As the novelist Alexander McCall Smith puts it,

[t]here's no reason why we should not see omissions to act as being as causally potent as positive actions. It's simply wrong to think that failures to act can't cause things—they do. It's just that our ordinary idea of how things are caused is too tied to ideas of physical causation, of pushing and shoving. But it's more subtle than that. (Smith 2005, p.105)

In sum, then, while we agree that Dowe is onto something in labeling omission-involving causation "parasitic," the nature of the parasitism remains too opaque at this stage for this consideration alone to warrant the rejection of the uniformity thesis.

2.4 Redundancy

Now we will examine a startling contrast between omission-involving and garden-variety causation. Begin with the observation that when we have a case of garden-variety causation that does not involve preemption or overdetermination, it is child's play to tweak it so that it does. Suzy throws a rock at the window, breaking it. Now add Billy, either poised to throw a rock if Suzy doesn't (early preemption), or throwing a rock a bit slower (late preemption), or throwing a rock that strikes the window simultaneously with Suzy's (overdetermination). By contrast, if we start with a case of causation by omission, it is not at all straightforward how to tweak it so as to introduce a preempted alternative (whether that alternative is itself an omission, or is rather an ordinary event).

Try it. Start with the case where Billy stands idly by, while Suzy throws a rock through the window. If he had intercepted the rock, the window would not have broken. Now try to add extra features to the case, so that (i) Billy's failure to intercept still counts as a cause of the window's breaking; but (ii) it preempts some alternative, so that now, if Billy had intercepted the rock, the window would have broken all the same. We submit that it is not at all clear how to complete this exercise. If you add a third party—say, Sally, who also throws a rock at the window, and whom Billy is in no position to stop—then it becomes natural to say that the window was doomed anyway, so that Billy's inaction made no difference to whether it broke; and, curiously, it becomes natural to infer that Billy's failure to intercept the rock is not, in this case, a cause of the breaking. "Curiously," because the natural inferences are so different in a case of ordinary preemption! That is: in our standard case of preemption (Suzy and Billy both throw, but her rock gets to the window first), it is likewise natural to say that Suzy's throw made no difference to whether the window broke, but to insist for all that, that her throw, and not Billy's, was a cause of the breaking.

It is perhaps less obvious, but still arguable, that we can have cases of redundant causation by omission, as in figure 38.

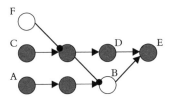

Figure 38

Arguably, the failure of neuron **F** to fire is a cause of E, since it is clearly a cause of D, which in turn causes E. But **E** would have fired, even if **F** had fired.

Consider what happens as we try to construct a better account. We might try to build upon the following observation about garden-variety causation. (a) When two events C and D occur at the same time, and (b) event E occurs at some later time, and (c) when in addition E depends on neither C nor D taken alone, but does depend on the two taken together—that is, had neither C nor D occurred, E would not have occurred—then (d) at least one of C and D must be a redundant cause of E. It might be that C and D jointly cause E, as D and B do in figure 16.

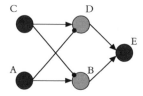

Figure 16

It might be that only one of C or D causes E, and does so in a way that preempts the other, as in cases of early, late, and (perhaps) trumping pre-emption. It might be that the two symmetrically overdetermine E. But what can be safely assumed is that at least one of them is somehow causally implicated in E's occurrence. Call this the "redundancy assumption." (Note that the assumption can be extended in an obvious way to cover not merely pairs of events C and D, but triples, quadruples, etc.)

We might hope that the redundancy assumption holds for omission-involving causation as well. If so, then we could see how at least to begin to construct a more adequate account of this kind of causation. We could start by taking (a)–(d) to provide a basis for sufficient (but not necessary) conditions on their respective kinds of causal relation. We could then extend these conditions by appealing to the redundancy assumption, hoping that in any case where that assumption applied, further tests would reveal what sort of redundancy was at issue, and which were the genuine and which were the pre-empted causal relata. For example, we notice in figure 38 that at the time at which **A** fires, **F** also fails to fire. We notice that E depends on neither A nor not-F, but does depend on the two taken together: had **A** not fired, but had **F** fired, E would not have fired. We conclude that at least one of A and not-F is causally implicated in E's occurrence. Further inspection reveals that not-F is a cause—because it causes D, which causes E—whereas A is not.

But there are at least two serious problems here. One problem—which we will not discuss in any detail—is that it is not at all clear that the strategies for handling and distinguishing the various kinds of redundancy discussed in chapter 3 will carry over neatly when omission-involving causation is at issue. A more fundamental problem is that the redundancy assumption is false (or at the very least, not clearly true) when applied to causation involving omission. Consider first redundant prevention. A version of a well-known and relevant example is this: Suzy throws a rock at a window, and Billy blocks the rock; but if he had not blocked it, the window still would not have broken, since it is protected by a high, thick, sturdy wall. It does not seem that Billy's block prevents the window from being broken; how can it, given that the window is never in any danger from Suzy's rock? And the wall doesn't do anything, so it can't be a cause. Yet we have the right pattern of counterfactual dependence: if Billy had not blocked, and the wall had not been there, then the window would have broken. McDermott (1995) reasons essentially on this basis that Billy's block does prevent the window from breaking: for between Billy and the wall, the rock is prevented from reaching the window; but since the wall doesn't do anything, Billy gets the credit. But the reasoning we just gave is at least as compelling. And that is enough to show that there is a phenomenon here that has no clear parallel in cases of ordinary causal preemption. In those cases, there is never any doubt about whether there is causation, nor about which of the relevant events is the genuine cause, and which the pre-empted alternative. Not so with our alleged case of redundant prevention, where, at the very least, intuitions prove vastly more malleable. Moreover, as we will see in the next chapter, cases that involve omission-involving causation with embedded redundancy figure significantly in puzzles surrounding the transitivity of causation. So, even if an account of omission-involving causation endorses the redundancy assumption without qualification, it must at least be supplemented by an explanation for why our intuitions about these sorts of cases can so easily be led astray. (For useful discussion, see Collins 2000, Maudlin 2004 and Lewis 2004a.)

An even more serious challenge to the redundancy assumption emerges when we reconsider the reasoning we engaged in about figure 38. It appears that this reasoning can be used to causally implicate any event C in the production of any later event E. Consider that at the time of C's occurrence, a certain other type of event fails to occur: namely, the appearance of a sufficiently powerful and knowing genie intent and capable of preventing E unless C occurred. (If this omission strikes you as too fanciful, you may take it on as an exercise to construct a more realistic one, or indeed a set of them.) Had C not occurred, and had this omission not occurred—that is, had such a genie appeared—then E would not have occurred. But it is crazy to think that either C or this omission is, for that reason alone, causally implicated in E's occurrence. That would be to claim that, simply because the circumstances of C's occurrence could have been such as to make E depend on it, it follows that E is caused by C, together with the failure of the circumstances to be this way. That's a terrible strategy. So too the redundancy assumption, in the unrestricted form that we are considering. It implies that a certain sort of redundancy is perfectly ubiquitous, and so the assumption ought to be rejected.

But this result leaves a very hard problem in its wake: How do we distinguish those cases in which we have genuine, as opposed to spurious, redundancy involving omissions? We think that no proper account of omission-involving causation will be forthcoming until this question receives an adequate answer. Happily for us, for our purposes here we can leave it wide open.

Let us now consider the serious problems that causation involving omissions presents for various treatments of causation.

3 Trouble with causation involving omissions

3.1 Transference and sufficiency accounts

For transference accounts the trouble is obvious: when an omission is involved either as cause or effect, there will either be nothing to send the appropriate stuff, or nothing to receive it. Philosophers who defend this approach must therefore dismiss causation involving omissions or find some other way to accommodate it. Observe that squeamishness about the ontological status of omissions gives the transference theorist little reason to prefer eliminativism, since causation involving omissions can nevertheless still (ultimately) be causation between perfectly ordinary events. Figure 29 reminds us of this fact.

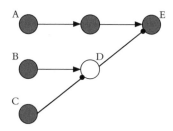

Figure 29

As we mentioned in §2.3, one denies that there is any such thing as causation of or by omission at some cost; and the price of denying that there can be no causation by double prevention is even higher. Schaffer (2000*a*) does an excellent job of weighing the cost, in part by showing how ubiquitous cases of double prevention are. An example along the lines of those he discusses will show why. Two pillars are leaning against each other. Suzy comes along and knocks one aside, thus causing the other to fall down. Deny that double prevention is causation, and you thereby deny, apparently, that she caused the second pillar to fall down: for her action prevented something—the continued presence of the first pillar in an upright state—which, had it occurred, would have prevented the second pillar from falling over. More generally, whenever two systems X and Y are stably interacting in such a way that the continued presence of X is inhibiting Y from behaving in a certain manner, then an event that "removes" X will thereby cause a change in Y, but do so by double prevention. It is safe to assume that that sort of causal relationship is extremely widespread. It is very bad news for a transference account if it must deny the existence of such relationships.

The trouble for minimal sufficiency accounts is just as pronounced, but takes more work to bring out. Begin by considering the account we offered in chapter 2. We suggested that C counts as a cause of E just in case C belongs to a set of co-occurring events that is minimally sufficient for E. Recall what this means: the set is such that, were only its members to occur at the given time, E would still occur, whereas the same is not true of any proper subset. We saw in chapter 2 that, on pain of rendering the wrong verdict about cases of preemption, this account must also require that the given minimally sufficient set be unique—and even then can only provide a sufficient condition on causation. Still, it would be a disaster if, for some particular kind of event, the minimally sufficient condition could not possibly be met. That is exactly the trouble we run into with omission-involving causation in all of its varieties.

Suppose, in figure 3, that we wish to count **A**'s failure to fire to be a cause of E that is contemporaneous with C.

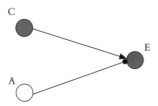

Figure 3

Indulging in a slight abuse of notation, let not-*A* be the omission that "is" (whatever exactly that comes to) **A**'s failure to fire at the relevant time. Then the set {*C*, not-*A*}, while sufficient for *E*, is obviously not minimally sufficient for it, since the set {*C*} is also sufficient for *E*. The point is perfectly general: Take any set S that is sufficient for some later event *E*. Suppose S includes some omission. Let S* be the proper subset of S that omits this omission. Then the counterfactual circumstance in which only the events in S occur at the given time is exactly the same as the counterfactual circumstance in which only the events in S* occur at the given time.[6] So S is sufficient only if S* is sufficient. So S is not minimally sufficient.

For exactly the same reason, our minimal sufficiency account cannot handle cases of causation by double prevention. Returning to figure 29:

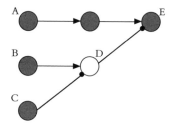

Figure 29

Letting *t* be the time at which **A** fires, we can see that any set of t-events that is going to be sufficient for *E* had better include *A*; but since {*A*} is already sufficient for *E*, it follows that there will be no set of *t*-events that is both minimally sufficient for *E*, and that contains *C*. Moreover, it is apparent that none of the strategies considered in the last section for augmenting our sufficiency account will succeed in connecting *C* up to *E*. So *C* will turn out not to be a cause of *E*.

Finally, consider prevention, focusing on figure 22 as an example.

---

[6] Alternatively, the requirement that only the events in S occur at the given time might be considered incoherent, namely if the events quantified over are taken to include arbitrary omissions. Suppose the set includes neither any event of type C, nor the failure of an event of type C to occur. Then it is impossible that only the events in set S occur at the given time, if this is taken to mean, inter alia, that no event of type C occurs at that time, and that the omission of an event of type C likewise does not "occur" at that time (i.e., some event of type C does occur). In the text, we are implicitly assuming that the "only events in S occur" clause is to be understood as saying that no ordinary events other than those in S occur.

Figure 22

Again, let t be the time at which **C** and **D** both fire. Clearly, if no events had occurred at t, then **E** would not have fired; it follows that the empty set is minimally sufficient for **E**'s failure to fire, hence that D is not a cause of this omission, hence (if we equate prevention with causation of omission) that D does not prevent E from firing.

The clear culprit is the account of sufficiency. It might also seem clear how to fix it. Recall that we settled on it because we had rejected a simpler account. According to this simpler account, a set of co-occurring events S is sufficient for a later event E just in case the occurrence of the members of S lawfully guarantees that E occurs. We rejected this account by reasoning that it was possible for the events in S to occur together with other events that acted to prevent them from bringing about E; in other words, a complete set of contemporaneous causes of E need not be sufficient for E *tout court*, but only under the additional assumption that nothing interferes with them. But why not say instead that such a possibility merely shows that the set S was not comprehensive enough? Suppose that the occurrence of an event of type Q would have prevented the events in S from bringing about E; all that shows is that we should have included in S the failure of an event of type Q to occur. Do so, and the original definition of sufficiency succeeds. What's more, so the claim goes, it does so in a way that shows that the sufficiency account that makes use of it can perfectly well accommodate causation by omission.

Unfortunately, matters are hardly so simple. To see why, consider figure 39.

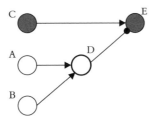

Figure 39

Let t be the time at which **C** fires. A and B are both Q-type events. As it happens, neither **A** nor **B** fire. If both of them had fired at time t—but only if both of them had fired at time t—then **D** (a stubborn neuron) would have fired, and therefore **E** would not have fired. Under the current proposal, if a set containing C is to be sufficient for E, it must therefore contain either not-A or not-B. The problem is that it need not contain both. And that means that there will be at least two distinct sets sufficient for E: one containing not-A (but not containing not-B), and one containing not-B (but not containing not-A). So there will be no unique sufficient set for E that contains C. If you like, you can think of the two omissions as "symmetrically overdetermining" E—and where there is redundancy like this, the uniqueness condition fails. What's more, the prospects for applying the strategy discussed in the last section for handling such overdetermination by way of the intrinsicness thesis seem dim: for reasons we will shortly discuss, it is doubtful that a suitable intrinsicness thesis can be formulated that will even be consistent with the claim that there is causation involving omissions.

The problem depends on nothing at all special about figure 39. Take any event C, and one of its effects E. It will always be possible to concoct multiple events that could have concurred contemporaneously with C and prevented E—but didn't occur—and which are such that, had all of them occurred contemporaneously with C, then they would have prevented C from bringing about E. Then their omissions will "symmetrically overdetermine" E, and so there will be no unique sufficient set for E containing C. There is a deeper point to which we will return shortly: if omissions can ever play the role of symmetric overdeterminers, then symmetric overdetermination involving them is rampant.

It was a bad idea to try to understand "sufficiency" in the simpler way; we should stick with the formulation that says that a set is sufficient for some event E just in case, were only the events in that set to occur (at the given time), then E would still occur. And we are therefore also stuck with the conclusion that the sufficiency account cannot straightforwardly accommodate causation involving omission. As noted above, however, sufficiency and transference theorists should not simply dismiss causation involving omission. So they had better find some way to accommodate it as a kind of special case.

3.2 Counterfactual accounts

In a simple case of ordinary causation involving events, according to counterfactual accounts, C will cause E because E depends on C; that is, because, had C not occurred, E would not have occurred. Now consider just causation by omission, that is, where an omission is a cause of an event. One might think that in a simple case of causation by omission, a "witnessing" counterfactual will simply be the following: had C occurred, E would not have occurred—where C is the event omitted. But as we have argued, the singular reference here to a nonexistent event is highly suspect, and at any rate ordinary reasoning involving causation by omission does not in general appeal to counterfactuals with this form. An example due to Sarah McGrath makes the point: she observes that her failure ever to compete in a triathlon will cause her athletically obsessed uncle to write her out of his will (well, not really, let us hope). But what is being omitted here is not some particular event (which one would it be?), but rather an event-type. The appropriate lesson is that the "witnessing" counterfactual for a claim of causation by omission needs to take the following form: had an event of type C occurred, event E would not have occurred. This is subtly but importantly different from the form of a witnessing counterfactual for a claim of ordinary causation.

So, it seems that when equipped with the right conditionals, a counterfactual analysis in any of the varieties we have considered can easily be extended to cover causation by omission. And note that for causation *of* omissions, we can take the witnessing counterfactual to be of the form, had C not occurred, an event of type E would have occurred. Contrastive versions of counterfactual accounts (chapter 2, §2.2.4), could hold that (for causation by omission) had an event of type C rather than type C* occurred, E would not have occurred, and (for causation of omission), had C not occurred, then an event of type E rather than type E* would have occurred. This makes the contrastive rendering of causation by omission less natural, but still acceptable. Although including omissions as causes greatly expands one's causal ontology, the fan of counterfactual accounts may think it is worth the cost. (And she will employ various strategies to distinguish mere causes from salient causes in an attempt to minimize the ontological pain.)

3.3 Intrinsicness

Recall from our discussion of late preemption (chapter 3, §4) that one attractive account of the structure of these cases turns on the:

Intrinsicness Thesis: Let S be a structure of events consisting of event E, together with all of its causes back to some earlier time t. Let S' be a structure of events whose intrinsic character matches the intrinsic character of S, and that exists in a world with the same laws. Let E' be the event in S' that corresponds to E in S. Let C be some event in S distinct from E, and let C' be the event in S' that corresponds to C. Then C' is a cause of E'.

As we discussed in chapter 3 (§4.3), an application of this thesis to the problem posed by late preemption requires some delicacy when laying out the relevant notion of "matching": perfect match of intrinsic character makes for a more readily defensible thesis, but at the cost of rendering that thesis useless as a cure for the late preemption disease. Never mind. For present purposes, just notice that the thesis has a great deal of plausibility when "match" is read as "perfect match." But it cannot apply to omission-involving causation.

The point is not that the event-structures the thesis concerns are structures of ordinary events (and not omissions); that is perfectly correct, but yields no conflict. It is rather that the thesis cannot hold, in general, when the structure S includes an event C that is a cause of E only by double-prevention. Start by comparing a case of late preemption with a case of double prevention to draw out the way that causation by omission can cause problems. In particular, juxtapose figure 18 with figure 29.

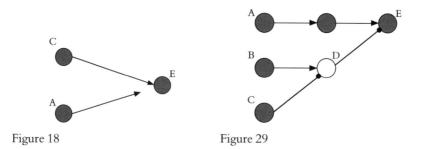

Figure 18   Figure 29

Figure 18, a case of late preemption, poses a problem that may be solvable only if appeal is made to some principle to the effect that the causal structure of a process is intrinsic to it. We offered one such principle based on our intrinsicness thesis. If a structure of events consists of some event E together with all of its causes back to some earlier time, then the fact that the earlier events in this structure are causes of E is guaranteed by the intrinsic character of that structure, together with the governing laws.

Now, as we saw in chapter 3, §4.3.1, that principle is inconsistent with the thesis, central to counterfactual analyses, that counterfactual dependence suffices for causation. Let's rehearse the argument using figure 29 to bring out the inconsistency. Suppose we count C in figure 29 as one of the causes of E, since, if C had not occurred, E would not have occurred. According to our intrinsicness thesis, this causal relation should remain stable under modifications of the situation that only change features extrinsic to the causal history of E. Among these features are the firing of **B**, and the passage of its stimulatory signal to **D**. Let us change these features dramatically, by removing them (figure 40).

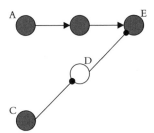

Figure 40

Doing so completely reverses the intuitive verdict about C. In figure 29, C got to be a cause of E (if at all) only because it canceled a potential threat to E's occurrence. In figure 40, there is no such threat; C is completely idle with respect to E. The case, more intuitively: David makes the coffee (A), and fills his cup (E). Meanwhile, Steffi scoops up James the cat (C). Steffi's scooping is causally idle with respect to the filling of the coffee cup. This means that something has to go: in particular, for those who hew to the thesis that counterfactual dependence always suffices for causation, intrinsicness has to go.

3.4 Structural equations

3.4.1 Counterfactual isomorphism with causal difference   Recently, counterfactual-based approaches involving causal models based on structural equations have become extremely popular. Given the ease with which counterfactual approaches handle causation involving omissions, it might seem that our discussion simply bolsters the case for adopting a causal modeling treatment of causation. But as we will see, although something is deeply right about the structural equations approach to these problems, causal modeling accounts that use structural equations as the basis for an analysis of causation also get something deeply wrong. We will start by raising a general problem for the structural equations approach that causation involving omissions creates, and then we will look carefully at one of the best recent attempts to harness the ideas behind the approach to give a reductive account of causation, Christopher Hitchcock's (2007a) approach using "self-contained networks."

We can make the case by recalling one of the principal objections to the de facto dependence treatment of late preemption. In §2.3.3 of chapter 3, we noted that when applied to figure 10, this treatment yielded the decidedly unwelcome consequence that C causes E—since E depends on C, holding B fixed.

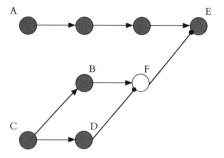

Figure 10

We are now in a position to point out a deeper purpose served by this example. But first we need to modify it slightly, by adding an extra neuron, **G**.

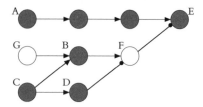

Figure 41

Since **G** does not fire, the original verdict stands: in figure 41, *C* is not a cause of *E*, notwithstanding the fact that *E* depends on *C* modulo *B*. But now consider figure 42:

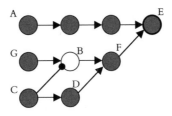

Figure 42

Here, **E** is a stubborn neuron requiring two stimulatory signals in order to fire. What's more, *C* clearly is, this time, one of the causes of *E*—a joint cause, with *A*. The crucial observation to make is that figures 41 and 42 are perfectly isomorphic with respect to counterfactual structure. One way to see this is to write down the appropriate structural equations for them, as follows.

Recall that the elements of a causal model based on structural equations consist of *variables*, a range of possible *values* for each of the variables, a specification, for each variable, of which other variables (if any) it immediately functionally depends on, and finally, "structural equations" that describe this dependence.

For figure 41, the structural equations are these:

$$A = 1 \qquad D = C \qquad\qquad E = A \;\&\; \neg F$$
$$G = 0 \qquad B = G \vee C$$
$$C = 1 \qquad F = B \;\&\; \neg D$$

For figure 42, they are these:

$$A = 1 \qquad D = C \qquad\qquad E = A \;\&\; F$$
$$G = 1 \qquad B = G \;\&\; \neg C$$
$$C = 1 \qquad F = B \vee D$$

To see the isomorphism, simply define, for the second set of equations, $G' = \neg G$, $B' = \neg B$, and $F' = \neg F$; then the set for figure 42, rewritten, becomes

$$A = 1 \qquad D = C \qquad\qquad E = A \;\&\; \neg F'$$
$$G' = 0 \qquad B' = G' \vee C$$
$$C = 1 \qquad F' = B' \;\&\; \neg D$$

Figures 41 and 42 thus display perfectly parallel patterns of counterfactual dependence; their causal models are exactly the same. But they are not causally isomorphic. There is an important point here, which is that our candidate model of the causal structure of these cases, fails. There is a second, more important point: any structural equations account of causation is going to fail, insofar as it commits itself to the view that the causal relations manifested in any situation are fixed by the correct causal model for the situation, together with the facts about which "variables" have which "values"—while admitting no causally relevant distinctions between different such values. But the third point is the most important one: causation involving omissions needs to be treated differently from causation that does not involve omissions. For there is no difference in the counterfactual structures of the two situations depicted. The manifest difference in their causal structures must therefore trace to something else, and it appears that the obvious feature to fix on is that, whereas in figure 41 we have causation involving omission in the relationship between D and E, in figure 42 we do not.

3.4.2 Causal modeling with default and deviant causal chains Hitchcock (2007a) attempts to respond to the problem we have raised for causal modeling accounts by partly—although only partly—incorporating the lesson we are urging. He argues that when we evaluate the causal structure of a situation, we ordinarily distinguish, in a context-sensitive way, between "default" and "deviant" values of the relevant variables. Often—though importantly not always—the default value of a variable is one that corresponds to an omission. According to Hitchcock, we can use this distinction to develop an analysis of causation that does an especially good job of explaining the intuitive differences between the deep structure of causation involving omissions and the deep structure of causation without omissions.

Modifying his presentation in ways to keep things simple (but in a way that will not affect our point), Hitchcock's view can be described like this: suppose variables C and E represent events that occur (C or E could represent an absence, so "occur" is a term of art here). A path is a sequence of variables such that each variable is connected to others by relations of immediate dependence, representing chains of dependence among the events or absences that are the values of the variables.[7] In order for the event represented by C to be a possible cause of the event represented by E, there must be at least one path from C to E. The *causal network* connecting C to E is the system of all these paths connecting C to E.

Hitchcock then combines his default/deviant distinction with a special sort of causal network: a *self-contained network*. In rough, intuitive terms, a self-contained causal network between C and E captures the idea that for many cases of causation, there is an important sense in which the event represented by C needs to make a positive contribution to whether or how the event represented by E occurs. As Hitchcock describes it, "[i]ntuitively, a network is self-contained when it is never necessary to leave or augment the network in order to explain why the variables within the network take the values that they do." (2007a, p.510)

More precisely, a self-contained network from C to E is a causal network from C to E such that, for any variable V in the network except for C, when all the other variables (including C) on all the paths connecting C to V take their default values, and any off-path variables keep their actual values, then V takes its default value. What we care about here is that if the network from C to E is self-contained, then we know that, when all the non-E variables including C on all the paths connecting C to E take their default values, E takes its default value too. (Assume that any off-path variables keep their actual values.) We can see this approach as one that exploits a contrast between default and deviant events, such that when causes take their default values, their effects take their default values rather than their deviant values. Now we can express Hitchcock's main thesis: if the network from C to E is self-contained, and E's value depends counterfactually on C's value, then according to Hitchcock's theory, C is a cause of E.

This prescription handles figures 41 and 42 nicely. Assume that default states for neurons are their non-firing states. (Don't worry about the way we are sliding between names for variables and their values and names for events or states—it won't matter for the purposes of our discussion.) In

---

[7] See Hitchcock 2001, 2004 for a detailed approach to causal modeling and his 2007a for a careful and complete presentation of his account.

figure 41, for example, if **C** and all the neurons on paths connecting it to **E** had not fired, then **E** would have fired all the same (for in particular, **F** would not have fired). So the network is not self-contained. By contrast, in figure 42, if these neurons had not fired, then, since **F** would not have fired, **E** would not have fired. Thus, *C* in figure 41 does not get counted as a cause of *E*, whereas *C* in figure 42 does.

But Hitchcock's account is supposed to do more than just get these cases right, since it is supposed to be an analysis of causation, and it is supposed to explain basic intuitions we have about cases such as the one depicted by figure 3.

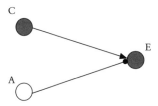

Figure 3

Let's look more closely at the view, building on what we've already covered.

Hitchcock does not present his account as a uniform treatment of causation, since he does not claim to be able to solve all cases in the same way, because not all networks are self-contained. So the account says nothing about many cases where the networks in question are not self-contained. However, although the account does not give definite answers in all cases, as we've noted, it is supposed to have the special virtue of getting the story about certain kinds of causation by omission—such as the type depicted in figure 3—intuitively right.

Unfortunately, there are several serious problems, even when we restrict the application of the self-contained networks account to cases involving omissions. The first problem is that it gives the wrong answer in typical cases of causation by double prevention. In figure 29, for example, if **C** and the neurons on paths connecting it to **E** take on their default, non-firing values, then in particular **D** does not fire, but **E** fires all the same. Hence, since the network from *C* to *E* is not self-contained, the account does not deliver the result that *C* is a cause of *E*. But surely it is.

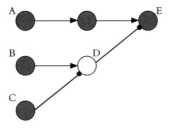

Figure 29

Of course, those who think that cases of double prevention are not clearly cases of causation will not be troubled by this result. But it remains a problem for those who share our view that C in figure 29 is clearly a cause and for anyone who aims to give a unified treatment of causation by omission.

Further problems become evident once we explore Hitchcock's account a bit further. Hitchcock's main argument for the importance of self-containment centers around the treatment of cases like those of figure 3.

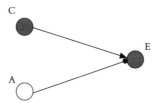

Figure 3

It is clear that C is a cause of E. What is less clear is whether the omission of A is a cause of E. As Hitchcock says—and we agree—there is a strong intuition that C is a cause of E. On the other hand, the intuition that the omission of A (call it A*) is a cause of E is much weaker. As Hitchcock characterizes the situation, there is an intuitive difference between the causal status of C and the causal status of A*: whether or not A* is a cause of E seems to depend on whether C is there to cause E, and in this sense, A*'s status as a cause is *parasitic* on C. So far, so good.

Now, how does Hitchcock treat figure 3? Remember, the claim is that if a network from X to Y is self-contained, and Y depends on X, then X is a cause of Y. There are two networks to evaluate for self-containment, one connecting C to E and one connecting A to E. Here is where the central importance of the default/deviant distinction kicks in, since what we are looking for is not just counterfactual dependence of values for E on values for variables in the network, but default-default dependence, i.e., when C (and the other non-E variables) all take their default values, E takes its default value. Thus: whether C is a cause of E will depend on how default and deviant values are assigned.

So let's look at what Hitchcock tells us about how to assign default and deviant status.

The default value of a variable is the one that we would expect in the absence of any information about intervening causes. More specifically, there are certain states of a system that are self-sustaining, that will persist in the absence of any causes other than the presence of the state itself: the default assumption is that a system, once it is in such a state, will persist in such a state . . . Temporary actions or events tend to be regarded as deviant outcomes. In the case of human actions, we tend to think of those states requiring voluntary bodily motion as deviants and those compatible with lack of motion as defaults. In addition, we typically feel that deviant outcomes are need of explanation, whereas default outcomes are not . . . (Hitchcock 2007a, pp. 506–7)

Consider first the network connecting C to E. To check for self-containment, we need to know what the default and deviant values of C and E are. If we assume, as we should, that a neuron's not firing is its default value, and a neuron's firing is its deviant value, we get the result that the network from C to E is self-contained, since (keeping the off-path variable A at its actual value) when **C** does not fire, **E** does not fire, and so when C takes its default value, E takes its default value. Moreover, E depends counterfactually on C, so Hitchcock's account tells us that C is a cause of E. And this is right: C is clearly and obviously a cause of E. However, when **A** does not fire, but we keep, as we should, the value of C as its actual value, **E** fires. Hence when A takes its default value (when A^* "occurs") E takes its deviant value and the network from A to E is not self-contained.

Hitchcock's diagnosis of the situation is that this result is thus exactly right: C is clearly a cause of E, and this fact is captured by the self-containment analysis. On the other hand, the omission of A is not clearly a cause of E, and if it is a cause, it seems to be so in some sort of dependent or parasitic way, i.e., it is only a cause because of what C does.

> This difference is captured by the difference between a causal network that is self-contained and one that is not. Whether we regard *parasitic dependence* as genuine token causation or not is a matter of brute intuition, and I will ... [offer] no pronouncement on this issue. (Hitchcock 2007a, p. 513)

It would seem that the self-containment approach gives us an illuminating account of the difference between causation involving events and causation (or "parasitic dependence") involving omissions, at least with simple cases like that of figure 3. Unfortunately, as soon as we move beyond the relatively staid arena of interpreting neuron diagrams as involving neurons firing, the account gets into serious trouble.

One obvious worry should crop up right away, since Hitchcock is explicit about the fact that the choice of default and deviant is pragmatic. If so, how can we preserve the objectivity of causation in a way that allows causal claims to play the role they do in the social and natural sciences? Another problem comes when we recognize that the definition of default seems to encode causal information, either implicitly or explicitly: "the default value of a variable is the one that we would expect in the absence of any information about intervening causes." (2007a, 506) If we are attempting to develop a reductive account of causation, how can we possibly incorporate these factors into our account?

Hitchcock attempts to mitigate these concerns by suggesting that "objectivity is retained at the level of token causal structure" (2007a, p. 504), but all this seems to mean is that facts about counterfactual dependencies between possible events and facts about which events actually occur are objective. We want more than this—we want objectivity at the "level" of *causation*, wherever that level is supposed to be (for Hitchcock, it doesn't seem to be at the level of these facts about counterfactual dependencies). A further suggestion is that we could allow only genuine (and presumably fundamental) laws of nature to determine default values of variables, but as we will see below, the most promising example of such an approach (Maudlin 2004) also relies on implicit causal assumptions, and as a result is explicitly nonreductive. Moreover, it is unclear how this approach could successfully treat objective macrolevel causal claims. A final idea is that our causal intuitions will vary with the change in context and the corresponding change in what is taken to be default and deviant, which suggests that the pragmatic element is intended to bolster the plausibility of the account by morphing its causal judgments to fit our changing causal intuitions.

But a serious problem with this last suggestion, and the deeper problem with the account of self-containment as a whole, can be illustrated by continuing our exploration of Hitchcock's view. Start with what is still a simple interpretation of figure 3, but involving a little more action than we normally see with neuron-firings. Here is the story.

Terminator, the prequel: The Terminator, a cyborg who is programmed to kill—relentlessly so, such that it is constantly attempting to kill its target— has been programmed to kill Victim. The Terminator has a large weapon and is shooting at Victim. The weapon is automatic, and so to shoot bullets continuously, the Terminator simply keeps its finger on the trigger. The Terminator keeps its finger on the trigger and kills Victim. This state of keeping its finger on the trigger is not temporary—it is easy to assume that from the beginning of its conscious existence, Terminator is continuously trying to kill Victim, and hence it keeps its finger on the trigger continuously. Policeman watches the whole episode but does not intervene. If the Terminator had taken its finger off the trigger or if Policeman had intervened, Victim would not have been killed.

Clearly, the Terminator's keeping its finger on the trigger is a cause of Victim's death. In some sense, Policeman's failure to intervene was a cause of Victim's death, but this causal fact (that the failure to intervene is a cause of the death) seems to depend somehow on the fact that Terminator causes Victim's death. How does Hitchcock's analysis fare?

We need to assign variables and their values, and then we need to check the causal networks to see if they are self-contained. One very natural way of making the needed assignments, and one which seems to be perfectly consistent with Hitchcock's stated criteria, is to take a variable C to represent Terminator's state, with the default value of C to be the Terminator's keeping its finger pressing down on the trigger. Keeping its finger pressing the trigger requires no change of bodily motion and is consistent with the Terminator's programming for it to always attempt to kill its victim. (As anyone who is familiar with the plots of the *Terminator* films will know, a Terminator can be programmed to be in a permanent state of trying to kill its victim.)

Take Policeman's state to be represented by variable A. Is Policeman's watching the whole episode but not intervening the default value or the deviant value of A? Policeman's job is to protect innocent citizens such as Victim, so it would seem that the default value should be the act of intervening. However, intervening would require bodily motion, and since Hitchcock's criteria for default values often (but again, importantly, not always) line up with omissions, perhaps the failure to intervene is the default. Let us assume the latter, since it more exactly meets Hitchcock's stated criteria and it won't matter much for what follows. But note that we have already run up against one problem of the account: the rules for what count as default or deviant are radically underdeveloped. We shall take Victim's state to be represented by V, and his death to be deviant, following Hitchcock's preferred interpretation (2007a, p. 506) of such situations: the default is that Victim will remain alive. Now we can check the causal networks from C to E and from A to E to see if they are self-contained.

A quick assessment of the case makes the problem clear. On this assignment of default and deviant, the causal network from C to E is *not* self-contained, since although (keeping the off-path variable A at its actual value) E depends on C, when C takes its default value, E takes its deviant value. Hence, the self-containment account tells us nothing about whether the Terminator's act is a cause, since it only tells us the causal facts for self-contained networks.

This result is destructive in two ways: first, we have a perfectly clear intuition that Terminator kills Victim, and the account fails to capture this. But worse, given that our intuitions here are parallel in relevant ways to the intuitions we have about the simple omission case of figure 3, the self-containment account fails rather spectacularly, since it gives us the opposite result in the case of the Terminator from the result it gave with the neuron case. According to Hitchcock's account, when we have a network that is not self-contained (but with the requisite dependence), our intuitions should be murky or somehow reflect some sort of indecision, or at least reflect our detection of facts about parasitic dependence. But we experience no such thing. It is just as clear in the Terminator case that the Terminator's keeping its finger on the trigger was a cause of Victim's death as it is in the neuron case that **C**'s firing is a cause of **E**'s firing. The self-containment account fails to give the intuitively right answer, and hence fails to perform as advertised.[8]

Perhaps one should be pragmatic and say that in one context of analysis we take the Terminator's keeping its finger pressing down on the trigger to be the default value of C and in another we take it to be the deviant value of C. In the first context, perhaps we are focusing on Terminator's programming and lack of bodily motion. In the second context, perhaps we are focusing on, say, how unusual it is to have murderous cyborgs attacking passers-by. But this just makes things worse, since it makes the analysis flip back and forth from treating the case as crystal clear—that Terminator's pressing the trigger is a cause of the death—to denying that a definitive judgment can be made. Yet our intuitions are just the opposite. In either context, our intuitions are perfectly clear: Terminator is a cause of the death of Victim. What this makes obvious is that the notion of self-containment does not capture our intuitions about causation or explain the special nature of causation by omission for the full range of causal cases. Moreover, as the possibility of flip-flopping shows, the pragmatic elements of the case do not always help the account to capture changes in our causal intuitions, strongly suggesting that natural, pragmatic choices about default and deviant outcomes crosscut causal intuitions.

Setting aside the question of whether Hitchcock succeeds in explaining distinctions we want to make (such as those between causation with omission and causation without), the nonreductive nature of Hitchcock's enquiry calls for a special mention. Since Hitchcock explicitly claims to disengage with the reductive causal project, it would be a mistake to see his account as making advances on treating just the problems that these accounts face: problems that focus on preemption, overdetermination and omission. Instead, it should be seen as an attempt to use a nonreductive account to gain a deeper understanding of the problems the reductionist faces, by explaining the differences in the causal factors that drive the differences in our causal intuitions. Such an account might initially proceed by working out the best causally nonreductive treatment of preemption and other stubborn problems. However, for it to be a player in the game of

---

[8] Moreover, the self-containment account has trouble with the cases like that depicted by figure 10. In figure 10, C is not a cause of E. But the self-containment account will not clearly judge that C is not a cause of E, since, on the usual interpretation where neuron firing is deviant and not firing is default, the causal network from C to E is not self-contained.

causal analysis, it must ultimately be able to provide a reductive analysis of the causal relations it relies upon.

We conclude that the self-containment account does not provide a suitably general or reductive account of why we make the causal judgments that we do. But, as we hope is obvious, we also think that identifying and developing views about default and deviant causal processes makes important progress in our quest to explain the nature of causation, and that Hitchcock's work on this has made an outstanding contribution to the debate. It helps us to understand causation in more depth even as it fails to successfully analyze its most problematic instances.

3.5 The default/deviant distinction and its connection to judgments about regularities

Much the same is true of Maudlin's (2004) treatment of causation. Maudlin is concerned to explain our causal claims and intuitions in a wide variety of cases, including those at the macrolevel, in terms of law-based judgments rather than counterfactual-based judgments. The project, as Maudlin develops it, is not one focused on analyzing causation. Rather, it is an examination of many of the intuitions underlying our basic causal judgments, in hopes of providing an explanation of some of these judgments in terms of assumptions involving "inertial behavior" and the laws. (Maudlin is content to remain agnostic about whether there even is a metaphysical or ontological relation of causation.)

In his discussion of causal judgments, he exploits a version of the default/ deviant distinction, dividing the laws governing cases into roughly two sorts.

Let us denominate laws *quasi-Newtonian* if they have this form: There are, on the one hand, *inertial* laws that describe how some entities behave when nothing acts on them, and then there are laws of *deviation* that specify in what conditions, and in what ways, the behavior will deviate from the inertial behavior. (Maudlin 2004, p. 431)

Obviously, "inertial laws" describe default behavior, while "laws of deviation" describe deviant behavior.

According to Maudlin, our everyday intuitions, at least about most of the causal claims we want to make about immediate causes in the actual world and in worlds relevantly similar to it, are determined by "lawlike macro-generalizations in quasi-Newtonian form." In worlds that we think can be adequately described using these sorts of lawlike generalizations, we judge causes to be, in effect, forces that bring about a deviation or change in an object from its inertial state.

Where a situation is conceptualized as governed by quasi-Newtonian laws, the laws will specify what counts as an inertial state and therefore what counts as a deviation from an inertial state (a first-class effect), and also what sorts of things or events (causes) bring about such deviations. The interfering factor is then the proximate cause of the deviation . . . (Maudlin 2004, pp. 438–9)

The idea is to be understood to be generally applicable in the sense that we can class a wide number of micro and macro level states as "inertial states," and whatever changes these inertial states are "first-class" (intuitively obvious?) causes.

We see three ways this account needs development if, ultimately, one wishes to employ it as part of a reductive analysis of causation—something, we again note, that Maudlin himself is not concerned to do. But for those of us engaged in this sort of project, Maudlin's exploration of the connections between causal judgments and quasi-Newtonian macrogeneralizations is potentially significant for an attempt to give a more reductive treatment of the default/deviant distinction.

So for those of us who are reductively inclined in this way, first, we'd need to know how quasi-Newtonian laws are supposed to be determined in a noncircular way, since classifying laws and states as "inertial" seems to require prior causal judgments about how laws govern events and states. Second, a reductive extension of the account would seem to fall victim to a problem that is similar to Hitchock's: a difficulty with handling certain sorts of states or events that do not involve much in the way of motion or action. Both accounts rely on the idea that facts about states or processes where not much is happening—the paradigmatic cases often involve omissions—often seem to be noncausal, or at best, causal in some intuitively trivial or derivative way. Hitchcock bases his account on default processes, and Maudlin requires that changes occur in inertial states. Third, some sort of noncausal naturalness constraint would need to be added in order to correctly identify what sort of event counts as a deviation and what sort of event counts as a cause of a deviation.

The trouble is that what we count as "inertial" or "default" can depend on factors that crosscut causal facts. At root, the problem is that non-changes at the macrolevel in states that we'd intuitively label "inertial" states don't always line up with non-causing: constant causation is different from the absence of causation. The point can be brought out by focusing on a different element of our Terminator example from §3.4.2. What we need to focus on now is what causes the shooting of the gun that (ultimately) kills the victim.

Recall the example: after initially pressing the trigger of the gun, the Terminator keeps the trigger depressed over a period of time such that the gun is constantly firing. Eventually, the shooting results in the death of the victim. Now, the Terminator's keeping its finger pressing down on the trigger seems to be a clear case of the Terminator being in an inertial state. Continuing to press the trigger requires no change of bodily motion, attitudes or of anything else relevant, and the automatic weapon simply spews bullets continuously. There seems to be nothing that could count as a perturbation or deflection from the inertial trajectory of the Terminator's state of keeping its finger on the trigger. Yet—and here is the problem—it is crystal clear that the Terminator's programmed disposition to always attempt to kill its victim is a (direct and immediate) cause of the Terminator keeping its finger on the trigger. So we have the disposition causing the Terminator to keep its finger on the trigger yet no deviation from an inertial state is required.

Perhaps there exist some contexts according to which we take the Terminator keeping its finger on the trigger as a deviation from its inertial trajectory and some in which we do not, but this, as with Hitchcock's account, would merely serve to highlight how easy it is to flip-flop from the right assessment of the case to the wrong one even while our causal intuitions remain the same. The existence of a simply-described context in which we can characterize causation without deviant change shows that we haven't got a general treatment of straightforward causal judgments of this type. While it may be true that in many cases set in quasi-Newtonian worlds our causal judgments align with deviations in inertial states, it is not always true.

In sum: Maudlin's view is richly suggestive, and surely gets something deeply right about our understanding of causal claims, the role of lawlike generalizations and the importance of change in inertial trajectories when making causal judgments. But before we could hope to use it as a basis for designing a reductive analysis of causation involving default and deviant events or processes, much more work would need to be done.

4 Methodology yet again

Why is it a serious mistake to think that the self-containment account (or, in fact, any of the main causal modeling approaches that have recently been developed), or a quasi-Newtonian account can function as a reductive analysis of causation? Answer: as we saw in our discussion of Yablo, a nonreductive account of causation (especially one that is explicitly pragmatic) is addressing a very different causal project. As we have tried to make clear, such a project is not without value, but it cannot be seen as an answer to the questions that reductionists have raised for treatments of problem cases. The nonreductive accounts are helping to excavate the nature of causation, but they help themselves to causal information, that, in the context of reductive analyses, is off-limits. Were reductive counterfactual and sufficiency theories to help themselves to the amount of causal information that these accounts rely upon, they could solve the problems with preemption and other issues with the greatest of ease.

5 Accommodating omission-involving causation

This completes our case that, first, extant accounts of causation fail to adequately handle causation involving omissions, and second, that such causation exhibits striking dissimilarities from ordinary causation. These dissimilarities run deep enough to at least render defensible the view—congenial to sufficiency and transference accounts—that it needs an analysis different from that which is appropriate for ordinary causation. This is a result that strongly favors sufficiency and transference accounts over their counterfactual rivals.

So where are we now in terms of being able to accommodate omission-involving causation using counterfactuals? Perhaps we should be optimistic. Perhaps the default/deviant distinction can be put to work using some of the insights from Hitchcock's and Maudlin's approaches, perhaps such a distinction could be employed as part of a contrastive theory of the causal relation, and—especially—perhaps it correlates with a distinction between analyses.

Perhaps. But it is too soon to celebrate victory. For we will close this chapter by briefly showing how an intuitive and attractively simple version of an approach based on counterfactual dependence does not work. This approach treats causation involving omission in the simplest possible way, in terms of straightforward counterfactual dependence, but the objection applies to all of our counterfactual variants, including contrastive interpretations of the causal relation. We will focus on the simple version to get the point across. Our simple counterfactual account claims that:

(1) Event *C* prevents an event of type *E* from occurring iff *C* occurs, no event of type *E* occurs, and, had *C* not occurred, an event of type *E* would have occurred.

(2) The omission of an event of type *C* causes an event *E* iff no event of type *C* occurs, *E* occurs, and, had an event of type *C* occurred, *E* would not have occurred.

(3) Event *C* causes event *E* by double prevention iff *C* occurs, *E* occurs, had *C* not occurred, *E* would not have occurred, and this relation of dependence holds because *C* prevents an event that, had it occurred, would have prevented *E* from occurring.

In short, all there is to causation involving omissions is some suitable relation of counterfactual dependence.

But that won't do. For observe that a range of cases of omission-involving redundant causation (see chapter 3 for an in-depth discussion of redundancy) still cause serious problems. In particular, (1)–(3) rule out as impossible any cases of redundant prevention, redundant causation by omission, or redundant causation by double prevention. But such cases surely are possible. For example, figure 43 appears to illustrate a clear case of redundant prevention.

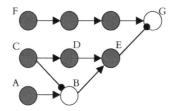

Figure 43

It seems undeniable that it is *C*, and not *A*, that prevents *G* from firing. Nevertheless, had *C* not occurred, **G** would have failed to fire all the same. The same example can be extended in an obvious way to show the possibility of redundant causation by double prevention: just let **G** be poised to prevent some other neuron from firing, etc.

It is perhaps less obvious, but still arguable, that we can have cases of overdetermined causation by omission, as in figure 38.

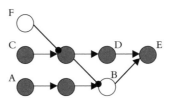

Figure 38

Arguably, the failure of neuron **F** to fire is a cause of *E*, since it seems to be a cause of *D*, which in turn causes *E*. But **E** would have fired, even if **F** had fired.

It would be convenient if we could respond to these examples by simply insisting that causation involving omission is exactly like garden-variety causation—since, after all, it can enter into all the same patterns of redundancy. But that would be to forget the features discussed above that starkly distinguish omission-involving causation from the garden variety. And at any rate, not every pattern of redundant causation can be reproduced: for example, there will be no analogue of virulent late preemption for omission-involving causation, simply because omissions, whatever they are, are not the sorts of things that can admit a wide range of variation in the manner of their occurrence. But matters are in fact quite a bit messier than even these remarks suggest, for the failure of the simple account contained in (1)–(3) leaves it entirely unclear what form a more adequate replacement should take. We thus find ourselves in the position of being unable to dismiss causation involving omissions, unable to assimilate it to garden-variety causation, and unable to give a decently unified or complete account of it using any of the standard approaches to causation that we have canvassed.

5

Cases that threaten transitivity

As we noted in the introduction to this guide, preserving transitivity seems to be a basic desideratum for an adequate analysis of causation; as noted at several points since, appealing to it has often seemed essential for handling one or another problem case; typically, a case involving some kind of preemption, and in chapter 4, we saw that it played a central role in making sense of our causal intuitions about prevention and double prevention. Here we will add that transitivity seems to underlie basic features of our causal reasoning: for it is typical to justify a claim that C causes E by pointing out that it causes D, which in turn causes E. Moreover, when we make causal judgments in black-box cases like the ones we discussed in chapter 3, §6, we assume that transitivity holds universally. So much the more astonishing, then, that recent work on causation has raised serious challenges to the claim that it is invariably transitive. (For a sampling, see McDermott 1995, Lewis 2004a, Hall 2000, Kvart 1991.) The challenges come in different varieties and need to be distinguished.

1 Double prevention

One important variety essentially involves causation by double prevention—which is made all the more interesting by the fact that the most natural understanding of the causal nature of double prevention relies on transitivity across omission-involving causation. Take Hartry Field's example (from an unpublished lecture): Suzy's enemy (Enemy) places an old-style bomb, fuse burning, outside her apartment door. But moments before the bomb would have exploded, Billy comes along and pinches out what is left of the fuse. Billy's act causes Suzy's survival (she was sitting next to the door, and would certainly have been killed by the blast). If causation is invariably transitive, then it seems as though Enemy's act of placing a bomb outside her door is among the causes of Suzy's survival. How so? As follows: placing the bomb was a cause of Billy's pinching out the fuse. Billy's pinching out the fuse was a cause of Suzy's continued survival. By transitivity, placing the bomb was a cause of Suzy's continued survival.

The abstract structure of this case can be characterized this way: *C* (the bomb, fuse burning, is placed outside the door) causes *D* (pinching the fuse). *D* prevents an event of type F (an explosion), which, had it occurred, would have prevented *E* (Suzy's continued survival). By doing so, *D* causes *E*. Hence, *C* causes *D*, and *D* causes *E*. If we pull back, we can see the case in even broader outlines: *C* threatens to prevent *E* (the lit bomb outside her door threatens to kill Suzy), but *C* also counteracts this threat by causing *D* (the lit bomb outside her door causes the pinching). But many seem to think that *C*, merely by, as it were, undermining its own attempt to prevent *E*, should not thereby qualify as a cause of *E*.

We have seen something close to this sort of case before—viz., figure 10.

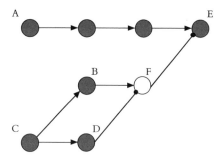

Figure 10

Note that a representation of the classic double prevention structure is embedded in figure 10 with neurons **D**, **F** and **E**. Earlier, we used an example like this to cast doubt on the thesis that counterfactual structure fixes causal structure, or at least that it does so in a way that need pay no attention to whether omissions are involved in the relevant relations of dependence. Now we see that figure 10 may also serve as a putative counterexample to transitivity: for *C* causes *D*, and *D* causes *E*, but *C* does not, so it seems, cause *E*. Whether the counterexample succeeds is not clear. As we have noted, an omission in the series from *C* to *E* plays a central role: if there were no causation by double prevention, there would be no threat to transitivity, since D would not count as a cause of E. So perhaps one should deny there is causation by double prevention (as Moore 2009 seems to want to do).

Well, there are more options than simply rejecting double prevention, a move which we find extremely unappealing—although, unfortunately, we don't find any of the other ways of dealing with the special problems raised by double prevention particularly happy either. We will review the options systematically.

1.1 Treatment options

1.1.1 First option We have noted the first option, which is to hold transitivity in an unrestricted form, but insist that double prevention is not causation. We already saw, in chapter 4, especially in §2.3 and §3.1, that accepting this option brings serious trouble: too many causal claims that are otherwise perfectly acceptable come out false.

1.1.2 Second option Our second option is to accept that double prevention is causation and that transitivity holds in an unrestricted form, and then argue that intuition errs when it says that C in figure 10 is not a cause of E, or that placing the bomb is not a cause of Suzy's survival. The challenge for those who defend this option is to explain how we could be inclined to make such a surprising mistake. Lewis (2004a) attempts to do so by noting that (i) the causation occurs in part by prevention; (ii) bombs aren't thought of as saving lives, but rather as endangering them; and (iii) Suzy's continued survival is not directly dependent upon the bomb being placed outside her door (but only step-wise dependent). So for reasons to do with salience and the peculiar structure of the case, according to Lewis, we easily misjudge its causal structure.

This response echoes a standard reply to objections to transitivity that involve long causal chains. A person's birth will almost certainly be connected, by a sequence of causes, to her death; but many balk at concluding that her birth is itself a cause of her death. Is transitivity the culprit? Arguably not; arguably, the odd-sounding conclusion ought to be accepted. A popular justification locates the difficulty in the pragmatics of explanation rather than the metaphysics of causation. Except in special circumstances, citing her birth is, for purely pragmatic reasons, a poor explanation for her death. Lewis's account of the bomb example might be defended in similar fashion: for pragmatic reasons, it would be a poor explanation of Suzy's survival that cited the placing of the bomb—but the one is a cause of the other, for all that.

We do not find these defenses of this second option especially compelling. As to the observation that the example partly involves causation by double prevention, that is grist for the mill of those who think such causation needs to be treated differently from the ordinary variety. As to the observation that bombs are not thought of as enhancing survival or saving lives, that can be rendered moot by tweaking the example, as figure 10 in fact shows: in figure 10, there is nothing about C per se that makes it the kind of event that should be thought of as threatening E. All we need to generate the counterintuitive result is a string of neurons related in the right way. As to the observation that Suzy's continued survival does not directly depend on the placing of the bomb outside her door, that sort of failure of dependence does not ordinarily lead us to question an attribution of causation, as witness any standard case of preemption: the intuitive verdict that C causes E, in such a case, is not weakened in the slightest by the fact that E fails to depend on C. And as to the appeal to the pragmatics of explanation, there is, at the very least, an important bit of unfinished business: for if this appeal is appropriate, then we ought to be able to exhibit some conversational context in which it would "sound right" to call the placing a cause of Suzy's survival, or C a cause of E.

Lewis provides just such a context for the ordinarily inappropriate claim that someone's birth causes her death (2004a, p. 101). Perhaps we could do the same: imagine that Billy is a double agent. He pretends to be the friend of Enemy, but in reality, he is loyal to Suzy. Enemy suspects Billy, and so sets a trap to find out the truth. He sets the bomb, and lets Billy know of his plot. Billy, desperate to save Suzy, rushes to her house and puts out the fuse, thus revealing his true colors to Enemy. In this context, we might be more willing to think that Enemy's setting of the bomb was a cause of Suzy's continued survival. (See Swanson 2010 for a developed discussion about the context sensitivity of our causal claims.) We are not convinced by this context-based defense of transitivity, although Paul is more sympathetic than Hall. (For further rebuttals, see Hall 2000 and Yablo 2004.)

1.1.3 Third option A third option is to flatly deny that causation is transitive (McDermott 1995). That would spell trouble for analyses that needed to invoke transitivity to handle, e.g., certain kinds of preemption, or any black-box cases. What's more, causation often seems transitive; for example, when you kick the ball towards the goalie, and the ball flies into the net, by transitivity, you caused the goal. As this brings out, it often seems perfectly appropriate to justify; a claim that C causes E by tracing a causal chain from the first event to the second, and this includes many cases involving double prevention. It won't do simply to say that all such inferences are invalid. How can we possibly embrace a theory of causation that says otherwise? (That observation, by the way, raises worries for anyone who thinks that the only ground for maintaining transitivity is as part of an ad hoc strategy for handling preemption.) What's needed is a more developed story, according to which the inference from "C causes D" and "D causes E" to "C causes E" is safe, provided such-and-such conditions obtain—where these conditions can typically be assumed to obtain, except perhaps in odd cases such as the problematic (original) version of our bomb example. For these reasons, the third option is untenable.

1.1.4 Fourth option The fourth option can be seen as a variant on the third, arrived at by spelling out the needed general conditions under which causation is transitive—or providing an account that spells out when and why causation can be safely inferred. We might put Hitchcock (2001) in this category, who argues that the cases that create problems for transitivity fail to involve appropriate "active routes" between the relevant events. Hall (2000, 2004) considers a view where, if C causes D in a way that does not involve omissions, and if D likewise causes E in a way that does not involve omissions, then we can safely conclude that C causes E. Otherwise, all bets are off: C may cause E, but that it does so is not guaranteed by the existence of the linking causal chain. We might put it this way: omission-involving causation is apples, and garden-variety causation is oranges, and apples and oranges don't mix. (See our discussion in chapter 4, §2.) Or at least, when they do mix, transitivity doesn't apply.

We will critically discuss Hitchcock's approach in a moment, when we discuss the way certain counterfactual-based analyses handle the challenge to transitivity posed by figure 10. First, we need to comment on the "apples and oranges don't mix" formula. For while it defuses the threat to transitivity posed by figure 10, it leaves us with a pile of unfinished business. In the first place, we still need some way of handling the black-box cases from chapter 3 where we do not know all the details of every step of the process under evaluation. In the second place, there are, as we will see in the next two sections, other challenges to transitivity that it does not address. In the third place, this response seems to require us to say that certain cases are not clear cases of causation when they are, in fact, perfectly clear. For example, consider figure 44:

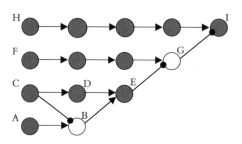

Figure 44

It seems clear that *C* causes *I*. Why? After all, *I* does not depend on *C*. A tempting response is this: *C* causes *D*, and *D* causes *I* (by double prevention); therefore *C* causes *I*. Is such an appeal to transitivity appropriate here? No, according to the "apples and oranges don't mix" reply. But then we need to provide some better response. Why does *C* cause *I*? If after all, against *prima facie* appearances, it doesn't cause *I*, why not? We might try to fix our rule about when transitivity fails by making the rider much more specific: when *C* causes *D*, and *D* causes *E*, then *C* causes *E*, unless *D* causes *E* merely by canceling a threat to *E* that was itself produced by *C*. That seems to do the trick, but is too precisely tailored to the kind of example we are considering to escape a charge of being ad hoc.

1.2 The problem analyzed

We have, it seems, run out of options. Consider now where the analyses on the table stand with respect to the options we have considered. It does not seem essential to transference fans that they endorse transitivity, since they do not need it to solve preemption, although they may wish to endorse it for independent reasons. But as we saw in the last section, causation by double prevention makes trouble for them anyway—and it is trouble that they can best deal with by giving some kind of special treatment of it and other kinds of omission-involving causation. Given that the special treatment needed is a special metaphysical treatment, not merely a special contextualist-explanatory treatment, something based on the fourth option is probably most appealing to such accounts.

Our minimal sufficiency account has less room for maneuver. Recall from chapter 3, §2.4 that this account appeared to require an appeal to transitivity in order to handle certain varieties of preemption. So option three is ruled out. Assuming option one is off the table, we are left with either the second or fourth option. But, since, like transference accounts, our sufficiency account must also treat omission-involving causation as a special metaphysical case, it would also seem to be far more natural and appealing for it to fix on the fourth option.

Finally, a counterfactual account can go a number of different ways, depending on which variation is under consideration. We should ask: (1) does the account make essential use of transitivity in order to handle preemption or other special cases? And: (2) does it aim to give a perfectly uniform treatment of ordinary and omission-involving causation? If the answer to the first question about essential use of transitivity is yes—as it is for the kind of covariation account championed by Lewis—then the account should endorse either the second or the fourth option. But if the answer to the second question, about uniform treatment, is *also* yes (as it is for Lewis), then the fourth option is ruled out. So it is no surprise that Lewis is at such pains in his (2004*a*) to defend the second option.

By contrast, de facto dependence accounts are explicitly designed to handle preemption cases without the need to appeal to transitivity. So their answer to the first question seems to be "no." Given that the extant versions of them also aim to give a uniform treatment of causation, it is no surprise if their defenders (Pearl 2000, Hitchcock 2001, Yablo 2004) take the third or fourth option. But notice that while de facto dependence accounts may happily deny transitivity, it does not automatically follow that they yield the result that C in figure 10 is not a cause of E. On the contrary: we saw in chapter 3, in §2.3.2 and §2.3.3, that Hitchcock's de facto account tells us that C in figure 10 is a cause of E, and in chapter 3, §2.3.3 we saw that Yablo's de facto dependence treatment of late preemption will get into deep waters if he is to avoid holding that C is a cause of E. It seems that, even if one rejects the view that transitivity holds universally, or has a general method of explaining when transitivity holds and when it does not, the way double prevention and transitivity are intertwined, as shown by cases with the causal structure of figure 10, creates problems.

This last point makes the issues with Hitchcock's (2001) de facto account worth looking at in more detail. Hitchcock tries to replace transitivity with an account of causation in terms of active routes. But the account does not always provide satisfying solutions. He discusses a case from Hall (2000):

Boulder: a boulder is dislodged, and begins rolling ominously toward Hiker. Before it reaches him, Hiker sees the boulder and ducks. The boulder sails harmlessly over his head with nary a centimeter to spare. Hiker survives his ordeal. (p. 276)

Recall from chapter 2, §2.2.3 that on Hitchcock's account, C is a cause of E when C and E are connected by an active causal route in an appropriate model. Whether a causal route is active is determined in part by the truth values of certain "explicitly non-foretracking" or ENF counterfactuals: roughly, counterfactuals where we hold certain effects, usually "side effects," of an event C fixed while we consider alternatives to C. The main idea is to use counterfactuals like "if c had not occurred, but e had occurred anyway, then . . ." to distinguish between active and inactive routes. As we showed in chapter 3, §2.3.2, Hitchcock's account gives us an elegant solution to problems with preemption.

Unfortunately, things are not so straightforward with *Boulder*. For here, we do find the requisite dependence of Hiker's survival on the falling of the boulder—giving us an active causal route between Hiker's survival and Boulder's fall—when we hold fixed the fact that at t, a split second before Hiker ducks, a boulder is falling towards his head. (Recall that Hiker ducks at $t + 1$ not because he notices the boulder at t, but because he sees it at an earlier time $t-1$.) Then, if the boulder had not been falling at $t-1$, Hiker would not have seen it at $t-1$, and so would not have ducked at $t+1$, a split second after t, but at t a boulder is falling towards his head, and so Hiker would have been crushed.

Hitchcock has two defenses against the unwelcome consequence that his account tells us that the boulder's fall is a cause of Hiker's survival. The first in effect argues that the result seems counterintuitive mostly because the relevant counterfactual is strange:

Must we then conclude that the boulder's fall did save Hiker's life after all? Perhaps this would not be so bad. On my account, unlike Lewis's, it is at least easy to explain why our pretheoretic intuition yields the "wrong" answer in this case. The interpolated variable B [the presence at t of the boulder near Hiker's head] is not easy to find, and the ENF ["explicitly non-foretracking"] counterfactual that reveals the active causal route from F [the boulder's fall] to S [Hiker's survival] is not at all intuitive. In words, the relevant piece of counterfactual reasoning would go as follows: suppose that the boulder had been present at a point one meter from Hiker's head and flying toward him, and suppose moreover that it had never fallen in the first place. Since it never fell, Hiker would not have seen it coming and would not have ducked; since it would have been there, one meter from his exposed head, it would have hit him and he would not have survived. This counterfactual reasoning is correct, but bizarre. If the boulder never fell, how did it get to be there, one meter from Hiker's head? We are to imagine, presumably, that the boulder was mysteriously and instantaneously transported to a position immediately in front of Hiker's head. This is the sort of counterfactual reasoning that only trained philosophers engage in; unaided intuition is not to be faulted for failing to "see" the relevant ENF counterfactual. (Hitchcock 2001, p. 297)

The second defense in effect denies that the model used above to reveal the active route is appropriate: in effect, it rejects the first interpretation of *Boulder* in favor of a simpler interpretation that tells us that the falling boulder does not save Hiker's life. In the simpler model, there is no representation of the fact that it takes Hiker some time to react to the boulder and duck, such that if Hiker waits too long it will be too late, and so there is no longer an active causal route from boulder's fall to Hiker's survival. Hitchcock's defense of this move hinges centrally on the following claim:

When we exclude the variable B [whose values represent the boulder's presence or absence at the point at which it is too late for Hiker to duck] from our model, it is not because we are unwilling to take seriously the possibility that the boulder was not present at that point (one meter from Hiker's head). We take that possibility seriously when we entertain the possibility that the boulder does not fall in the first place. Rather, we are not willing to take seriously the possibility that the boulder (or *a* boulder of similar size and shape) comes to be in that position *even though the boulder does not fall in the first place*. This possibility is just too far-fetched. (Hitchcock 2001, p. 298, italics in the original)

Excluding the variable B essentially forbids us from appealing to the relevant ENF counterfactual in order to exhibit the de facto dependence of Hiker's survival on the boulder's fall, allowing us to say the boulder's fall is not a cause of Hiker's survival after all.

Both of these defenses strike us as initially plausible but ultimately unsuccessful. Our response to both defenses is to remind the reader that it is not that broadly pragmatic or contextual factors can never have an influence on our off-the-cuff judgments about what causes what—of course they can. But these factors don't seem to be responsible for our judgments in closely related cases, and thus cannot provide the foundation for a general strategy for setting aside cases that remain problematic even after we've rejected transitivity. Trying to set them aside by minimizing the fact that we get an unpleasant result or changing the model so that we can no longer see the result is not a good strategy.

Consider first a somewhat melodramatic variant on our standard case of preemption from chapter 3, where Suzy's throw breaks the bottle. This time, instead of throwing a rock at the bottle, Billy has planted a bomb near it, which he causes to go off a split second after Suzy's rock breaks the bottle. Thus, had Suzy not thrown, the bottle would have shattered as a result of the explosion. According to Hitchcock, the counterfactual that is supposed to testify to the fact that it is Suzy's throw, and not Billy's triggering of the bomb, that causes the shattering is something like this: had Suzy not thrown, and had the shockwave from the bomb's explosion somehow failed to strike the bottle in its intact state, then the bottle would not have shattered. But do we really need to engage in this sort of counterfactual reasoning in order to know that it is Suzy's throw, and not Billy's triggering of the bomb, that causes the shattering? We doubt it.

Second, we think the discussion is better served by focusing not on the boulder case, but on figure 10, which has essentially the same structure as *Boulder*. Recall that in chapter 3, at the start of §2.3.3, we show how Hitchcock's de facto view tells us that, in figure 10, C is a cause of E.

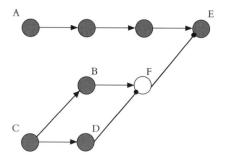

Figure 10

With Hitchcock's defenses in mind, we point out that the rules that govern the operation of neuron diagrams are clear enough that anyone can engage in the relevant bit of counterfactual reasoning, lack of philosophical training notwithstanding: clearly, in figure 10, if we hold fixed the fact that **B** fires, then if **C** had not fired, **E** would not have fired. This reasoning is no less perspicuous than the reasoning we needed to engage in with respect to our old preemption case of figure 1, namely, that if we hold fixed the fact that **B** does not fire, then if **C** had not fired, **E** would not have fired.

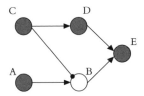

Figure 1

And in the case of figure 10, the relevant "explicitly non-foretracking" counterfactual is also easy enough to see: we hold the occurrence of *B* fixed while considering alternatives to *C*. And the possibility that in figure 10 **B** fires—even though **C** does not—is not at all far-fetched, certainly no more far-fetched than the possibility, when we consider figure 1, that **B** does not fire, even though **C** does not fire. So we can't claim that figure 10 should simply be ignored. If you are not convinced, recall figure 41 (which is just a slightly emended version of figure 10).

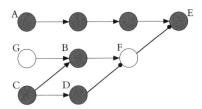

Figure 41

Perhaps we could employ the "bizarre counterfactual" argument against figure 10 by holding that, if **C** had not fired, then **B** *could* not have fired (since there was nothing else are around to cause it to do so). But we can't say this with respect to figure 41. For if **C** had not fired, then **B** could still have fired, namely if **G** had also fired. Observe, however, that the shift from figure 10 to figure 41 does not increase the intuitive plausibility that C is a cause of E. To be sure, if **G** had fired, we might happily count C a cause of E—although that would also be a case in which E depends on C *simpliciter*. But **G** does not fire. And since it does not, the only relation C bears to E is that of initiating a threat that it itself cancels—which, as figure 41 makes intuitively clear, does not seem to be enough to promote C to the status of cause of E.

So, a de facto account like Hitchcock's, which in effect employs special counterfactuals instead of transitivity to get the right answer in cases involving preemption and other kinds of redundancy, gets into trouble using those same types of counterfactuals with cases that have the structure of figure 10 and figure 41. We conclude that this trouble is just as bad as the trouble that transitivity-based accounts get into. And as a result, we suspect that, given the loss of systematicity that goes along with a rejection of transitivity, his denial of transitivity costs more than it is worth.

What about a counterfactual account based on a contrastive response to cases that embed double prevention? While Schaffer (2005) does not propose his contrastive account of causation as complete or reductive analysis—since it doesn't handle preemption—he defends a version of option two as a response to troubles with transitivity. Recall from chapter 2, §2.2.4, that Schaffer takes the causal relation to be a four-place relation between events and classes $\{C^*\}$, $\{E^*\}$ of contrast events, and describes difference-making as "a useful heuristic." While this heuristic can become complex when we have large classes of contrast events, we can get the idea by focusing on cases where $\{C^*\}$ is a class of a single contrast event, and likewise $\{E^*\}$: in such cases, difference-making is understood to be the idea that C rather than C^* is a cause of E rather than E^*. So causation in such cases is contrastive such that C rather than C^* is a cause of E rather than E^* iff C^* had occurred instead of C then E^* would have occurred instead of E. According to Schaffer, by understanding our problem cases of causation in terms of contrastive difference-making, we make it natural to accept both that double prevention is causation and that transitivity holds in an unrestricted form. The claim is that the contrastive account gives a natural resolution of problematic cases involving double prevention (what he calls "causation by disconnection") and the supposed counterexamples to transitivity.

Let's look at this possibility in more detail. Can the contrastive account really handle our troublesome cases of embedded double prevention? Perhaps one could provide something along the following lines as a contrast-based description of Field's case of Enemy and the bomb: Suzy's enemy (Enemy) places an old-style bomb, fuse burning, outside her apartment door, in contrast to placing it there unlit. But moments before the bomb would have exploded, Billy comes along and pinches out what is left of the fuse, in contrast to not pinching it out. Enemy's placing the bomb with its fuse burning in front of Suzy's door, in contrast to placing it there unlit, was a cause of Billy pinching out what is left of the fuse, in contrast to not pinching it out. Billy's pinching out what is left of the fuse, in contrast to not pinching it out, was a cause of Suzy's survival, in contrast to her dying in an explosion. By transitivity, placing the lit bomb in front of Suzy's door in contrast to placing it there unlit was a cause of Suzy's survival in contrast to her dying in an explosion.

As we can see, this contrastive rendering doesn't give us a happy result. Either the contrastive account fails to handle the example, or these seemingly natural contrasts are not the right ones to use in constructing the causal chain. Now, if these contrasts are not the right ones, it is reasonable to ask why they are not—and in general, what sort of (noncircular) rules we are supposed to follow when selecting contrasts for our causal chain.

Schaffer has a response available. As he develops contrastivism, it denies that Enemy's placing the bomb with its fuse burning in front of Suzy's door, in contrast to placing it there unlit, was a cause of Billy pinching out what is left of the fuse, in contrast to leaving it burning. This is because of the role of difference-making in selecting the relevant contrasts: recall that we are to hold in general that C rather than C^* is a cause of E rather than E^* iff C^* had occurred E^* would have occurred. In the rendition of the case above, it isn't true that if the event C^* had occurred then the event E^* would have occurred, for if Enemy were to place an unlit bomb in front of Suzy's door (C^*), Billy would not leave the fuse burning (E^*)—because there is no burning fuse for Billy to leave. And so the initial causal step in Field's case fails.

Let's try a different rendering of the story: Enemy places an old-style bomb, fuse burning, in plain sight outside Suzy's apartment door, in contrast to hiding it behind a curtain next to the door. But moments before it would have exploded, Billy comes along, sees the bomb and pinches out what is left of the fuse, in contrast to not pinching it out. This causal claim works because we have the right contrasts for difference-making: if Enemy had hidden the bomb, Billy would not have pinched out the fuse. Enemy's placing the bomb with its fuse burning in front of Suzy's door, in contrast to hiding it, was a cause of Billy pinching out what is left of the fuse, in contrast to leaving it burning. Billy's pinching out what is left of the fuse, in contrast to leaving it burning, was a cause of Suzy's survival, in contrast to her dying in an explosion. Now, by transitivity, placing the lit bomb in front of Suzy's door in contrast to hiding it was a cause of Suzy's survival rather than dying in an explosion.

Endorsing transitivity here makes sense—because we can see, from the contrastive details included in the causal claim, that part of what Enemy did was place the bomb in a place where Billy could see it. After all, he placed it in front of Suzy's door, not in some hidden place. And thus, his act of placing the bomb in front of Suzy's door was a cause of her survival. This would seem to count as a good example of how the contrastive account's method of building contrasts into the causal chain itself can give us a satisfying explanation of why we want to accept that Enemy's act was among the causes of Suzy's survival.

We agree that this version of the story allows one to mix double prevention with transitivity in a reasonably satisfying way. But a puzzle remains: why can't we simply say that Enemy's placing the bomb with its fuse burning in front of Suzy's door was a cause of Billy pinching out what is left of the fuse? Why must we go contrastive in the simple case, where it seems irrelevant to build contrasts in? And *if* we must go contrastive, why can't we say that Enemy's placing the bomb with its fuse burning in front of Suzy's door, in contrast to his placing it there unlit, was a cause of Billy pinching out what is left of the fuse, in contrast to leaving it burning? If we accept that causation is supposed to involve contrasts, both of these causal claims seem very natural, yet Schaffer must deny them, or at least must accept that his approach, when faced with these examples, falls silent. So while he can resolve some examples where double prevention is embedded in a case raising a worry about transitivity, the resolution is not sufficiently general.

In particular, we need to be able to resolve cases that exhibit the perfectly clear and plausible structure of figure 10. In such a case the contrasts should be given in terms of neurons firing or not firing.

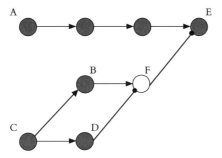

Figure 10

C's firing rather than not firing causes **D**'s firing rather than not firing. **D**'s firing prevents **F**'s firing, so **D**'s firing rather than not firing causes **F**'s not firing rather than firing. And **F**'s not firing rather than firing causes **E**'s firing rather than not firing. Thus, **D**'s firing rather than not firing causes **E**'s firing rather than not firing. Since **C**'s firing rather than not firing causes **D**'s firing rather than not firing, and **D**'s firing rather than not firing causes **E**'s firing rather than not firing, if we admit transitivity, **C**'s firing rather than not firing causes **E**'s firing rather than not firing. And so the contrastivist seems to have the same problem handling figure 10 as other accounts do: *C* causes *D*, and *D* causes *E*, but *C* does not, so it seems, cause *E*.

Schaffer has an account of how he prefers to handle figure 10's exemplar, *Boulder*. In *Boulder*, recall, a boulder falls towards Hiker. Take the boulder's rolling to correspond to **C**'s firing. Hiker's ducking corresponds to **D**'s firing, and his avoidance of death-by-crushing corresponds to **F**'s failure to fire. Finally, Hiker's uneventful lunch under a tree corresponds to **E**'s firing.

Understood contrastively: the falling of the boulder rather than its remaining motionless causes Hiker to duck rather than walk upright, Hiker's ducking rather than walking upright causes him to survive rather than be crushed, which causes him to have an uneventful lunch rather than a grisly death. Result: if we endorse transitivity, it would seem that, according to the contrastivist, the falling of the boulder rather than its remaining motionless causes Hiker to have an uneventful lunch rather than a grisly death.

How does Schaffer avoid this conclusion? As follows: he argues that we need to distinguish between two different contrast events that can be picked out by the same event nominal. According to Schaffer, when we say "the falling of the boulder rather than its remaining motionless causes Hiker to duck rather than walk upright," we pick out a contrast event such that Hiker's walking upright is a walking-upright-with-the boulder-remaining-still. But when we say "Hiker's ducking rather than walking upright causes him to survive rather than be crushed," we pick out a contrast event where Hiker's walking upright is a walking-upright-with-the-boulder-falling, and according to Schaffer, these contrast events are different events. And if these are different events, then there is no chain of causes from C to D to E, and so the transitivity worry simply doesn't apply. So the falling of the boulder rather than its remaining motionless does not cause Hiker to have an uneventful lunch rather than a grisly death after all.

Something along the same lines could be tried with figure 10. The part of the original version of the contrastivist account that got us into trouble was the part that told us that **C**'s firing rather than not firing causes **D**'s firing rather than not firing, and **D**'s firing rather than not firing causes **F**'s not firing rather than firing.

Let's look at how we'd apply the solution to *Boulder* to a contrastivist rendering of figure 10. We'll need to be very careful about selecting the appropriate contrasts. The new version of the story is something like this: **C**'s firing rather than not firing causes (**D**'s firing with **B**'s firing) rather than (**D**'s not firing with **B**'s not firing). But it isn't (**D**'s firing with **B**'s firing) rather than (**D**'s not firing with **B**'s not firing) that causes **F**'s not firing rather than firing, because it is not the case that if (**D** had not fired with **B** not firing) that **F** would have fired. Instead, it is (**D**'s firing with **B**'s firing) rather than (**D**'s not firing with **B**'s firing) that causes **F**'s not firing rather than firing. Thus, transitivity doesn't apply.

For us, the central question is: why think that the event of Hiker's walking upright with the boulder remaining still would be a different event from Hiker's walking upright with the boulder falling, or for that matter, different from Hiker's walking upright while the Queen of England drinks her second cup of tea? Correspondingly, why think that the absence of **D**'s firing is such that **D**'s not firing when **B** is not firing would be a different absence from **D**'s not firing when **B** is firing, or for that matter, from **D**'s not firing while some event on the Moon occurs? We don't normally think that such extrinsic differences would be sufficient to give us different events or different absences. We simply don't individuate using such extremely extrinsic properties. Holding otherwise forces us to endorse extremely fragile events, events that can be individuated merely extrinsically.

Without relying on extreme extrinsic individuation, the contrastivist ends up in the same boat as everyone else with regard to figure 10, and by extension, its exemplar *Boulder*. Now, since the contrastivist does not claim to provide a reductive analysis of causation, she may prefer to fall silent about cases with the structure of figure 10 (and figure 41) rather than try to solve them with a controversial theory of event individuation. But in any case, it's worth noting that endorsing the view that events can be individuated by extrinsic properties involving other events in their surroundings denies the intuition at the heart of our intrinsicness thesis from chapter 3, §4.3.1. And thus, we go right back to the worries that have dogged several versions of counterfactual accounts, namely, worries about how deeply counterintuitive it is to hold that, merely by varying the extrinsic surroundings of a causal structure of events running from C to E, we can vary whether C causes E.

Now, bickering between partisans of the various approaches should not obscure an important fact about the examples we are considering, which is that they raise puzzles about causation that are of deep interest, regardless of one's commitments about how best to analyze or characterize that relation. Indeed, even those who reject the project of providing a reductive analysis of causation (cf. Tooley 1990, Schaffer 2005) appreciate that it is a hard but fascinating question what best to say about these putative counterexamples to transitivity. As our discussion here should make clear, they are everyone's problem.

That puzzle is about to get harder. For what is essential to the examples we've focused on—what makes them tick—is that they involve at a crucial stage a relation of causation by double prevention. So one might think that what they reveal is a tension between a commitment to the view that causation is transitive and a commitment to the view that double prevention is (a kind of) causation—which is not the same as rejecting causation by double prevention. That might be right. At the end of the day, it will certainly turn out to be a defensible position to take, although what to do once we've recognized this tension requires further elucidation. That said, it is not clearly and uncontroversially right, nor can it serve up a complete solution to the problem of transitivity. For there are other putative counterexamples to transitivity that make no use of omission-involving causation, as we are about to see.

2 Switching

2.1 Basic switches

Omissions are not the only source of worries about the transitivity of causation. *Switches*—cases where C initiates an alternative causal route to E, without, intuitively, itself being a cause of E—also generate perplexity. (See Paul 2000.) A train rushes along a track towards the point where the track forks. Suzy flips a switch, directing the train along the left-hand side of the fork. If Suzy hadn't flipped the switch, the train would have taken the right side of the fork. A few miles later, the left and right tracks converge, and a mile after this point Billy robs the train. Assume that taking the left side of the fork rather than the right makes no difference to the train's manner or time of arrival. Does Suzy's flip cause Billy's robbery?

The intuitive answer is that it does not. The train would have been where it was, when it was, no matter which side of the fork it took to get there. So how could the flip be a cause of the robbery? It had nothing to do with it. However, if the flip caused the train to take the left-hand track, and the train's journey on the left-hand track was among the causes of it being on the track at the time and place of the robbery, then by transitivity the flip was a cause of the robbery after all.

If that reasoning sounds at all suspicious—perhaps because "being on the track at such-and-such time and place" doesn't sound like it names a proper event—then observe that the example can easily be sanitized, as figure 45 shows.

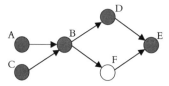

Figure 45

Let us stipulate that C acts as a "switch," causing the signal leaving **B** to travel on the upper path rather than the downward path. (Figure 46 shows what happens if **C** doesn't fire.)

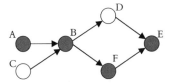

Figure 46

It looks like C is a cause of D. And D, clearly, is a cause of E. But to many, it seems intuitively wrong to count C a cause of E. One wants to say, rather, that C merely helps determine the route to E. And surely something can help determine the causal route to an effect, without itself being among that effect's causes.

You will be tempted, perhaps, to assimilate these examples to the examples discussed in the previous section—to suppose, that is, that what we have here is really one class of putative counterexamples to transitivity. That would be hasty. It may well be that when the dust settles, we will clearly and distinctly see that fundamentally the same phenomenon is driving the two kinds of examples. But at this early stage, a number of considerations suggest otherwise. We will discuss two; see Hall (2000) for a more detailed treatment.

First, the structure of the case is more complex than a simple diagnosis of switching indicates. Although a superficial assessment might indicate that the flip is not a cause of the robbery—since merely changing the causal route to the robbery doesn't seem like enough to make the source of the change a cause—a closer look shows us that the flip might play a more important role than simply that of determiner of causal route.

If an event C merely helps determine how E occurs, but is not directly linked by any causal process to E, then this may not suffice for causation. Example (from Hall 2000): Suzy and Billy are competing to see who can break the bottle first. Suzy is preparing to throw her rock when she gets a muscle cramp, and drops it. Consequently, Billy's rock breaks the bottle. Had the cramp not occurred, the bottle still would have broken—but as a result of Suzy's throw, and not of Billy's. The cramp thus determines the causal route to the breaking. But, intuitively, (i) it does not help cause the breaking, and (ii) the causal processes it initiates do not link it to the breaking.

By contrast, the flip appears to initiate a causal process terminating in the robbery, and so perhaps it is a candidate for a cause of this event. More generally, perhaps any switching case in which the "switch" changes the way the effect is brought about by initiating an alternative causal process that terminates in that effect is one in which the switch thereby itself counts as a cause—however unintuitive this result may seem at first glance. And even if we disagree, we can still recognize here a feature absent from, e.g., the example depicted in figure 10.

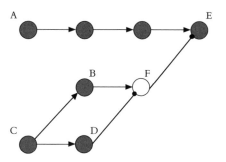

Figure 10

Here, we might be willing to call C a "switch"—since, thanks to C, the causal route to E includes D—but not the kind that initiates a process connecting it to the effect in question. For the link between D and E, causal though it may be, is not secured by an intervening process. Or so it seems. But one might object that a suitable "process" does connect D with E: namely, one consisting in part of omissions. If we are prepared to be generous in what counts as a process, then an interesting possibility arises: one might claim that our cases from §1 are all cases of switches, and use this to argue, in the style of option two, that transitivity holds after all.[1] Perhaps. But there is another feature that distinguishes examples like Suzy's flip from examples like those discussed in the previous section.

To see this feature, consider an alternative situation in which large portions of the right-hand track are missing such that if Suzy had not flipped the switch, the train never would have reached the point of re-convergence, and so would not have been robbed. That is a situation in which it seems intuitively clear that Suzy's action is a cause of the robbery. Or, thinking in terms of neuron diagrams, consider figure 47.

---

[1] But see Hall 2004 for discussion and critique of such a proposal, in a slightly different context.

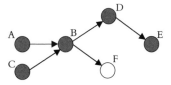

Figure 47

The stimulatory connection between neuron **F** and neuron **E** is now absent, and that alteration clearly reverses the intuitive verdict about C: by sending the stimulatory signal up the top branch, C does indeed count as a cause of E.

Observe now that the difference between the members of each pair of cases is a difference purely extrinsic to the causal processes that lead up to the effect. Simply by tinkering with the environment of these processes, we reach a situation in which the "switch" clearly is a cause of the given effect. Some (such as Hall 2000) take that to be a strong reason for counting the switch a cause of the effect, even in the original case, because they endorse some kind of intrinsicness thesis; observe in this regard that the intrinsicness thesis introduced in chapter 3, §4.3 plainly requires us to project the causal structure of figure 47 (in particular, the fact that C causes E) onto figure 45.

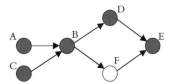

Figure 45

But even if one were to disagree that C is a cause of E, we can see that there is a feature here absent from the examples considered in the last section. Recall that in figure 10 there is no way to simply delete stimulatory and/or inhibitory connections between neurons in such a way as to make C a clear intuitive cause of E in every case. Similarly with the bomb example: there is no way to "remove" features from the environment of the processes leading up to Suzy's survival in such a way as to make it clearly intuitive, in every causal context, that the placing of the bomb is a cause of the survival.

Whether these and perhaps other differences between the two kinds of putative counterexamples to transitivity run deep enough to warrant giving them quite different treatments remains an open question. But it is noteworthy in this regard that certain of the analyses on the table seem committed to treating them differently. For example, transference accounts seem to have no choice but to count Suzy's flip a cause of the robbery, or C in figure 45 a cause of E. (Unless, perhaps, they would fail to count C a cause of D—a worse problem, in our view.) And our minimal sufficiency account, wedded as it is to an intrinsicness thesis (in order, remember, to properly handle preemption), will likewise count Suzy's flip a cause of the robbery: for as we have seen, the process connecting the two is just like a process existing in alternative circumstances in which the flip clearly is a cause of the robbery.

Counterfactual accounts have more room to maneuver, at least if they do not automatically endorse transitivity as a way of solving preemption problems. But whether they will always exploit this room to maneuver is another question. For example, the de facto dependence accounts we have considered appear to have the result that the flip is a cause of the robbery: for, holding fixed that no train is ever on the right hand track, it seems that if Suzy had not switched the train to the left hand track, it would not have reached the scene of the robbery. Again, in figure 45, holding fixed that neuron **F** never fires, it seems that if **C** had not fired, the signal would somehow have to have died as it followed the downward path, and so would not have stimulated **E** to fire. But matters are far from clear, in part because, as we have already seen, it is difficult to know how to systematically and rigorously evaluate the relevant counterfactuals. (For example, do the relevant counterfactuals involve worlds where events are cleanly excised versus worlds where events are replaced with somewhat similar events?) See Swanson 2010 for related discussion.

There is, finally, the alternative strategy we discussed earlier, which is to develop an account of causation that does not imply that there is a causal chain from the flip to the train's journey on the left hand track to the robbery. If no two- (or multi-) step chain from the flip to the robbery exists, we need not hold that transitivity has ever been violated in this case. There are different ways to construct the details; we will give just one illustrative example (drawn from Paul 2000; for others, see McDermott 1995, Schaffer 2005 and Kvart 2011). Arguably, the difference between the journey down the left-hand side of the fork and the journey down the right-hand side of the fork is minimal enough to hold that although the flipping causes the journey to be down the left-hand side of the fork, it does not cause the journey itself; add that it was the journey—and not that it was a journey down the left-hand side of the fork—that was a cause of the robbery, and we see that transitivity gives no reason to hold that Suzy's flip was a cause of the robbery. While we doubt that this strategy will effectively handle all switching cases (for reasons given in Hall 2000), and we refuse the strategy if it is couched in terms that require controversial individuations of events, there are promising moves to be made whenever the actual and "backup" causal routes to the effect are sufficiently similar (see Paul 2000 for details). At any rate, if spelled out carefully enough it seems particularly well-suited to addressing the third class of alleged counterexamples to transitivity, to which we now turn.

2.2 Mis-match of aspects

Suzy reads an interesting article just before her morning constitutional. As she takes her walk, she thinks about the argument put forward in that article. While on her walk, she suffers a terrible sunburn on her nose, having absent-mindedly applied hair product instead of sunscreen to her face before departing. So: reading the article was a cause of her thoughtful walk, which in turn was a cause of her sunburn. But, apparently, it does not follow that reading the article was a cause of the sunburn. If her absent-mindedness resulted from thinking about the article, then it was. But in fact, she wasn't thinking about the article when preparing to depart: her absent-mindedness was due to entirely different factors. Perhaps we have here yet another kind of counterexample to transitivity.

Before trying to decide the matter, let us first try to get clear on the structure of the case. It seems that reading the article was responsible for one aspect of the walk: namely, that it was a thoughtful walk. Similarly, Suzy's absent-mindedness was responsible for a different aspect, namely that it was a walk without sunscreen. But it was in virtue of the second aspect, and not the first, that the walk led to the sunburn. Now that we see the trick, it is easy to construct more examples. As usual, we will let a neuron diagram serve as an archetype:

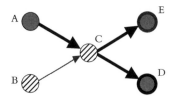

Figure 48

In figure 48, neurons **A** and **B** simultaneously stimulate **C**. But their effects on **C** are different. Had **A** not fired, **C** would not have fired at all. By contrast, if **B** had not fired, **C** would still have fired, but in grey. Moreover, the intensity with which **C** fires (15 units, say), which is represented by the thickness of the arrow, is due entirely to the signal from **A**. **C**, when it fires, thus sends out an intensity-15 signal along the stimulatory channels to **D** and **E**. Finally, neuron **D** is so constructed that it will fire iff it receives an intensity-15 signal, whereas **E** is so constructed that it will fire iff it receives a signal from a striped-firing neuron. We would thus like to say that B causes E, but does not cause D. Figure 49 shows what would have happened if **B** had not fired:

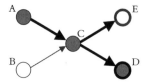

Figure 49

Prima facie trouble for transitivity now emerges from the following line of reasoning about figure 48: B causes E. But as it does not somehow do so at a spatiotemporal distance, there must be a spatiotemporally continuous causal chain connecting B to E. The only available such chain passes through C. Therefore, B must in fact be a cause of C. That is already surprising: we would have liked to say that B is not among the causes of C, but rather merely helped to determine the manner of C's occurrence. But matters are worse. For C, it seems clear, is a cause of D. Hence, by transitivity, B is a cause of D after all. But that is a mistake: the only initial event causally responsible for D is A.

One response to this sort of problem is to adopt a theory of events that implies that C is not one event but (at least) two: there is the firing-of-a-certain-intensity, and there is the firing-in-a-certain color-and-pattern.[2] Then we could say that B causes the second of these, but not the first, and that it is the first, but not the second, that causes D. The apparent threat to transitivity thus vanishes. Similarly, the walk was not one event but two: there was the walking-without-sunscreen, and there was the thoughtful walking. The absent-minded preparations for departure caused the first—which alone caused the sunburn—while the reading of the article merely caused the second. Hence, the reading was not a cause of the sunburn.

But unless the theory of events is exceedingly fine-grained—packing an enormous multitude of numerically distinct events into the exact spatio-temporal region of the walking—other examples are easy to generate. (Kim 1980 is the best source for such fine-grained theories of events, and see Lewis 1986a for a variation on the same theme.) Likewise for our neurons: for any aspect of the firing of C, we can postulate a "downstream" neuron that is sensitive to just that aspect, and an "upstream" neuron that is responsible for just that aspect—thus forcing the introduction of a C-firing somehow corresponding to just that aspect. And such a fine-grained theory of events, in addition to being suspiciously ad hoc without further motivation, is controversial for other reasons.

Jonathan Bennett (1988) focuses on an important reason: the ontological extravagance makes serious trouble for the project of giving a sensible semantics for causal sentences. "The spark caused the fire." To which of the (large) infinity of coincident events does the term "the spark" refer to? To which does "the fire" refer to? Resolve these indeterminacies one way, and you may get the sentence to come out true, according to your favorite analysis. But there will almost certainly be other ways to resolve them that will get it to come out false. The result: no causal sentence will ever be determinately true. (It's also worth noting that one could raise a similar worry for the contrastivist who is permissive about which events count as contrast events.)

It is unclear how much of a problem this result is. Some will find a fine-grained theory attractive nevertheless, if its ontological excessiveness can be balanced by other attractive features of the overall view. But apart from this,

---

[2] What distinguishes them? One suggestion comes from Lewis (1986a) and Yablo (1992a): the events differ with respect to the possible conditions under which they could have occurred. Thus, the first could have occurred if C had fired in a different color and pattern, but not if it had fired with a different intensity; for the second, the reverse is true.

there is nothing else especially attractive about the view, and nothing even approaching consensus in the literature on the correct theory of events, so to tie one's account of the transitivity of causation to a controversial theory of events seems unwise unless no better alternative presents itself.

Especially because there seems to be a better alternative. We will give a sketch of the form it might take (see Paul 2000 for more discussion). Start by taking the basic causal facts to be expressed not by sentences of the form "event C caused event E," but rather by sentences of the form "event C's having property F caused event E to have property G." We could, perhaps, count C a cause of E *simpliciter* just in case sufficiently many of C's properties—or sufficiently many of its non-accidental properties—cause sufficiently many of E's (non-accidental) properties; that might explain why, in figure 48, we count A a cause of C (since it was responsible for C's being a firing), whereas we only consider B to have been causally responsible for one aspect of C's occurrence (its pattern). We could then take transitivity to apply to these event-property pairs: when C's having property F causes D to have property G, and D's having property G causes E to have property H, then C's having property F cause E to have property H. Hence, that Suzy's preparation was absent-minded caused her walk to be a walk without sun protection, which in turn caused her sunburn. But reading the article, while it caused her walk to be thoughtful, did not cause it to be a walk without sun protection. So the example poses no threat to transitivity; rather, transitivity simply does not apply.

This, of course, is the same result that an appeal to fine-grained events would deliver, and the same result that the contrastive account delivers. But notice that the approach under consideration delivers it without needing to endorse any particular theory of events, whether fragile, coarse-grained, fine-grained, or what-have-you. A final advantage is that this move, or one relevantly like it, but where the causal relata are simply property instances or tropes instead of events-having-properties, provides a natural underpinning for accounts of mental causation and other debates where event-talk has quite naturally given way to property instance-talk.

So the way to see the point is this: it doesn't seem right to individuate events in exceedingly fine-grained ways. Yet any theory of events that relies on a more natural coarse-grained approach packs enough into each event to create false puzzles—seeming "counterexamples" to transitivity involving the mismatch of different aspects of the events. The solution: divorce the theory of events from the theory of causation, and take property instances to be the causal relata instead. Property instances can be as fine-grained as you like, and they fit naturally with the usual understanding of laws of nature as relations between properties. (When we say, e.g., that force is proportional to velocity, this is most naturally understood as a relation between properties, not events, and links causation to nomic subsumption in a clear and straightforward manner.)

Refining our approach to transitivity in this way can also weed out some of the more troublesome switching cases discussed earlier. Recall the case of the train that is diverted to the left side of the fork and then (later) robbed. If flipping the switch only causes the train's subsequent journey to have the property of occupying the left-hand track, and does not cause the train's journey *simpliciter*, then, since this difference in location is not a cause of the robbery, endorsing transitivity does not, after all, require us to conclude that the flip was not a cause of the robbery.[3] This fits our intuitions better than accepting the flip as a cause.

Unfortunately, not all switching cases can receive this kind of treatment. Consider a different version of the train case: when the train is diverted to the left-hand track, it is stopped, taken apart, oiled, and reassembled before continuing down the track. This may make the train's journey so different from what it would have been that in fact the flipping is a cause of the journey *simpliciter*, and not merely a cause of the journey's change in location. Transitivity may then count the flip as a cause of the robbery (or more carefully, as a cause of the robbery's having the property of occurring when, where and how it actually did). However, to the extent that the properties of the events in the new causal process initiated by the "switch" are substantially different from what they would have been otherwise, our intuitions follow suit: we are more inclined to call the flip a cause (cf. Hall 2000).

---

[3] An appeal to fine-grained events won't necessarily get the same result. Suppose for instance that we hold that counterfactual dependence suffices for causation, and try to avoid the awkward conclusion that the flipping causes the robbery by distinguishing a version of the train's journey that is only accidentally along the left-hand track from a version that is essentially along the left-hand track. We get that the flipping causes the second of these, but not the first; so far, so good. But the prohibition on backtracking counterfactuals will guarantee that the robbery depends on both. So there is a chain of step-wise dependence linking the flipping to the robbery. So the flipping turns out to be a cause of the robbery, after all.

We will leave it an open question whether the best way to handle the examples under discussion here is to appeal to a particular theory of events, to revise our assumptions about the basic causal relata, or to pursue yet some other strategy. But one thing, at least, is clear: the apparent threat to transitivity posed by the examples is only that—apparent. It seems clear that what grounds our judgment that reading the article is not a cause of the sunburn, or that B in figure 48 is not a cause of D, is that the two events are not connected up in the right way: there is, at the intermediate stage, some crucial mismatch. So these examples do not, in the end, pose a real challenge to transitivity. Instead, they challenge standard ways of constructing causal chains between ordinary events.

Let's look briefly at whether we have the resources to exploit this fact. Since officially we are married to a treatment of event causation, we will set aside the divorce proposed above and content ourselves with pointing out some problems for the approaches we've been considering that arise under the assumption that we need to accept a fine-grained theory of events, according to which perfectly coincident events are distinguished by their modal profiles, i.e. by the possible conditions under which they could have occurred.

To begin, it seems that transference theories can make little use of such distinctions. Consider figure 48. There is a firing of **C** that is essentially a firing in the striped pattern, but only accidentally an intensity-15 firing. And then there is a firing that is only accidentally a firing in the striped pattern, but essentially an intensity-15 firing. Having drawn this distinction, we presumably want to put it to use by saying that the first but not the second causes E, whereas the second but not the first causes D. The problem for transference accounts is now obvious, for this difference in "essences" evidently will not translate into a difference with respect to what sorts of stuff—energy, momentum, tropes, or what have you—is transmitted. We do not suggest that this result is a clear disaster for the transference theorist, for she is within her rights to contrapose, and insist that what we have revealed is the irrelevance of these modal distinctions to giving a proper account of fine-grained causation. But, of course, that response only has teeth if she can offer a rival proposal. We will not speculate further about what such a proposal might be (although Ehring's 1997 may help here).

Our other accounts seem better placed to handle fine-grained causation in the manner indicated, if only because they at least provide frameworks that can, in principle, exploit the difference between, for example, the proposition that intensity-15-C occurs and the proposition that striped-C occurs. But subtle pitfalls remain. We will point out just one, that applies to certain versions of a counterfactual analysis. It parallels the problem that faces the transference account, for what emerges is that these analyses likewise erase the causal distinction between striped-C and intensity-15-C, and more generally any causal distinction between events that differ merely in their modal profiles.

A way in which this happens is by way of a certain reading—curious, but often insisted upon—of the antecedent in the counterfactual "if C had not occurred, then E would not have occurred," an issue we discussed in detail in chapter 3, §4.2.8 and §4.2.9. Here for example is Lewis (2004a, p. 90): "When asked to suppose counterfactually that C does not occur, we don't really look for the very closest possible world where C's conditions of occurrence are not quite satisfied. Rather, we imagine that C is completely and cleanly excised from history, leaving behind no fragment or approximation of itself."

It is far from obvious what it means to "cleanly excise" an event, but this much is clear: whatever it means, the result of cleanly excising striped-C will be exactly the same as the result of cleanly excising intensity-15-C. *Pace* Lewis's motivation for this reading of the counterfactual, this seems to be a clear mistake. For surely, if striped-C had not happened, then one thing that we would like to conclude might have happened in its place is a grey but equally intense firing of **C**. Surely if we are attracted to a counterfactual analysis, then admitting that counterfactual possibility is exactly what we need to do if we want our analysis to conclude correctly that striped-C is not a cause of D.

The covariation account recently defended by Lewis runs into exactly the same difficulty. To see why, we need to correct one inaccuracy in our statement of it in chapter 2, §2.2.2. We gave the following rendition of the key idea: C causes E iff E counterfactually covaries with C to a sufficient extent, where E counterfactually covaries with C just in case (and to the extent that) variation in the manner of C's occurrence would be followed by corresponding variation in the manner of E's occurrence. But in fact, Lewis quite explicitly leaves it open whether the counterfactual circumstance in which a C-like event occurs, but in a manner slightly different from that in which C actually occurs, is a circumstance in which it is C itself—as opposed to some qualitatively similar but numerically distinct event—that is occurring. Introducing a bit of technical terminology, he says only that an "alteration" of C occurs; he sees it as an advantage of his account that it does not settle whether alterations of an event are in fact possible versions of that very event, or different events altogether. But in the present context this feature does not look so advantageous. The trouble, once again, is that the alterations of striped-C will be exactly the same as the alterations of intensity-15-C. So once again, no difference with respect to their causal properties will be forthcoming.

One of us (Paul) thinks that this simply adds ballast to the idea that we should dispense with events as the causal relata. For again, if we move to properties, we find ourselves in a better position, for we can cleanly excise the stripeyness of C without excising its intensity. Issues remain, to be sure, especially with double prevention and other cases involving omissions. But given the problems with transitivity we've discussed, if we can avoid a significant class of counterexamples while simultaneously ridding ourselves of suspect commitments to fine-grained or fragile events, what's not to like?

6

Concluding remarks

1 A deep divide

We have now navigated our way through many of the main points of interest for those who wish to engage with the metaphysics of causation. Focusing critically on many of our own contributions to the causal literature, as well as on exemplary contributions by others, most notably, those by Dowe, Halpern, Hitchcock, Lewis, Maudlin, Pearl, Schaffer, and Yablo, we looked in detail at straightforward (and not so straightforward) counterfactual analyses, de facto approaches, causal modeling approaches, nomic sufficiency accounts, contrastive accounts, and theories based on transfers of conserved quantities. In order to assess the central problems and prospects for a reductive theory of the causal relation, we worked through a series of outstanding problems and puzzles, contemplating a range of causal structures that represent the central features of causation, most notably, structures involving preemption, overdetermination, and causation involving omissions. Along the way, we considered treatments of causal puzzles founded on distinctions between intrinsicness constraints and dependence constraints, distinctions between garden-variety and omission-involving causation, and distinctions between default and deviant processes.

What has emerged from our discussion is that there is a deep divide in our intuitions about causation, and correspondingly, in how to handle two very central issues: problems with redundant causation, most notably with late preemption and overdetermination, and problems with causation involving omissions. As we discussed, the intuition captured by our intrinsicness thesis—that we detect, embedded within the complex structure of various cases, a basic causal structure that is causal regardless of its extrinsic surroundings—seems to be a key factor in the way that we want to interpret cases of late preemption and overdetermination. For example, we suggest that, once we see the basic causal structure between C and E of figure 20, that this plays an important role in our causal judgments. Accordingly, we judge C to be a cause of E in figure 18 and again in figure 11.

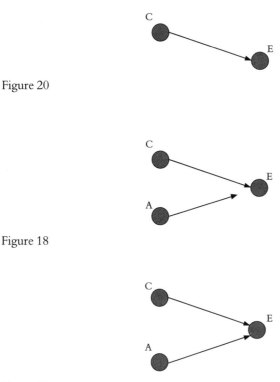

Figure 20

Figure 18

Figure 11

On the other hand, when we are faced with omission-involving causation, our intuitions can change. What we find especially interesting is that for certain cases involving additional structure, in particular, cases of double prevention that involve omissions embedded in a causal chain, what seems decisive for our causal judgment is something entirely different from intrinsicness. That is, in such cases, what is decisive for our judgment that C causes E is that the requisite dependence exists—not that there exists some intrinsic fact involving an embedded causal structure. Look again at figure 29:

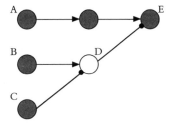

Figure 29

Here, we conjoin a prevention structure to another causal line to create a case of prevented prevention, or "double prevention," and suddenly, dependence plays a central role in our causal judgments: *C* is unambiguously judged to be a cause of *E*.

Figure 10 then rachets things up, to dramatic effect—causation involving omission is fitted together with a double instance of preemption to create havoc with our overall causal judgments.

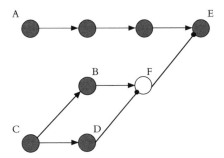

Figure 10

This confusion then shows up in the debate over transitivity, as witnessed by the way that structures embedding figure 10 or a variant thereof exhibit some of the most difficult cases for those who would defend transitivity.

How are we to adjudicate this conflict between intrinsicness and dependence? Given our strong sense that the causal relation is intrinsic, brought out by our consideration of cases of preemption, the sensitivity to extrinsic detail we see with dependence raises deep and difficult problems for any analysis of causation defined in terms of counterfactuals. But the simple, clean and appealing way that counterfactual dependence fits with causation involving omissions, in addition to the central role it plays in causal modeling, makes dependence hard to give up.

So we see a deep intuitive tension in the way we want to judge these cases, one that creates serious trouble for any reductive treatment that wants to approach causation in a uniform manner. And as our discussion in chapters 4 and 5 brought out, even if we dispense with uniformity we are still in serious trouble. First, because there is still no acceptable, suitably reductive treatment of causation involving omissions, uniform or not. Second, if our approach to causation involving omissions is not uniform, we need some reductive way of drawing distinctions between the types of causal structures that are to be analyzed in different ways, and we need some method by which to combine different types of causal substructures into a larger causal structure that generates the correct causal result. As chapters 3, 4 and 5 attest, such combinations can radically change our causal judgments for reasons that causal theorists do not fully understand, and thus a view that embraces multiple kinds of causation faces the difficult task of specifying in detail—as it must be able to do—exactly how the different kinds of combined causal structures are to be interpreted. Finally, we need to decide whether transitivity applies uniformly, and if it does not, to be able to decide, when examining causal structures and combinations of structures, just when transitivity is supposed to apply and when it isn't.

Apart from the outstanding problems canvassed in the preceding chapters, then, open questions that deserve further study include questions about whether it is desirable or even possible to try and fit together an account of causation that puts all varieties of causation under one roof, let alone one that captures causation involving omission and makes causation transitive only when we think it should be. This point brings us right up against the wall: can we settle whether causation is transitive? And if it isn't, when it isn't? Advocates of the view that causation is not transitive have done little or nothing to address the central problem for their view, which is that nearly all of our ordinary, philosophical and scientific causal claims and inferences rely on the assumption that causation is transitive. If this assumption is false, when exactly is it false? How are we to protect and refine our ordinary and scientific reasoning processes?

Puzzles about omissions raise similar worries. Given that all kinds of inferences—moral, legal, ordinary and scientific—rely on the assumption that there is causation involving omissions, how are we to make sense of omissions and determine, precisely, when and how causation involves them? These are outstanding questions that extend far past metaphysics and the philosophy of physics, and they need much more attention in the literature. That said, some have made a start on these questions. Recent work by Sartorio (2009, 2010) develops our understanding of the way causation is involved with moral questions, especially with respect to transitivity and omissions. Applications of some of the features of causal overdetermination to moral responsibility are discussed by Bernstein (forthcoming), and Swanson (2010) discusses the way our causal talk is connected to our theories of causation, including omission-involving causation. Other prospects for further work include the question of whether reductionism about causation is a desirable or even a viable goal, the role of nonreductive approaches in helping to further reductive projects, whether there is vagueness of some sort infecting our concept of causation (or worse, some sort of ontological indeterminacy), and the semantics of counterfactuals needed for causation (see Hajek forthcoming for some recent discussion of Lewis's semantics).

After surveying the literature in some depth, we conclude that, as yet, there is no reasonably successful reduction of the causal relation. And correspondingly, there is no reasonably successful conceptual analysis of a philosophical causal concept. No extant approach seems able to incorporate all of our desiderata for the causal relation, nor to capture the wide range of our causal judgments and applications of our causal concept. Barring a fundamental change in approach, the prospects of a relatively simple, elegant and intuitively attractive, unified theory of causation, whether ontological reduction or conceptual analysis, are dim.

2 The method by counterexample

This pessimistic conclusion is not wholly a cause for dismay, however, since we have also seen how the search for a reductive theory of causation, and its sister search for an analysis of the concept of causation, generates an enormous bounty by opening up a number of interesting and potentially fruitful lines of enquiry. As part of the search for an analysis of causation, philosophers have discovered new causal features and developed richer, more nuanced treatments of the causal relation. Subtle questions about what causal processes are and what the roles of intrinsicality, transitivity, and dependence must arise by examining causal cases from the perspectives of several different analyses of the causal relation. The main tool we have used to gather this bounty is what we dubbed, early on, the *method by counter-example*. The method consists primarily of using sample cases and fictional examples to evaluate the philosophical claims made by a theory, and exploring and isolating various features of the causal relation by proposing counterexamples to extant theories.

In applying our method by counterexample, we have relied heavily upon neuron diagrams and other simple descriptive cases to highlight features of the causal relation. For the simple, clean and quick representation of examples and puzzles in causation, neuron diagrams are unparalleled. (Of course, as neuron diagrams can also oversimplify, conflate properties, and allow the willing mind to overinterpret, we have also noted that they must be used with care. With great power comes great responsibility.)

Using the neuron diagrams, we have employed the method by counter-example to: (i) bring out how the causal relation might not be transitive even though many theories of causation need to rely upon transitivity to avoid compelling counterexamples; (ii) show how causal modeling and de facto accounts can be at sea once causally nonreductive assumptions (such as those about default/deviant determinations or counterpart needs) are dis-allowed; (iii) show how preemption does not require events to go missing; (iv) show how causation involving omissions causes problems for nearly every theory of causation; (v) show how we need to be clearer about what we take causal processes to be; (vi) illustrate ambiguities in treatments of a causal default/deviant distinction; (vii) highlight, using black-box cases, the importance of knowing the deep level structure of a case before deciding what it supposedly shows; and, finally, (viii) illustrate the tension between causal judgments involving dependence, as in cases of double prevention, and causal judgments where intrinsicness plays a central role, as in preemp-tion. The method by counterexample has also been extremely useful in helping to show the value (as well as the cost) of adopting an approach that investigates the nature of the causal relation only in a nonreductive context. One should not simply take causal facts for granted and then apply them to other metaphysical puzzles without having done the work to see what ontological and conceptual facts are buried in the causal facts one has accepted. Our discussions of preemption, overdetermination and black-box cases, and of the nonreductivity problems for causal modeling, are particularly salient demonstrations of this point.

Another general point we have noted concerns the fact that theories of causation are often intertwined with other theories, such as theories of laws, theories of the metaphysics of the causal relata, theories of the truth conditions for counterfactuals, and theories of the correct semantics and pragmatics for causal claims. These theories can be related in ways which affect the development of one's theory of causation. If, for example, we want to endorse a default/deviant distinction as the basis for a theory of causation, what sorts of worlds would create trouble for such a view? Imagine a Conway world (from Conway's Game of Life) without any state that counts as an empty state. Without any clear candidate for what counts as an omission, how do we evaluate counterfactuals about such a world? What are the laws, and do they support causation? What counts as the default state in such a world?

As the results of our extended application of the method show, one must work through the examples in order to understand the constraints and the applications involved in fitting causal facts into one's overall ontology. Our use of the method by counterexample is intended as a corrective to philosophical skepticism about the value of counterexamples involving fictional situations, even when constructing theories of the metaphysics of the causal relation in the actual world. To dismiss the working through of such counterexamples as unproductive "epicycling" is to dismiss a valuable research tool, and to betray a lack of understanding of how many philosophical, especially metaphysical, advances are made.

Of course, while we think the method by counterexample is extremely valuable, there is an art to using it properly. One must not appeal cavalierly to just any intuitions or concepts. It just isn't true that any counterexample-qua-interpreted-by-X needs to be taken seriously, especially if the counterexample is taken outside of its methodological context. Williamson (2007) and Hitchcock (2007b) address some of the constraints on counterexamples and counterfactual-based reasoning, and Paul (2012) shows how some uses of counterfactuals and counterexamples can be understood in terms of philosophical modeling.

3 The causal method

In light of the competing intuitions we have about the nature of causation and the internal tensions this generates, especially for unified accounts, we believe that philosophers working on causation need to be very sensitive to the different ways of approaching the problem of causation in the literature.

One must keep track of the different distinctions that come out when analyzing cases in order to develop causal theories from a broader, distinction-sensitive viewpoint. For example, when is dependence essential and when is it sufficient? When is nomic sufficiency essential and when is it sufficient? One must also be clear about the philosophical prerequisites needed to build a theory of causation. Why do we want to build a theory of causation? What is the value of having a theory of causation? What kind of theory does one want to build, and how should it be done?

Another thing to keep track of is differences in methodological approach, in particular, between conceptual and reductive analyses of causation, between reductionist and nonreductionist accounts, and between observer-independent and observer-dependent treatments of causation. The importance of keeping track is highlighted when we notice that what count as theoretical desiderata and potential counterexamples are dependent on the sort of account being targeted. Counterexamples involving magic and wizards may not be relevant for an account purporting to capture only the subtleties of actual-world causation rather than the full content of our causal concept. Counterexamples involving ordinary common-sense judgments may not be relevant for an account that purports to be truly observer-independent and hence free of observer-dependent constraints. And so on. A lack of clarity about which approach is being taken, and what each such approach requires, can sow confusion in the philosophical literature, since the requirements for success vary across different types of analyses.

In this vein, we discussed how the causal literature exemplifies different ways of approaching different sorts of analyses. Some approaches use causal modeling to draw out facts about the causal relation, and do not scruple to make causal or pragmatic assumptions while doing so. Others explicitly rule out anything causal or nonobjective in an attempt to grasp the Holy Grail, a reductive analysis of the causal relation to more fundamental entities, or a noncircular analysis of our fundamental causal concept. We saw tensions in the literature over the different approaches, especially when authors are not perfectly clear about which approach they are adopting (as in Maudlin 2004), or when they use the nonreductive approach to try to solve problems of omissions, preemption and overdetermination for reductive approaches (as in Hitchcock 2007a). We also saw these issues surface in our discussions of preemption, overdetermination and black-box cases, and we strongly suspect they also lurk behind some of our perplexity with causation involving omission and transitivity. We tried to contribute some clarity to the overall discussion by laying out our methodological rules in chapter 2 and by pointing out, in various places in the preceding chapters, where we saw the rules being violated or where certain claims created confusion.

Our exploration of the varied and esoteric features of causation brings out another methodological point. One might have thought, once upon a time, that the only goal of a metaphysical treatment of causation that was worth its salt was to provide an analysis of the metaphysical relation that determined whether or not the world contained some sort of deep metaphysical necessity. But as our discussion about the features of causation brings out, even when we put a premium on reductive theorizing, there is much more to the project of exploring the metaphysics of causation than the search for deep metaphysical necessity. In particular, if we separate the project of determining whether there is the right sort of metaphysical necessity in the world from the project of determining what sorts of causal structures and properties the world has, we can see clearly that one can pursue the second project independently of the first. For example, questions about the nature of preemption, overdetermination, joint causation, transitivity and omission are all independent of one's position about the ontological thickness of causal necessitation. Even if one has a metaphysically speaking, very thin notion of what metaphysical necessity might amount to in ontological terms, one can—and should—explore the features of the causal relation and the many forms it can assume.

With all this in mind, then, we can distinguish between different sorts of approaches to the metaphysics of causation. One approach takes the problem of causation to involve ontology, that is, to be a problem centered on determining the features or properties of the causal relation (or its instances) itself, in the actual world and in worlds that resemble our world in relevant respects. A different approach takes the problem of causation to center on the explication of a concept of causation, whether the concept approximates some folk or ordinary notion of causation or whether it captures some more sophisticated, philosophically refined concept. One could also take a mixed approach, one that focuses on both of these ways of thinking. A mixed approach tries to thread a path through the causal landscape, mapping the objective structure of dependence relations and the intrinsic properties of the world at some suitably fundamental ontological level while recognizing that our understanding of causation comes from the application of a causal concept that selectively draws on features of this landscape in conjunction with pragmatic considerations, including norms about default and deviant events and processes.

Although we have focused mostly on the ontological part of the project, we like the idea of a mixed approach for a final theory. Such an approach would be sensitive to the need to give a suitably objective account of the causal structure of the world, yet recognize that any account that can do justice to our causal intuitions will have to have some pragmatic features drawn from our ordinary causal judgments, at least enough of such features to accommodate our causal explanations.

But beware. The description we just gave of the mixed approach is consistent with least four different ontological stances towards causation. A philosophically respectable account of causation based on the mixed approach must be clear about which treatment is being defended. While we won't pretend to have identified all the different ways of making sense of the mixed approach, here is a sketch of some different ways to approach the ontological part of it.

The *inflationary realist* holds that causation is an objective relation that exists as an ontological addition to the fundamental structure of the world, including the existing counterfactual (or other) structure of the world. We take Michael Tooley (1987, 1990) to be a good example of such a realist. The inflationary realist can adopt a mixed approach by simply adopting two different kinds of irreducible, fundamental causal relations.

The *conservative realist*, by comparison, denies that there is any such additional relation, or anything more than a certain amount of ontological minima. All that exists are atoms (or the equivalent) in a space of some sort. A fan of Humean supervenience like David Lewis can count as such a realist: he holds that there is nomic possibility, but this reduces to patterns of events (i.e., arrangements of atoms in the space), and reduces counterfactual dependence to similarity relations between worlds along with a few other details. The conservative realist has a much more minimal ontology than the inflationary realist, choosing to accommodate our causal judgments by inflating her ideology rather than her ontology.[1] Compare the dispute between the inflationary realist about spacetime who holds that material objects are ontological additions, numerically distinct from the points of spacetime they occupy, to the conservative realist approach of the supersubstantivalist who identifies material objects with such points (or regions).

A *moderate realist* about causation extends the position of the conservative realist, yet falls short of inflationary realism by admitting only certain sorts of additional non-causal properties and relations into her ontology. She accepts the contents of the ontology of the conservative realist, and adds in a little bit more, but not as much as the inflationary realist. In particular, she does not add in anything causal. The additional properties she adds are, at least by her lights, more acceptable than primitive causal properties and relations. For example, perhaps she has a view about nomic possibility that is less conservative than that of the conservative realist, yet does not admit primitive causation. Or perhaps she accepts irreducible chances, or a primitive temporal arrow, again, without admitting primitive causation. She also extends her ideology instead of her ontology to accommodate our ordinary ways of understanding causation, but, given her relatively permissive ontological standards, thinks there is an interesting ontological question about whether, for example, we need to endorse more than the existence of relations of counterfactual dependence in order to have an ontologically complete underpinning for causation. Both the conservative realist and the moderate realist could adopt our mixed view, and one of us counts herself as a moderate realist (Paul). The other inclines towards conservative realism (Hall).

A different sort of approach one might take can be described as *soft pragmatism*. The soft pragmatist infects his ontology with pragmatic notions, in contrast to the three varieties of realist we have described. Each of these realist positions also holds that we cannot describe or understand the notion of causation in any sort of observer-dependent way. In contrast, while the soft pragmatist will agree with the realist that the counterfactual structure of

---

[1] Or, one might be a conservative realist about causation while being more inflationary about the causal relata (see our discussion of causal overdetermination in chapter 3, §5).

the world is objective, he will argue that the causal relations that are built from counterfactuals involve more than this, and this more is partly observer-dependent. Such a pragmatist could adopt a mixed approach, balancing ontology and conceptual analysis, as well. (We are not sure whether anyone has adopted soft pragmatism in print, although we have heard it aired in various discussions. It is worth asking whether this is the place on the landscape where certain advocates of causal modeling would locate themselves.)

Thinking carefully about the different ontological stances one could take brings up another central issue for the metaphysics of causation: whether or not the project is reductionist, that is, does it reduce the causal to the non-causal. Inflationary realism gives up on the reductionist project, but has the virtue of being explicit about its capitulation. Moderate and conservative realism lend themselves most naturally to reductionist interpretations: causal relations are reduced to the other, more fundamental entities that the realist admits in the world. On such views, causal theories are to be given in noncausal terms, and our ability to determine whether there is causation is not dependent on having independent cognitive access to any irreducibly causal facts. The soft pragmatist might also be reductionist, but in a different way: for example, by reducing his observer-dependent "causal" properties to other sorts of observer-dependent non-causal properties. The reductive moderate, conservative and soft pragmatist ways of approaching causation can be contrasted to nonreductive versions of such views where causal notions, causal properties or other causal entities are fed into the theories of causation at various levels.

For the other part of the mixed approach, the conceptual analysis, while traditional philosophical approaches are relevant here, there is an important role for certain types of experimental work on our folk and philosophical concepts of causation. At the very least, consulting experimental work will help to constrain and guide our intuitions about folk and philosophical concepts, and work in cognitive science on the psychology of causation needs significantly more attention in the philosophical literature.

This is not the place to go into further detail.[2] Our point here is merely that the different ways these questions can be approached needs to be given

---

[2] For a detailed treatment of the role for a posteriori reasoning in metaphysics, see Paul 2012 and 2010a, for a more general methodological discussion see Hall 2006.

more care and attention in the literature, for they have significant implications for the development and potential success of our treatments of causation. For a sample of interesting experimental philosophical work on causal concepts see Hitchcock and Knobe (2009); for a sample of work tying the philosophy and psychology of causation together see Siegel (2009); Walsh and Sloman (2011), Woodward forthcoming, and Rose and Danks 2012. For samples of recent work in the psychological literature on causation, see Lombrozo (2010), Gopnik and Schulz (2007), Goodman et al. (forthcoming), Newman et al. (2008), Saxe and Carey (2006), Steyvers et al. (2003) and Kushnir et al. (2010). (And for classic work on the psychology of causal perception see Michotte 1946/tr. 1963.)

4 Cognate debates

We will close with the observation that the sort of exploration we've conducted in this manuscript isn't just of interest to metaphysicians. Having a detailed understanding of the twists and turns in the discussion of causation is crucial for a number of cognate debates in related areas of philosophy, and should also be of interest to those working in computer science, economics, history, law, political theory, psychology, and sociology.

Take, for example, issues in legal liability. In the law, legal liability is intimately connected to causal judgments, and judge and jury decisions involving legal responsibility and attendant consequences are often developed and justified based on the causal chains leading to various events. Now consider our puzzles involving causation with omissions, preemptive prevention and transitivity, and our concerns over the correct way to individuate events. One needs to know how to navigate the deep structure of these puzzles in order to determine the correct causal judgment—this is so, even if we are willing to infuse our judgments with pragmatic features. If we are trying to determine who is legally responsible for the collapse of a building or the death of a patient, where the collapse or the death involved, say, circuitous causal paths, multiple possible events, or a series of prevented preemptions, having a clear sense of the causal contributions made by omissions, of the events that are supposed to be caused, and of the delicate issues surrounding transitivity will clarify and constrain the legal analysis and the subsequent judge or jury's decision.[3] See Moore (2009) for an extensive treatment of the relationships between legal reasoning and the philosophy of causation, and Schaffer (2010) for further contributions to this discussion.

Another place where the metaphysics of causation can be important comes into play in our understanding how to make sense of partial individual responsibility for an ostensibly collective action, for example, how to make sense of the relationship between voting for an outcome and causal responsibility for that outcome. Many voting outcomes involve causal redundancy, in the sense that the outcome (or the winner of the election, etc.) is not decided by a margin of a single vote, but by a margin of many votes. In such a case, for any particular voter, if she had not voted, the outcome would have been the same. Consider Suzy, who voted for candidate A, who won by a landslide. Does this mean Suzy is not causally responsible for A's win? Our answer depends, at least in part, on the structure of the case, and on our preferred interpretation of that structure. Such a case might be understood as a case of symmetric overdetermination, where each overdetermining cause counts. But such a case may also be understood as a case of preemption (say, where the tie-breaking vote for candidate A preempts all subsequent votes for candidate A, including Suzy's, from causing A's election, given that all the votes for candidate B have already been counted). The interpretation supporting preemption is not at all far-fetched.

[Consider] the case of the United States, where several time zones are involved. By the time voters in California or Hawaii go to the polls, the earlier-voting states may have already determined the victor. (Goldman 1999, p. 212)

Of course, once we understand the potential causal structure involved, there are ways to organize elections or to count votes differently so that such a preemptive situation does not arise, or to find a way to ascribe responsibility for voting even if strictly speaking, the vote is causally preempted. Our point here is simply that a clear account and interpretation of the causal

---

[3] For example, there was an intense debate over insurance payouts for the collapse of the two towers of the World Trade Center, for the amount of the payout depended on whether the collapse involved two attacks or just one single attack, and thus whether there were two causal paths and two collapse events, or just one. A federal appeals court held that there was just one attack and one effect, but allowed a jury to review the case and make a final decision. The jury decided that there were two attacks. (See, e.g., *BBC News*, "Battle over Twin Towers insurance," 9 February 2004.)

structure is an essential part of designing an election model that properly distributes voter responsibility.

A final example comes from the long debate over the causal efficacy of mental substances, states and properties. To make progress in the debate over mental causation, one needs a clear understanding of the distinction between symmetric overdetermination and joint causation, of the guidelines concerning the relationship between causes and the laws that link them to their effects, of whether and how counterfactual dependence is sufficient for causation, and what the rules are for counterparts that determine the truth of the relevant counterfactuals. Without this clarity, work on mental causation may slur over many of the subtle metaphysical issues that are essential to the proper understanding of the problem.

These are just a few of the places where a deeper understanding of the causal relation and its associated concepts play an essential role in giving a fully developed treatment of a philosophical topic. We hope that our discussion in the preceding chapters provides a jumping-off place for those who wish to approach philosophical topics in a causally sophisticated way, and for nonphilosophers to get a sense of the philosophical issues involved in understanding and making use of causal notions.

This completes our guide to the philosophical terrain of the metaphysics of causation. For all the questions and problems we have raised, we remain convinced that the pursuit of a reductive account of causation—both of its ontology and its concept—is a valuable enterprise. There is still much to be learned about the metaphysical nature of the causal relation and its attendant causal concepts.

References

Albert, David. 2000. *Time and Chance*. Cambridge MA, Harvard University Press.

Anscombe, G. E. M. 1971. *Causality and Determination: An Inaugural Lecture*. Cambridge: Cambridge University Press.

Armstrong, D. M. 1983. *What Is a Law of Nature?* New York: Cambridge University Press.

——. 2004. "Going Through the Open Door Again: Counterfactual vs. Singularist Theories of Causation." In Collins et al. 2004a, 445–57.

Beebee, Helen. 2004. "Causing and Nothingness." In Collins et al. 2004a, 291–308.

Bennett, Jonathan. 1988. *Events and their Names*. Indianapolis: Hackett.

Bennett, Karen. 2003. "Why the exclusion problem seems intractable, and how, just maybe, to tract it." *Noûs* 37: 471–97.

——. 2007. "Mental Causation." *Philosophy Compass* 2 (2): 316–36.

Bernstein, Sara. Forthcoming. "Moral Overdetermination."

Campbell, John. 2010. "Independence of Variables in Mental Causation." In *Philosophy of Mind: Philosophical Issues*, edited by Ernest Sosa and Enrique Villanueva, 20: 64–79.

Cartwright, Nancy. 1983. *How the Laws of Physics Lie*. Oxford: Clarendon Press.

——. 1999. *The Dappled World*. Cambridge: Cambridge University Press.

Casati, Roberto and Achille Varzi, eds. 1996. *Events*. Aldershot: Dartmouth Publishing.

Chalmers, David. 2011. "Verbal Disputes." *Philosophical Review* 120 (4): 515–66.

Collins, John. 2000. "Preemptive Preemption." *Journal of Philosophy* 97: 223–34. Reprinted in Collins et al. 2004a, 107–17.

Collins, John, Ned Hall, and L. A. Paul, eds. 2004a. *Causation and Counterfactuals*. Cambridge, MA: MIT Press.

——. 2004b. "Introduction." In Collins et al. 2004a.

Correll, Shelley J., Stephen Benard, and In Paik. 2007. "Getting a job: Is there a motherhood penalty?" *American Journal of Sociology* 112: 1297–338.

Davidson, Donald. 1967. "Causal Relations." *Journal of Philosophy* 64: 691–703.

——. 1969. "The Individuation of Events." In *Essays in Honor of Carl G. Hempel*, edited by Nicholas Rescher. Dordrecht: Reidel, 216–34. Reprinted in Davidson 1980, 163–80.

——. 1970. "Events as Particulars." *Noûs* 4: 25–32. Reprinted in Davidson 1980, 181–7.

——. 1980. *Essays on Actions and Events*. Oxford: Clarendon Press.

Dowe, Phil. 2000. *Physical Causation*. New York: Cambridge University Press.

Dowe, Phil and Noordhof, Paul, eds. 2004. *Cause and Chance: Causation in an Indeterministic World*. London: Routledge.

Eells, Ellery. 1991. *Probabilistic Causality*. Cambridge: Cambridge University Press.

Ehring, Douglas. 1997. *Causation and Persistence*. New York: Oxford University Press.

Elga, Adam. 2000. "Statistical Mechanics and the Asymmetry of Counterfactual Dependence." *Philosophy of Science* (suppl. vol. 68, PSA 2000): 313–24.

Fair, David. 1979. "Causation and the Flow of Energy." *Erkenntnis* 14: 219–50.

Fine, Kit. 2003. "The Non-identity of a Thing and its Matter." *Mind* 112 (446): 195–234.

Frick, Johann. 2009. "'Causal Dependence' and Chance: The New Problem of False Negatives." ms.

Ganeri, Jonardon, P. Noordhof, and M. Ramachandran. 1996. "Counterfactuals and Preemptive Causation." *Analysis* 56: 219–25.

——. 1998. "For a (Revised) PCA-analysis." *Analysis* 58: 45–7.

Goldman, Alvin. 1970. *A Theory of Human Action*. Englewood Cliffs, N. J.: Prentice-Hall.

——. 1999. "Why citizens should vote." *Social Philosophy and Policy* 16 (2): 201–17.

Goodman, Noah D., Tomer D. Ullman, and Joshua B. Tenenbaum. Forthcoming. "Learning a Theory of Causality." *Psychological Review*.

Goosens, William K. 1979. "Causal Chains and Counterfactuals." *Journal of Philosophy* 76: 489–95.

Gopnik, A. and L. Schulz. 2007. *Causal Learning: Psychology, Philosophy and Computation*. New York: Oxford University Press.

Gopnik, A., C. Glymour, D. M. Sobel, L. E. Schulz, T. Kushnir, and D. Danks. 2004. "A Theory of Causal Learning in Children: Causal Maps and Bayes Nets." *Psychological Review* 111: 1–30.

Hajek, Alan. Forthcoming. *Most Counterfactuals are False*.

Hall, Ned. 2000. "Causation and the Price of Transitivity." *Journal of Philosophy* 97: 189–222. Reprinted in Collins et al. 2004a, 181–203.

——. 2004. "Two Concepts of Causation." In Collins et al. 2004a, 225–76.

——. 2006. "Philosophy of Causation: Blind Alleys Exposed; Promising Directions Highlighted." *Philosophy Compass* 1: 86–94.

——. 2007. "Structural Equations and Causation." *Philosophical Studies* 132: 109–36.

——. Forthcoming. "Humean Reductionism about Laws of Nature."

Hall, Ned and L. A. Paul. 2003. "Causation and Preemption." In *Philosophy of Science Today*, edited by Peter Clark and Katherine Hawley. Oxford: Oxford University Press.

Halpern, J. and J. Pearl. 2001. "Causes and Explanations: A Structural-model Approach—Part I: Causes." In *Proceedings of the Seventeenth Conference on Uncertainty in Artificial Intelligence*. San Francisco: Morgan Kaufman, 194–202.

——. 2005. "Causes and Explanations: A Structural Model Approach." *British Journal for the Philosophy of Science* 56: 889–911.

Hausman, Daniel. 1998. *Causal Asymmetries*. New York: Cambridge University Press.

Hitchcock, C. 1996. "The Role of Contrast in Causal and Explanatory Claims." *Synthese* 107: 395–419.

——. 2001. "The Intransitivity of Causation Revealed in Equations and Graphs," *Journal of Philosophy* 98: 273–99.

——. 2004. "Do All and Only Causes Raise the Probabilities of Effects?" in Collins et al. 2004a, 403–17.

——. 2007a. "Prevention, Preemption, and the Principle of Sufficient Reason." *Philosophical Review* 116: 495–532.

——. 2007b. "What's Wrong with Neuron Diagrams?" In *Causation and Explanation*, edited by J. K. Campbell, M. O'Rourke, and H. Silverstein. 69–92. MIT Press, Cambridge, MA.

Hitchcock, C. and J. Knobe. 2009. "Cause and Norm," *Journal of Philosophy* 106: 587–612.

Horwich, Paul. 1993. "Lewis's Programme." In *Causation*, edited by E. Sosa and M. Tooley. Oxford: Oxford University Press.

Kim, Jaegwon. 1973. "Causes and Counterfactuals." *Journal of Philosophy* 70: 570–2.

——. 1980. "Events as Property Exemplifications." In *Action Theory*, edited by M. Brand and D. Walton, 159–77. Dordrecht: Reidel.

——. 1998. *Mind in a Physical World*. Cambridge, MA: MIT Press.

Kitcher, Philip. 1981. "Explanatory unification." *Philosophy of Science* 48: 507–31.

——. 1989. "Explanatory Unification and the Causal Structure of the World." In *Scientific Explanation*, edited by P. Kitcher and W. Salmon, Minnesota Studies in the Philosophy of Science, vol. 13. Minneapolis: University of Minnesota Press.

Kushnir, Tamar, Alison Gopnik, Chris Lucas and Laura Schulz. 2010. "Inferring Hidden Causal Structure." Cognitive Science 34, 148–60.

Kvart, Igal. 1991. "Transitivity and Preemption of Causal Relevance." *Philosophical Studies* 64: 125–60.

——. 2004. "Causation: Probabilistic and Counterfactual Analyses." In Collins et al. 2004a, 359–86.

——. 2011. "Causal Relevance." *New Studies in Exact Philosophy: Logic, Mathematics and Science, Vol. II.,* John Woods and Bryson Brown (eds.), Hermes Scientific Pub. Co., pp. 59–90.

Langton, Rae and David Lewis. 1998. "Defining 'Intrinsic'." *Philosophy and Phenomenological Research* 58: 333–45.

LePore, Ernest and Barry Loewer. 1987. "Mind Matters." *Journal of Philosophy* 84: 630–42.

——. 1989. "More on Making Mind Matter." *Philosophical Topics* 17: 175–91.

Lewis, David. 1970. "How to Define Theoretical Terms." *Journal of Philosophy* 67: 427–46. Reprinted in Lewis 1983: 78–95.

——. 1973a. "Causation." *Journal of Philosophy* 70: 556–67. Reprinted in Lewis 1986b, 159–72.

——. 1973b. *Counterfactuals*. Cambridge: Harvard University Press.

——. 1979. "Counterfactual Dependence and Time's Arrow." *Noûs* 13: 455–76. Reprinted with postscripts in Lewis 1986b, 32–66. Citations are from the latter printing.

——. 1983. *Philosophical Papers*, Vol. I. Oxford: Oxford University Press.

——. 1986a. "Events". In Lewis 1986b, 241–69.

——. 1986b. *Philosophical Papers*, Vol. II. Oxford: Oxford University Press.

——. 1986c. "Postscripts to 'Causation'." In Lewis 1986b, 172–213.

——. 1991. *Parts of Classes*. Oxford: Blackwell.

——. 2000. "Causation as Influence." *Journal of Philosophy* 97: 182–97.

——. 2004a. "Causation as Influence." In Collins et al. 2004a, 75–106; this is an expanded version of Lewis 2000.

——. 2004b. "Void and Object." In Collins et al. 2004a, 277–90.

Loew. Forthcoming. PhD dissertation for the Department of Philosophy at the University of North Carolina at Chapel Hill.

Loewer, Barry. 2007. "Counterfactuals and the Second Law." In *Causation, Physics, and the Constitution of Reality: Russell's Republic Revisited*, edited by Huw Price and Richard Corry. Oxford: Oxford University Press, 293–326.

——. 2012. "Two Accounts of Laws and Time." *Philosophical Studies* 160 (1): 115–137.

Lombard, Lawrence. 1986. *Events: A Metaphysical Study*. London: Routledge and Kegan Paul.

Lombrozo, Tania. 2010. "Causal-explanatory Pluralism: How Intentions, Functions, and Mechanisms Influence Causal Ascriptions." *Cognitive Psychology* 61: 303–32.

Mackie, J. L. 1965. "Causes and Conditions." *American Philosophical Quarterly* 2: 245–64.

Marshall, Dan and Josh Parsons. 2001. "Langton and Lewis on 'Intrinsic'." *Philosophy and Phenomenological Research* 63 (2): 347–51.

Maslen, Cei. 2004. "Causes, Contrasts, and the Nontransitivity of Causation." In *Causation and Counterfactuals*, edited by John Collins, Ned Hall, and L. A. Paul. Cambridge, Mass.: MIT Press, 341–57.

Maudlin, Tim. 2004. "Causation, Counterfactuals, and the Third Factor." In Collins et al. 2004*a*, 419–43; reprinted in Maudlin 2007*c*.

———. 2007*a*. "A Modest Proposal Concerning Laws, Counterfactuals, and Explanation." In Maudlin 2007*c*.

———. 2007*b*. "On the Passing of Time." In Maudlin 2007*c*.

———. 2007*c*. *The Metaphysics Within Physics*. Oxford: Oxford University Press.

McDaniel, Kris. 2009. "Ways of Being," In *Metametaphysics*, edited by David Chalmers, David Manley, and Ryan Wasserman. Oxford: Oxford University Press.

McDermott, Michael. 1995. "Redundant Causation." *British Journal for the Philosophy of Science* 46: 523–44.

McGrath, Sarah. 2005. "Causation by Omission," *Philosophical Studies* 123: 125–48.

Mellor, D. H. 2004. "For Facts as Causes and Effects." In Collins et al. 2004*a*, 309–23.

Menzies, Peter. 1996. "Probabilistic Causation and the Pre-Emption Problem." *Mind* 105: 85–117.

Merricks, Trenton. 2001. *Objects and Persons*. Oxford: Oxford University Press.

Michotte, A. (1946/tr. 1963). *La Perception de la Causalité*, Institut Supérieur de Philosophie. English translation of updated edition by T. Miles and E. Miles, *The Perception of Causality*. New York: Basic Books.

Moore, Michael S. 2009. *Causation and Responsibility: an Essay in Law, Morals, and Metaphysics*. Oxford: Oxford University Press.

Newman, G. E., H. Choi, K. Wynn, and B. J. Scholl. 2008. "The Origins of Causal Perception: Evidence from Postdictive Processing in Infancy." *Cognitive Psychology* 57 (3): 262–91.

Northcott, Robert. 2008. "Causation and Contrast Classes." *Philosophical Studies* 139 (1): 111–23.

Paul, L.A. 1998*a*. "Keeping Track of the Time: An Emended Counterfactual Analysis of Causation." *Analysis* 58 (3): 191–8.

———. 1998*b*. "Problems with Late Preemption." *Analysis* 58 (1): 48–53.

———. 2000. "Aspect Causation," *Journal of Philosophy* 97: 235–56. Reprinted in Collins et al. 2004*a*, 205–24.

———. 2002. "Logical Parts." *Noûs* 36 (4): 578–96.

———. 2004. "The Context of Essence." *Australasian Journal of Philosophy* 82 (1): 170–84.

———. 2006. "Coincidence as Overlap." *Noûs* 40 (4): 623–59.

Paul, L. A. 2007. "Constitutive Overdetermination." In *Topics in Contemporary Philosophy*, Vol. IV: *Causation and Explanation*, 265–90.

———. 2010a. "A New Role for Experimental Work in Metaphysics." *European Review of Philosophy and Psychology* special issue, edited by Joshua Knobe, Tania Lombrozo and Edouard Machery vol. 3, 461–76.

———. 2010b. "Counterfactual Theories of Causation." In *The Oxford Handbook of Causation*, edited by Helen Beebee, Christopher Hitchcock and Peter Menzies. Oxford: Oxford University Press, 158–84.

———. 2010c. "Temporal Experience." *Journal of Philosophy* 107: 333–59.

———. 2012. "Metaphysics as Modeling: The Handmaiden's Tale." *Philosophical Studies* 160 (1): 1–29.

Pearl, Judea. 2000. *Causality: Models, Reasoning and Inference*. Cambridge: Cambridge University Press.

Pereboom, Derk. 2002. "Robust nonreductive materialism." *Journal of Philosophy* 99: 499–531.

Ramachandran, Murali. 1997. "A Counterfactual Analysis of Causation." *Mind* 151: 263–77.

———. 1998. "The M-set Analysis of Causation: Objections and Responses." *Mind* 107: 465–71.

———. 2004. "A Counterfactual Analysis of Indeterministic Causation." In Collins et al. 2004a, 387–402.

Rose, David and David Danks. 2012. "Causation: Empirical Trends and Future Directions." *Philosophy Compass* 7 (9): 643–53.

Salmon, Wesley. 1994. "Causality Without Counterfactuals." *Philosophy of Science* 61: 297–312.

Sartorio, Carolina. 2005. "A New Asymmetry between Actions and Omissions." *Noûs* 39 (3): 460–82.

———. 2009. "Omissions and Causalism." *Noûs* 43 (3): 513–30.

———. 2010. "The Prince of Wales Problem for Counterfactual Theories of Causation." In *New Waves in Metaphysics*, edited by Allan Hazlett. Basingstoke: Palgrave Macmillan.

Saxe, R. and S. Carey. 2006. "The Perception of Causality in Infancy," *Acta Psychologica* 123: 144–65.

Saxe R., J. B. Tenenbaum, and S. Carey. 2005. "Secret Agents: Inferences about Hidden Causes by 10- and 12-month-old Infants." *Psychological Science* 16 (12): 995–1001.

Schaffer, Jonathan. 2000a. "Causation by Disconnection." *Philosophy of Science* 67: 285–300.

———. 2000b. "Overlappings: Probability-Raising without Causation." *Australasian Journal of Philosophy* 78: 40–6.

——. 2000c. "Trumping Preemption," *Journal of Philosophy* 97: 165–81. Reprinted in Collins et al. 2004a, 59–73.

——. 2001. "Causation, Influence, and Effluence." *Analysis* 61: 11–19.

——. 2003. "Overdetermining Causes." *Philosophical Studies* 114: 23–45.

——. 2005. "Contrastive Causation." *The Philosophical Review* 114: 327–58.

——. 2010. "Contrastive Causation in the Law." *Legal Theory* 16: 259–97.

Shoemaker, Sydney. 2001. "Realization and Mental Causation." In *Physicalism and its Discontents*, edited by Carl Gillett and Barry Loewer. Cambridge: Cambridge University Press, 74–98.

——. 2007. *Physical Realization*. Oxford: Oxford University Press.

Sider, Theodore. 2001. "Maximality and Intrinsic Properties." *Philosophy and Phenomenological Research* 63: 357–64.

——. 2003. "Maximality and Microphysical Supervenience." *Philosophy and Phenomenological Research* 66: 139–49.

Siegel, Susanna. 2009. "The Visual Experience of Causation." *The Philosophical Quarterly* 59 (236): 519–40.

Simons, Peter. 1987. *Parts: A Study in Ontology*. Oxford. Oxford University Press.

Sloman, S. A. 2005. *Causal Models: How People Think about the World and its Alternatives*. New York, NY: Oxford University Press.

Smith, Alexander McCall. 2005. *Espresso Tales*. New York: Random House.

Steyvers, M., J. Tenenbaum, E. Wagenmakers, and B. Blum. 2003. "Inferring Causal Networks from Observations and Interventions." *Cognitive Science* 27: 453–89.

Strevens, Michael. 2003. "Against Lewis's New Theory of Causation." *Pacific Philosophical Quarterly* 84: 398–412.

——. 2009. *Depth: An Account of Scientific Explanation*. Cambridge: Harvard University Press.

Swanson, Eric. 2010. "Lessons from the Context Sensitivity of Causal Talk." *Journal of Philosophy* 107: 221–42.

Thomson, Judith. 2003. "Causation: Omissions." *Philosophy and Phenomenological Research* 66: 81–103.

Tooley, Michael. 1987. *Causation: a Realist Approach*. Oxford: Clarendon Press.

——. 1990. "Causation: Reductionism versus Realism." *Philosophy and Phenomenological Research* 50, Supplement: 215–36.

Turner, Jason. 2010. "Ontological Pluralism." *Journal of Philosophy* 107: 5–34.

Walsh, C. and S. Sloman. 2011. "The Meaning of Cause and Prevent: The Role of Causal Mechanism." *Mind and Language* 26: 21–52.

Weatherson, Brian. 2001. "Intrinsic Properties and Combinatorial Principles." *Philosophy and Phenomenological Research* 63 (2001): 365–80.

Williamson, Timothy. 2007. *The Philosophy of Philosophy*, Oxford: Blackwell.

Wilson, Jessica. 2011. "Non-reductive Realization and the Powers-based Subset Strategy." *The Monist* 94: 121–154.

Wolff, P. 2007. "Representing Causation." *Journal of Experimental Psychology: General* 136: 82–111.

Woodward, J. 2005. *Making Things Happen: A Theory of Causal Explanation*. Oxford: Oxford University Press.

——. Forthcoming. "Causal Reasoning: Philosophy and Experiment." *Oxford Studies in Experimental Philosophy*.

Yablo, Stephen. 1992a. "Cause and Essence." *Synthese* 93: 403–49.

——. 1992b. "Mental Causation." *Philosophical Review* 101: 245–80.

——. 2004. "Advertisement for a Sketch of an Outline of a Proto-Theory of Causation." In Collins et al. 2004a, 119–37.

Index of Names

Subject Index